EIGHTEENTH CENTURY

EDITED BY

George Rudé

UNIVERSITY OF ADELAIDE

THE FREE PRESS, NEW YORK

Collier-Macmillan Limited, London

For information, address:

The Free Press
A DIVISION OF THE MACMILLAN COMPANY
60 Fifth Avenue, New York, N.Y. 10011

Collier-Macmillan Canada, Ltd., Toronto, Ontario

DESIGNED BY ANDOR BRAUN

Library of Congress Catalog Card Number: 65–11892

Second Printing June 1965

SOURCES IN
WESTERN
CIVILIZATION

The Eighteenth Century

THE

Sources in Western Civilization

GENERAL EDITOR, *Herbert H. Rowen*

RUTGERS UNIVERSITY

CONTENTS

INTRODUCTION

The conclusion of the wars of the late seventeenth century brought a threefold settlement of Europe in the early years of the eighteenth: the Treaty of Utrecht and allied treaties (1714–1715), for Western Europe; the Treaty of Nystad (1721), for Northern Europe; the Treaties of Karlowitz (1699) and Passarowitz (1718), for Southeast Europe. This rescrambling of the settlements of 1648–1659 (Westphalia and the Pyrenees) put a stamp of legality on the notable shift in the balance of power that had taken place in the intervening years through diplomacy, wars and economic expansion. By the Utrecht treaty, England increased her colonial empire at the expense of France and Spain and gained a virtual colonial supremacy over her rivals; the United Provinces, though protected against French expansion by regaining her "barrier" in the Southern Low Countries, had ceased to be a great power. By Utrecht, Austria acquired the old Spanish Netherlands in the North and former Spanish principalities in Italy, and, by Karlowitz and Passarowitz, she recovered Transylvania and Hungary and gained parts of Bosnia and Serbia from the Turks. Russia gained Azov from Turkey and by the treaty of Nystad extended her frontiers westwards at the expense of Sweden and Poland. The electorate of Brandenburg emerged as the kingdom of Prussia and added new lands in the east, and was soon to be reinforced by the conquests of Frederick the Great. Thus the significant results of these peace treaties were the emergence of Britain as the leading colonial and commercial power, with some claim to ascendancy in Europe; an extension of the power and dominions of Austria; the decline of Turkey in Europe; the eclipse of the United Provinces, Spain, and Sweden as great powers; the temporary decline of France; and the sudden appearance of Russia and Prussia as European great powers.

1. "LAW OF NATIONS" OR "REASON OF STATE"?

Could any logical system in the relations between states be deduced from this violent reshuffling of the balance of power? Did treaties and settlements mark the just balancing of the claims of the contending parties, or were they nothing but the temporary seal set on fresh conquests promoted by dynastic ambitions, economic self-interest and "reason of state"? Generally speaking, philosophical sceptics joined hands with the practical statesmen in insisting that all attempts to find an underlying "law of nations" to regulate the relations between the powers were illusory, and that the actions of governments in their external relations were prompted purely by *raison d'état* and the opportunity for expansion at the expense of weaker neighbors. "The times," wrote Voltaire, "the occasion, custom, prescription and force — it is from these alone that the rights (of nations) derive." On the other hand, there were Utopian dreamers and international jurists who believed that the relations between states were, or should be, governed by a "law of nations," deriving from "natural law."

Among the former was the versatile Abbé de Saint-Pierre, whose numerous schemes for promoting human happiness included a *Projet de paix perpétuelle* ("Plan for Permanent Peace," 1715). Among the latter, one of the most persuasive and coherent was the Swiss lawyer and diplomat, Emmerich Vattel, author of a posthumously published *Law of Nations* (1773). Vattel differed from his great seventeenth-century predecessor Grotius in maintaining that "natural law" entitled subjects to withdraw their allegiance from an oppressive sovereign; his book [1]* also had the advantage of combining the speculations of the theorist with the practical experience of the diplomat. In this respect his concern for the implications of an enlightened self-interest in the relations between nations anticipate both the efforts of the peacemakers of 1815 and the utilitarian philosophy of Jeremy Bentham.

2. MONARCHY, COURT, AND GOVERNMENT

The prevailing form of government in Europe until the French Revolution was the absolute monarchy; yet (to quote the historian Albert Sorel) "every form of government existed . . . and all were

* *Numbers in full brackets refer to the numbers of selections in the text.*

considered equally legitimate." Political theorists divided these forms into "monarchical", "aristocratic" and "democratic", but there were wide variations within each category. There were evident differences among the absolute monarchies of France, Spain, Prussia and Austria; Britain and Sweden were "limited" monarchies; Poland's monarchy was in practice what the Austrian was in theory — elective; the autocracy of Russia reproduced neither the absolute monarchy of France nor the Oriental despotism of Turkey; and the Republics of Switzerland and Venice were very differently constituted from the Republic of the United Provinces, where the rule of aristocratic "States" was sometimes absolute and sometimes tempered by the quasi-monarchy of the stadholderate. In none did "democracy" extend a voice in government to the common people, as it did in France in 1793 and in Europe, Australia and America in the nineteenth century.

From its "glorious revolution" of 1688 England had acquired a "balanced" or "mixed" Constitution. "And herein," wrote Sir William Blackstone in 1765, "consists the true excellence of the English government, that all parts of it form a mutual check upon each other. In the legislative, the people are a check upon the nobility, the nobility a check upon the people, by the mutual privilege of rejecting what the other has resolved; while the king is a check upon both, which preserves the executive power from encroachments." Yet the Constitution, consisting largely of unwritten conventions, remained fluid and the respective roles of King, Lords and Commons were not precisely determined. The king, however, remained the effective head of administration and retained considerable initiative in selecting ministers and promoting the policies of his choice. While these powers were generally recognized, opinion differed widely as to how they should be exercised. Among the more conservative of the politicians presuming to give the king advice on the matter was the former chief minister and Jacobite leader, Henry St. John, Viscount Bolingbroke. Dissatisfied with the operation of the "Whig Supremacy" under Sir Robert Walpole, Bolingbroke retired from active opposition to write *The Idea of a Patriot King* (1738). Bolingbroke's pamphlet [2a] is important both because it presents a Tory view of the constitutional role of the king and because it was widely believed (probably incorrectly) to have influenced George III's conduct of affairs in the early years of his reign.

In France the absolute monarchy, founded by Henry IV and

Cardinals Richelieu and Mazarin and consolidated by Louis XIV, lost a great deal of its vigor after the Regency and the early years of Louis XV. The king, devoted to hunting and the amorous pursuit of ladies of the court, allowed the affairs of state to drift after the death of Cardinal Fleury in 1743. Leadership of the government was disputed by rival factions, with secretaries of state, pretenders to office, princes of the blood and royal mistresses (particularly the intelligent and artistic, if not always wise Madame de Pompadour) all played their part. The Marquis d'Argenson, who served as foreign minister between November, 1744, and January, 1747, became one of the most bitter of the court's critics. The passage quoted [2b] was written a month after his fall from favor. Elsewhere, he wrote of the royal council of this time as "a republic not of citizens assembled to take counsel concerning the well-being of the state, but of heads of factions, each thinking only of his own concern, one of finance, another of the navy, another of the army, and each achieving his own ends according to his greater or lesser facility in the art of persuasion."

In Prussia, the absolute monarchy had been founded in almost self-conscious imitation of that of France, but it still retained the full vigor of its creators. The real founder of the state had been Frederick William, the Great Elector of Brandenburg; on his death in 1688, he bequeathed to his successor increased territory, a standing army of 27,000 men, a well-stocked treasury and a strong central government. His son, Frederick I, achieved his ambition of converting the electorate into the kingdom of Prussia, but otherwise he was (in the words of his grandson, Frederick the Great) "great in small things and small in great" — he spent his money on luxuries and the arts and allowed himself to be ruled by his ministers. His successor, Frederick William I — known as the "Sergeant King" — had a very different record. He reasserted the royal authority, built an efficient civil service, and greatly increased his revenues, both by his drastic pruning of expenditure on "luxuries" and his decision to combine the departments of war, finance and domains under a single board. Thus everything was geared to his objective of building one of the strongest armies in Europe. The king became his own recruiting sergeant, chose his guardsmen from men at least six feet tall, horsewhipped his troops into obedience, and left a military force of 70,000 men. His son, Frederick the Great, who had suffered from his brutalities but yet had cause to appreciate his qualities, gave a description of his father's military government in his *Memoirs of the House of Brandenburg* [2c].

Unique among the states of Europe was Poland [2d]. In name a monarchy, it was actually ruled by a sort of democracy of nobles or country gentlemen (*szlachta*). They exercised their power by controlling the Diet (legislative assembly), where their elected representatives acted as instructed by their electors and an absolute unanimity of votes (the so-called *liberum veto*) was required to make a law. The executive authority was weakened by its division between king and senate and above all because the crown was elective and the king had only meager revenues and no standing army at his disposal. The result of this system, while it safeguarded the privileges and liberties of the nobility at large, was to paralyze both legislative and executive authority and to expose Poland, at a time when her power was waning, to the predatory ambitions of more powerful states. Such occasions arose in 1733, when rival claims to the elective throne provoked the War of the Polish Succession, and again after 1772, when Austria, Russia, and Prussia resolved their differences at Poland's expense, divided her territory between them in three partitions, and effectively wiped the Polish state off the map for years to come.

In Russia, on the other hand, the absence of an hereditary aristocracy and the disappearance of the *Zomski Sobor*, the Russian representative institution, placed the Tsar on a lonely peak of absolute authority above the laws and every class of his subjects. This was true in theory; in the case of so vigorous a ruler as Peter I, theory was matched by practice. It was also true fifty years later of Catherine II. Fifteen years after she assumed power, John Williams, an English traveler in Russia, had reason to write in *The Rise, Progress and Present State of the Northern Governments*, that "the sovereign of the Russian Empire is absolute and despotic in the utmost latitude of these words and master of the lives and properties of all his subjects who, though they are the first nobility . . . , may nevertheless for the most trifling offence be seized upon and sent to Siberia . . . and have all their goods confiscated." But, mindful of the disputed succession and the weak government that had followed the death of Peter the Great, and no less of the fate of Peter II, Catherine's murdered husband, Williams wisely added "the sovereign is in many respects in a more disagreeable situation than any person in his domains . . . a bold and enterprising person who can gain over

6

a party of the guards may in two hours' time dethrone the sovereign and overturn the whole system of government." Catherine herself, while she was the most powerful ruler since Peter, was in no position to weaken the autocracy by engaging in far-reaching social and political experiments, even had she wished to do so. [2e; see also 9].

Similar problems faced the Sultan, or Grand Signior, of the Ottoman Empire, though in an acuter form. "The transmission of absolute authority displays itself in Turkey," wrote Lord Broughton in his *Travels in Albania and other Provinces of Turkey* (1809–1810), "by the total annihilation of every lower dignity in the presence of superior rank . . . The Caimacan would, in an instant, lost his supremacy before the Vizier-Azem . . . whilst that absolute prince is himself shorn of his beams, and degraded into a nonentity, by the appearance of the Sultan . . . There is one master — the rest are slaves without individual or aggregate dignity." This was true in theory and of the stronger Sultans in practice; but Turkey was also a theocratic and a military state, in which the ruler had either to impose his authority on both janissaries (army) and ulemas (priests), or face the danger of being torn forcibly from the corrupting comforts of the seraglio (harem) and flung to the wolves. Lady Mary Wortley Montagu saw this side of the problem when she wrote from Constantinople in 1717:

> The government here is entirely in the hands of the army . . . When a minister here displeases the people . . . they cut off his head, hands and feet, and throw them before the palace gate, with all the respect in the world; while that Sultan, to whom they all profess an unlimited adoration, sits trembling in his apartment, and dare neither defend nor avenge his favourite.

A few years earlier, however, Aaron Hill, another English traveler, gave a somewhat different picture of the power of the Sultan and the vast authority exercised in his name by his creature, the Grand Vizier [2f].

3. THE PEOPLE OF EUROPE

Eighteenth-century society was predominantly "aristocratic." In most countries of Europe an aristocracy of birth, wealth, or legal status lorded it over their fellowmen as governors and magistrates, feudal *seigneurs*, monopolizers of fiscal privilege and high office in army, Church, and state, or merely in their display of ostentatious living, cultural attainments, and foreign travel. "In all the states of Europe," wrote the Abbé Raynal, "there are a sort of men who assume from their infancy a pre-eminence independent of their moral character." Yet this international brotherhood differed widely in status, wealth and power from one country to another. In Western and Central Europe there were important distinctions of rank among the nobility. In Spain, the great land-owner or grandee [3b] had a very different status from that of the *hidalgo*, or impoverished country squire; in France, similarly, the court nobility looked contemptuously upon the rural *hobereaux*, while the English lower gentry were separated by a deep social gulf from the great landed magnates who held high Cabinet office, sat in the Lords and manipulated elections to the House of Commons. In Eastern Europe, on the other hand, the division of property at death and the deliberate policies of rulers prevented the emergence of a powerful hereditary aristocracy. In Poland, all members of the *szlachta* claimed social and political equality. In Russia, from Peter I's time, aristocrats claimed social status and privilege by service to the state rather than by title-deeds or the possession of great landed wealth. In Turkey this "leveling" had gone further, and the nobility had only such temporary status and authority as was conferred on its members by the Sultan.

Yet in many countries "aristocratic" society was being progressively undermined by the challenge of a merchant class, enriched by trade or moneylending and claiming social privilege by the purchase of offices or by intermarriage with the nobility. In no monarchy had this "invasion" gone so far as in England. In England alone there were no restrictions on the freedom of the aristocracy to engage in trade, and the commercial operations of aristocracy and gentry insured a higher degree of social mobility than elsewhere. By the end of the seventeenth century, it had become common for large landowners to derive considerable wealth from real estate, docks, mines, and trading investments, while merchants, grown prosperous from banking and overseas trade and with daughters married into the nobility [3e], began to lay claim to a share in their political power and social status. Similar claims would be made by manufacturers and tenant farmers after the "revolutions" in industry and agriculture a century later.

In all countries of Europe, the living conditions of the mass of the people remained — to adapt the famous phrase of Hobbes — "nasty, brutish and short." Readers of the literature, memoirs, parliamentary reports and political tracts of the period may well be astonished by the lack of genuine concern for the material welfare — as distinct from the morals or submissiveness — of the poor. The great majority worked on the land. Peasant families accounted for eight in ten of the population in France and perhaps for nine in ten in Russia. Outside Britain, the Low Countries, Switzerland, Norway and Sweden, and parts of France and Italy, the mass of the peasantry were tied to the soil and were subject to varying degrees of seignorial authority and jurisdiction. In Poland and Hungary the aristocracy enjoyed virtual power of life and death over their peasants. In East Prussia the peasant worked three days a week — sometimes even five or six — for his lord. In Russia he could be sold with his landlord's estate like a chattel and be let out for hire. In Turkey a more direct form of slavery persisted and human life was at the continual mercy of the whim of pasha and janissary [3c]. In France, although only a minority of peasants were subject to personal serfdom, manorial dues and obligations persisted until the Revolution and the majority of the rural population, whether sharecroppers (*métayers*), small proprietors or landless workers, were dependent for their survival above the lowest depth of poverty on the price of bread [3d]. Even in England, where feudalism had long since vanished and social progress and prosperity were considerably more advanced than in other monarchies, the "lower orders" of journeymen, laborers, cottagers, paupers, common seamen and vagrants — who accounted for nearly three in four of the population — lived on low wages or on public charity, fought a losing battle against high mortality and disease, were hounded by recruiting sergeant, squire, and parson, and drowned their earthly sorrows in strong drink and the exercise of brutal sports. It was not until the French Revolution that such conditions began to be the constant concern of press, governments and popular assemblies.

4. ECONOMIC CHANGES: AGRICULTURE AND INDUSTRY

The great political changes in Europe took place at the end of the eighteenth century; those in industry and agriculture, which laid the foundations of capitalist industry and large-scale farming, began much earlier. The birthplace of the so-called agrarian revolution was the Low Countries. French and English noblemen and agronomists went there at the turn of the century to learn the new methods of soil cultivation and rotation of crops to bring back to their own countries. The main problems were to improve the yield of the soil, to overcome the wastage of the old, traditional system of the open field, and to produce and feed fatter cattle and sheep. In France these problems were tackled by the combined efforts of enterprising noblemen, who developed their estates by new farming methods, Physiocrats, who believed that the soil was the source of all wealth, and the government itself, which set up a Department of Agriculture in 1761, and encouraged the formation of local societies to promote the new ideas. In England private initiative played by far the greater part. There Viscount ("Turnip") Townshend, a former secretary of state, devoted himself to cultivating hay, clover, and turnips on his Norfolk estates and bequeathed the new method of four-crop rotation known as the "Norfolk course" to his disciple, Thomas Coke of Holkam. Meanwhile Jethro Tull showed in *The Horse-Hoeing Husbandry* how seed could be sown without waste by the use of his invention, the mechanical seed-drill, and Robert Bakewell gave an impressive demonstration of how to improve the quality of sheep and cattle by selective breeding and improved use of grass crops.

Though George III himself took an active interest in these proceedings and turned them to good use on his own estates at Windsor, the British government only actively intervened in 1793 when it set up a Board of Agriculture. Its first secretary was Arthur Young, who had already won an international reputation as a propagandist of the new agriculture. He had successively toured England's Southern, Northern and Eastern counties, Ireland and France in search of new ideas and as an outlet for his own conceptions [4a]. His insistent refrain was the need to make profitable use of all available areas of cultivation and to replace such open fields as persisted by compact fields enclosed by hedges and fences. But he severely criticized the methods whereby enclosures were often carried through; and in later years he deplored some of the social consequences of the very system he had done so much to promote — the concentration of land in fewer hands and the expulsion of many small freeholders and yeomen from the soil.

While most countries in Western Europe felt the effects of these innovations in agriculture, it was only Britain that experienced a transformation on a similar scale in industry. In no other country in Europe did there exist at this stage the peculiar combination of factors that made an industrial "revolution" possible. Britain alone had the necessary technical skill and experience, capital available for investment, a large, expanding, and unfettered market, a tolerable system of communications, easy access to raw materials, and a sufficient quantity of mobile labor. Even in France, a "revolution" of this kind only came about during the next century after the social transformation accomplished by the Revolution and Napoleonic Empire.

Apart from its social consequences, which were to be realized in the future, the most significant results of the industrial revolution in England were the application of steam power to production and the gradual emergence of the factory system in the place of home industry. There were three main lines of development. One was the radical change made in textile machinery, leading to a vast expansion of the cotton industry; the main center was Manchester and its surrounding districts. Second was the improvement in the processing of iron by smelting with coke instead of charcoal. Third was the succession of improvements in the steam engine, which was used to drive textile, mining and other machinery. Though it has long been the fashion to date the industrial revolution from the accession of George III to the throne in 1760, these processes did not really get fully under way until the 1780's. It was then that the iron industry was transformed by Cort's new methods of puddling and rolling, that James Watt's steam engine began to be applied to industry, and that textile manufacturers were first able to make full use of the new "water machines" after the expiration of Richard Arkwright's restrictive patent. Thus, John Aikin was able to describe a revolution that was already in full swing when he wrote his book about Manchester [4b].

5. MERCANTILISM AND FREE TRADE

During the greater part of the eighteenth century, as in the seventeenth, the commerce of the great trading nations of Europe was regulated by the principles of mercantilism. While its operation varied from one country to another and from one century to the next, its central and common aim was as expressed by one of its earliest theorists, Thomas Mun, in 1622. "The ordinary means to increase our wealth and traesure is by *Fforraign Trade,* wherein we must ever observe this rule: to sell more to strangers yearly than we consume of theirs in value." A hundred years later, Matthew Decker wrote in his *Essay on the Causes of the Decline of Foreign Trade* (1739):

> Therefore if the Export of Britain exceed its Import, Foreigners must pay the Balance in Treasure and the Nation grow Rich; But if the Import of Britain exceed its Export we must pay the Foreigners the Balance in Treasure and the Nation grow poor.

In practice this doctrine meant that every country saw its material strength in terms of the weakness of its neighbors, that colonies were needed to promote the particular interests of the "mother" country, that a rival trading nation must be compelled if possible to import more than it exported, that it was in the interest of neither France nor Britain to have goods carried by Dutch merchant fleets, and that a favorable balance of "treasure" must be insured by its accumulation in its most convenient form, bullion.

At a time when it seemed plausible that world trade was not expandable, the mercantilist system was believed to be in the best interests of both rulers and merchants. But towards the middle of the eighteenth century its underlying assumptions came under fire from two quarters — from the growing school of *philosophes* and humanists, who believed that it was an offense against "natural law" to interfere in economic affairs, and from the growing number of "interloping" merchants, many of them in the colonies, who as late comers on the scene found the existing regulations harmful to their interests. Thus the theory of "free trade" and noninterference by governments in economic matters won advocates in France and Britain. The earliest exponent of this view in France was Boisguilbert, who wrote in the time of Louis XIV, but the most complete and consistent critic of mercantilism was the Scot, Adam Smith. His *Inquiry into the Nature and Causes of the Wealth of Nations* [5] appeared in 1776 and won an early convert in Britain's prime minister, William Pitt the Younger, himself the grandson of an "interloping" India merchant.

6. THE COLONIAL SYSTEM

Closely linked with the commercial policies of mercantilism was the old colonial system. Ever since the Portuguese Vasco da Gama sailed to India and Cortès conquered Mexico for Spain, a major purpose of European overseas expansion had been to extract trade and treasure from the new dependent territories of East and West. As trade and colonization spread European settlers found that home parliaments and governments were insisting that their produce, trade, and manufactures serve primarily the interests of the "mother" country. England's Navigation Laws were devised both to cripple the Dutch and to ensure that colonial goods carried in English or colonial ships should be landed only at such ports as Parliament determined. In 1719 the British Parliament resolved that "erecting manufactures in the colonies tended to lessen their dependence upon Great Britain," and the Molasses Act of 1733, passed at the instigation of West Indian planters, was intended to stop the export of competing French and Dutch sugar to North America. While such laws were enforced with greater or less severity according to the prevailing interest of the metropolis, they became a growing source of irritation to the colonists. The extent and effectiveness of their protests of course depended on the degree of their dependence on the mother country. In the case of the West Indies, such dependence was almost absolute [6a]. The Americans, however, felt sufficiently independent once the French had withdrawn from Canada to carry their protests against the old system to the point of separation [12].

Another aspect of the old colonial system was the direct political control exercised by the home government or parliament over the colonists. The system was by no means rigid or narrowly authoritarian. West Indian planters and New England settlers enjoyed the right to vote supplies through their colonial assemblies, yet their freedom of action was considerably reduced by the overriding powers of governors. The great turning point came with the American revolution, but even earlier the old system had been breached and new horizons in colonial administration opened up by the Quebec Act of 1774 in which Britain granted a measure of freedom to her French Canadian subjects [6b]. The original Proclamation of 1763 binding the newly conquered territory of Canada to the British crown had provided for the complete subordination of the Canadian provinces, though colonial assemblies were to be set up in the manner of New England. But the fear that the French might attempt to regain them persuaded the British government to conciliate the French Canadians by restoring French customs and civil law. This was an important precedent for the future. Though American colonists and

English radicals denounced the measure as "establishing Popery and French laws" in Canada, it served as a model for later developments in colonial self-government within the British Empire.

7. METHODISM

Though the eighteenth century has been termed with some justice an Age of Reason, it was also an age of pietism and religious revival. The paradox is not so great as it may appear. Religious skepticism and toleration were mainly the preserve of aristocratic society. In England Horace Walpole deplored "enthusiasm"; in France courtiers and government officials read Voltaire and the Encyclopedists, and "enlightened" monarchs like Frederick II and Catherine of Russia combined religious indifference with toleration in welcoming to their dominions those persecuted in other countries for their religious beliefs. Yet the mass of the people were little touched by the ideas of skeptics and rationalists. It was to these ordinary folk that the new religious sects and societies made their appeal. In France Jansenism lost its support among bishops and courtiers, but made new converts among the lower clergy and common people. Scenes of religious frenzy were enacted in 1727 by crowds which gathered at the burial of the saintly Jansenist deacon Pâris at the tomb of St. Médard. In Germany Zinzendorf founded the Moravian Brothers, and Pietists under August Francke revived Luther's earlier ideas of ecclesiastical democracy and gave the first impetus to Protestant overseas missions. Emanuel Swedenborg promoted a new apocalyptic religion which found ardent disciples. In America Jonathan Edwards revived an austere and mystical Calvinism.

No other revivalist movement made such a lasting impression as the Methodist Societies founded in England by George Whitefield and John and Charles Wesley. Even before the rise of Methodism the established Church of England had begun to mend its ways and to show a new spirit that would lead ultimately to an evangelical revival, but by and large the eighteenth century remained the age of sporting parsons and political bishops, who abhorred "enthusiasm" and were more concerned to police the poor than to offer them lively sermons or spiritual guidance. It was to the poor, particularly to the new communities of town-workers and miners, that George Whitefield and John Wesley, after his "conversion" in 1738, addressed their new "vital religion." It was among these and among a growing volume of middle-class supporters that the Wesleys built up their Methodist Societies with their distinctive organization of classes, circuits, lay preachers and ministers [7]. During more than fifty years of pastoral activity John Wesley traveled 224,000 miles through England and Wales and preached 40,000 sermons. Before he died in 1791 more than 350 Methodist chapels had been built, and the movement soon spread to America and the new Australian colonies.

8. THE ENLIGHTENMENT

In striking contrast with all forms of religious revivalism was the great intellectual movement of the age, the Enlightenment. It expressed itself in various guises — in scientific treatises, philosophical and political tracts, the social sciences, sensational psychology, and the writings of physiocrats, free-traders and "economists." But in all these guises it had a general tendency to explain the universe, nature and man in secular and rational terms, to eschew mysticism and the belief in sin, to see man with all his imperfections as susceptible of indefinite improvement, and to apply the laws of science to human psychology and society. Subtly combining rationalism with empiricism, it was militant, didactic, and widely influential.

The Enlightenment reached into all countries of Europe outside the Ottoman Empire, but its natural home was France. It was from France that sprang Montesquieu's great political treatise *The Spirit of the Laws*, the *Encyclopedia* of D'Alembert and Diderot, Rousseau's *Social Contract*, and Voltaire's histories, political satires, and correspondence. Yet England was the birthplace of these great philosophical and scientific ideas that spread all over Europe and North America from France as their main distributive center. It was from England that the first attacks on religious orthodoxy were made by the deists of the early eighteenth century, from England that John Locke's philosophy and his *Treatises on Civil Government* passed to France and inspired political theorists from Montesquieu to Rousseau.

Of equal influence was Sir Isaac Newton, the great prophet of the rational explanation of the universe. In his *Mathematical Principles on Natural Philosophy* (1687), he propounded the laws governing the motions of the earth and the heavenly bodies; in his *Optics* (1704), he developed a corpuscular theory of light in place of the prevailing wave theory, favored by Descartes. Yet the determined support of Descartes' theories by Fontenelle and the French Academy

long held up acceptance of Newtonian physics in France. None
played a greater part in breaking down this opposition than Voltaire.
During his visit to England in 1726 he became intimately acquainted
with Newton's work and extolled its merits in *Letters concerning
the English Nation* [8]. It was another twenty years before "the
mania of (gravitational) attraction" won the day in Paris, whence
it spread through Europe. It had a profound effect on the course
of the Enlightenment. The *philosophes* argued that if the mysteries
and chaos of the universe could be shown to be subject to the
harmony of natural law, so could man's social relations and political
institutions.

9. "ENLIGHTENED" DESPOTISM

Political writers, as we have seen, tended to divide governments
into "monarchical," "aristocratic" and "democratic"; they also tended
to stress the particular virtues of one or other of these elements in
the constitution according to their fancy. Montesquieu favored a
"mixed" constitution, Rousseau a "democratic," while Voltaire and
Diderot pressed the claims of "enlightened" absolute monarchy.
These writers, particularly those who favored a "monarchical" solution, had considerable influence upon the rulers of their day. Between
1740 and the French Revolution there appeared in Germany, Austria, Russia, Denmark, Spain and Portugal a generation of monarchs
and ministers who have been termed "enlightened despots"; the
historian Lord Acton called it the age of "the Repentance of Monarchy." Foremost among these rulers were Frederick the Great, King of
Prussia, Catherine II, Empress of Russia, and Joseph II, Holy Roman
Emperor. These monarchs dipped deeply into the works of the
philosophes, even emulated them in their own writings and invited
them to their courts. They had — or thought they had — the general
welfare of their subjects and of their states at heart and tried to rule
according to the best "philosophical" principles; they were tolerant
in religion and waged war on religious fanaticism within their
borders; they abolished torture, built roads and canals, and modern-
ized their governments and civil service. Yet the limitations of their
reformatory zeal are equally evident. The most genuinely "enlightened" of them all, the "crowned socialist" Joseph II of Austria,
alienated his subjects by his highhanded methods and lived to see
the destruction of most of his work. When faced with peasant revolt
led by Pugachev, Catherine turned her back on reform and earned

the name of "Great" far more for the extension of her dominions and the strengthening of the monarchy in Russia than for promoting the welfare of her people. Frederick, who called himself "the first servant of the state," is chiefly remembered for the brilliance of his campaigns and for having thrust Prussia upon Europe as a great military power.

The very term "enlightened despot" reveals the contradictory position in which these rulers found themselves. How could fundamental reforms be made without destroying the very social structure on which their "despotism" rested? The dilemma is well illustrated by Catherine's much publicized attempt to consult her subjects on needed reforms by convening a great assembly in Moscow in 1767. Her *Instructions* to her Commissioners [9] are strongly imbued with the ideas of Montesquieu and she sincerely sought the advice of Diderot on their implementation. Yet, to Diderot's chagrin, the autocracy was left untouched ("there ought to be *some to govern* and *others to obey*"), there was not a whisper of emancipation of the serfs, and the assembly yielded no practical results.

10. LITERATURE AND THE ARTS

Imaginative literature and the fine arts tended to change their form and content according to the audience to which they were addressed. As long as "aristocratic" society was everywhere well intrenched, the old art forms of classical and baroque — the latter with its subsequent variation in rococo — persisted. In architecture, it was the age of conscious imitation of the Italians and the Versailles of Louis XIV; in painting, of the dainty fantasies and elegance of Tiepolo in Italy and Watteau and Fragonard in France. In poetry, there persisted an even more wholehearted veneration for classical antiquity, as illustrated by the odes of J.-B. Rousseau in France, and Pope's literary criticism and translations from Homer in England. Yet new ideas, forms and fashions were developing almost imperceptibly in response to new tastes and new social demands. The great battle of "the ancients and the moderns" had already been engaged before the turn of the century; in France Fontenelle was a hardy champion of the "moderns." Newspapers, magazines and the new art of satire, in which Pope joined with Swift and Voltaire, were addressed to a new reading public. Above all the novel found a wider audience with its realistic portrayal of everyday life, its high moral tone and its propagation of middle-class values. Hard on the heels of the novel followed the "comedy of tears," Diderot's art criticism and Greuze's sentimental painting in France, and in England Grey's *Elegy* and Hogarth's realistic portrayal of the vices and virtues of the age. In Germany, which had little classical tradition to guide it, the explosion was more violent; the young Goethe and Schiller and other contributors to the *Sturm und Drang* ("Storm and Stress") movement in the 1760's and '70's deliberately turned their backs on the classics and took their models from the long despised Middle Ages. Indeed, in its fully developed form, the Romantic movement — already in full bloom in Germany before 1800 — was to seek its inspiration in medieval folklore, chivalry and Gothic cathedrals rather than in Homer's and Vergil's epics, Horace's odes and Grecian columns.

These developments sooner or later found expression in the literary criticism of the age. "First follow nature," enjoined Pope [10*a*] — but it was a nature "restrained" and "methodized" and seen through the eyes of the "ancients." Schlegel, though partial to the "moderns," was anxious to give both sides their due [10*b*].

II. THE PARLIAMENTARY REFORM MOVEMENT IN
    ENGLAND

The movement for parliamentary reform in England had its origins in the opposition to Sir Robert Walpole in the 1730's. It was revived in London in the '60's and only saw its aims substantially realized in the Reform Act of 1832. The British parliament of the eighteenth century, though enjoying liberties envied in other countries, was elected on a restricted franchise of privileged burgers and county freeholders. In 1780, there were only 214,000 electors in all England and Wales. Many boroughs were the property of men of wealth (the "pocket boroughs") or votes in them were easily bought and sold ("rotten boroughs"). A further grievance was that the king, or his aristocratic ministers, was able to build up majorities in parliament by bribing or intimidating the numerous "placemen" who sat in it. Finally, under the Septennial Act of 1716, Parliaments lasted for seven years without new elections.

The demands of reformers tended to be piecemeal and empirical. In Walpole's day the Septennial Act came under fire; and during a heated debate in March 1734, the opposition moved that a return be made to three-year parliaments [11*a*]. Walpole survived the attack, but the movement revived in London in 1760 with demands for shorter parliaments and "a more equal representation of the people." It received fresh impetus from the stormy career of John Wilkes [11*b*], who, on being excluded from parliament and imprisoned for publishing attacks on the king and the government, persuaded the Middlesex electors to re-elect him repeatedly in defiance of parliament's ban; he eventually took his seat in 1774 to the acclamations of a large part of the electorate. As member for Middlesex, Wilkes supported the demand of the London M.P.'s for shorter parliaments; in 1776 he broadened the attack by urging, in a memorable speech [11*c*], that not only should an end be put to "corruption" and "rotten boroughs," but that the vote should be given to "the meanest mechanic, the poorest peasant and day labourer." This oblique call for male adult suffrage was formulated more clearly a few years later by the Duke of Richmond in the Lords and by Major John Cartwright, author of the radical pamphlet *Take your Choice* and founder of the Society for Constitutional Information. After that the movement attracted both moderate reformers like Charles James Fox and Earl Grey and the radical followers of Thomas Paine, but it suffered severe repression during the wars with revolutionary France. The eventual Reform Bill of 1832 was conceived in the image of Fox and Grey rather than of Paine, and the full program of Wilkes and Cartwright was not realized until 1884.

12. THE AMERICAN REVOLUTION

Before the French Revolution the most notable breach in the European state and colonial system was made by the thirteen English colonies of North America in their declaration of independence. All the grievances there voiced by the colonists had been latent under the system that had governed their relations with the home country for the previous hundred years, but the Seven Years' War (1756–63) brought them into the open. The expulsion of the French from Canada gave the colonists a new sense of independence, while the heavy expenditure that victory had entailed led the British parliament to tighten up the restrictive economic regulations and to impose new taxes by which the colonies would contribute to the upkeep of a military establishment. One of these new measures was the Stamp Act of March 1765, which was widely resented in America as an infringement of the principle that freeborn subjects of the crown should not be taxed without the consent of their own representatives. The colonial legislatures were invited by that of Massachusetts to send delegates to a congress in New York; nine states were represented and on October 19, 1765, passed "declarations," moderate in tone but firm in the demand that the Stamp Act be repealed [12a]. They were supported by opposition groups in the British parliament and by the merchants of Bristol and London. In March 1766 a new government under the Marquess of Rockingham repealed the stamp duties, though Parliament insisted in a Declaratory Act on its sovereignty over the colonies. A change of government led to more vigorous policies: in 1767 the Townshend duties were imposed to raise revenue by the direct taxation of glass, paper and tea. After the New England merchants had declared an embargo on British imports, the new duties (excepting those on tea) were withdrawn by the North government in 1770.

Meanwhile Boston had become the center of a popular radical movement in New England. When troops sent there in 1768 to restore order fired on a riotous crowd, the resulting "massacre" deeply stirred patriotic feelings and made reconciliation more difficult. Yet it was not until after North's Tea Act, the Boston "Tea Party" of 1773 and the retaliation that followed in the "Intolerable Acts" of 1774 that decisive steps were taken which led to the eventual breach. The most significant and far-reaching of these was the summoning of a continental congress. The First Congress met at Philadelphia in September 1774, attended by delegates from all the colonies except Georgia. It proved a battleground between the popular leaders, who were beginning to look to a republican solution, and conservative groups, whose chief concern was to prevent a popular revolution. The outcome was in the main a victory for the popular party — a proposed "plan of union" was decisively rejected; a general embargo was declared on all trade with Britain and the West Indies; and Congress adopted a militant Declaration of Rights. Local committees set up to implement these decisions soon fell into the hands of the popular party and by April 1775, Congress resolved to establish an army for its defense. In England, too, despite conciliatory gestures, war now seemed inevitable. But even after the first fighting at Lexington and Concord (April 1775), some months passed before the growing demand to break off all relations with Britain was debated in Congress. The main motion in favor of independence came from

Virginia, and Thomas Jefferson's notes on the debates that followed show the division of opinion and the opposition that was still voiced, in June 1776, by conservative leaders and the delegates of the "middle" colonies of Pennsylvania, Maryland and others [12*b*]. Among the most forceful and consistent opponents of an immediate declaration of independence was John Dickinson of Pennsylvania [12*c*]. But by early July these differences had been largely resolved, and the Declaration of Independence of July 4 received the assent of the delegates of all thirteen colonies [12*d*].

13. THE FRENCH REVOLUTION

The French Revolution was one of the great cataclysmic events of history. Within ten years it completely changed the social and political order of the France of the old regime, and its impact reached far into Europe. The feudal order in France, though greatly modified under the great cardinal-ministers and Louis XIV, remained basically in being until 1789. In fact, since Louis' time, a "feudal reaction" had extended the privileges of the higher clergy and nobility. The main achievement of the Revolution was to destroy this order lock, stock and barrel; it did so more quickly than had ever been done elsewhere before. The Declaration of the Rights of Man adopted by the National Assembly on August 27, 1789 [13*b*] already laid down the principles of equality before the law, equal taxation and equal eligibility to public office. A great program of legislation followed, much of which was incorporated in the Constitution of 1791. By this time the old feudal system of justice had been swept away, the army had been "purged" and reformed, the lands of the Church had been declared national property and put up for auction; local government had been recast, and titles of nobility, venal offices, feudal guilds and internal tolls and customs barriers had been done away with. Most spectacular of all was the declaration of August 4, 1789, which voted away a great part of the feudal land system; this measure was completed by the Jacobin Convention in July 1793 when it declared the peasants' redemptive debts null and void.

Other far-reaching legislation such as the declaration of the Republic and the institution of male adult suffrage followed later, but the mass of the permanently significant legislative work of the Revolution was completed in these early years. It bore in both its triumphs and its limitations the distinctive imprint of the *bourgeoisie* and the liberal aristocracy that enacted it. Yet the Revolution moved progressively leftwards for the next four years: the constitutional monarchists of 1789–91 gave way to the Girondins and they in turn to the Jacobin Convention and the Committee of Public Safety. This was due in part to the intrusion of such external factors as the war with Europe; but even more it was due to the active intervention of the non-propertied or small-propertied classes, the peasants and urban *sans-culottes* — the craftsmen, shopkeepers, small workshop masters and journeymen, who were most heavily concentrated and most strongly organized in Paris. Their intervention changed the whole course of the Revolution and in important respects influenced its final outcome. The dual nature of the Revolution — both *bourgeois* and *sans-culotte* — that was one of the results of this intervention already appeared in the more or less spontaneous movements that shook Paris and the provinces in the summer and autumn of 1789; it was strikingly evident, for example, in the march of the women to Versailles in October, which had the twofold object of getting food for their families and bringing the king to the capital [13*a*]. As the *sans-culottes* became organized in clubs and sectional assemblies, their pressure became more insistent. The Jacobin Constitution of 1793 was accompanied by a new Declaration of Rights [13*c*], which made some concessions to the *sans-culottes* by extending the boundaries of both political and *social* democracy beyond those conceived in that of 1789. (Robespierre's proposed Declaration of April 23, 1793, which was not adopted, went considerably further in this direction.) Again it was the Paris *sans-culottes* who a few months later compelled the reluctant Jacobins to impose controls on the price and supply of food and raw materials (the Law of the Maximum). Outside Paris their influence is evident in the "instructions" of the "temporary commission" set up to restore revolutionary authority in Lyons after its rebellion had been crushed in the autumn of 1793 [13*d*]. While a great deal of this influence was short-lived and became negligible after the fall of Robespierre, it had far-reaching consequences for the future and gave the French Revolution its own peculiar stamp.

14. THE DEBATE ON THE FRENCH REVOLUTION

The ideas of the Revolution spread to other countries in Europe and in many exerted a profound influence. England was notable among the countries in which the Revolution was hotly debated and which saw the emergence of two distinctive parties of supporters and opponents. The outbreak of revolution in France was at first welcomed by all classes; by some, because it seemed the dawn of a new age, by others, because they hoped that revolution and anarchy would weaken a traditional enemy. This general consensus was disturbed by the appearance in 1790 of Edmund Burke's *Reflections on the Revolution in France* [14a], in which the author castigated the Revolution and all its works and warned his readers of the contagion that might spread from France to other countries. The occasion for the onslaught was the claim made a few months earlier by Dr. Richard Price in a sermon preached at the Old Jewry in London that the French in their revolution were merely carrying on the traditions and principles of England's "glorious revolution" of 1688–89. Burke argued in reply that the English revolution, far from attempting a general transformation of society, had patched up the existing constitution and strengthened the relations of church and state and the rights of property. The French, on the other hand, by proclaiming "the rights of man," were proposing to tear down the social fabric and to leap blindly along a path of total renovation. "It is with infinite caution," he asserted, "that any man ought to venture upon pulling down an edifice, which has answered in any tolerable degree for ages the common purposes of society."

Burke's attack provoked spirited replies from radicals, Dissenters and parliamentary reformers. The most vigorous came from Thomas Paine in *The Rights of Man* [14b]. To Burke's apology for the French court and clergy, Paine retorted: "He pities the plumage, but forgets the dying bird." Striking at the core of his opponent's argument, he claimed that "the vanity and presumption of governing beyond the grave is the most ridiculous and insolent of tyrannies" and that "that which may be thought convenient in one age may be thought wrong and found inconvenient in another."

The debate thus opened was to have great and distant consequences. In the first place, it divided England on the immediate question of the attitude to be adopted to the revolution in France. Events soon favored Burke as the progress of the Revolution estranged the propertied classes and much of liberal opinion in England, and as the growing conflict of interest between the two countries led to the outbreak of war in February 1793. Charles James Fox and the shrinking Whig opposition continued to defend the Revolution, but Pitt made the war a pretext for silencing and persecuting both parliamentary reformers and sympathizers with revolutionary France. Yet in the long run Paine's writings and French ideas gave a fresh stimulus to the reform movement in England by bringing its discussion back to "first principles." In a wider sense still, Burke's restatement of Tory principles on progress and revolution in the *Reflections* profoundly influenced the development of conservative political thinking, while Paine's writings, which were eagerly read by reformers and by London craftsmen and the new factory workers of the North, played their part in shaping the direction of the radical movement of the nineteenth century.

15. NAPOLEON

Napoleon Bonaparte both crowned and consolidated the work of the Revolution, and he renounced it. In his own words spoken in exile at St. Helena: "I closed the gulf of anarchy and cleared away the chaos. I purified the Revolution, dignified Nations and established Kings." As the young commander-in-chief of the Army of Italy in 1796–7 [15*a*], he overthrew feudal governments, closed the ghettoes of Venice and Rome, promoted republicans and liberals to office, and imposed by force of arms the ideas, laws and constitutions of France on the conquered and liberated peoples. As Emperor, he hacked through the ancient tangle of feudatories and princes in Germany and created in their place a Confederation of thirty-nine states governed by French laws, which became the nucleus of the future united Germany. In France he maintained the land settlement of the Revolution, refusing to restore the estates either of the nobles or of the Church to their old owners; he erected his code of civil laws (the Code Napoléon) on foundations already firmly laid by the National Convention, and created his new institutions of both central and local government from the "representatives on mission," the communes and the departments of the Revolution.

At the same time his first act as consul after his *coup d'état* of the eighteenth Brumaire (November 1799) was to proclaim that "the Revolution . . . is ended." Under his military dictatorship there was little room for the "liberties" of 1789, still less for those of the Jacobin Republic of the Year II. His generals and marshals and men enriched by the purchase of "national property" and by military contracts under the Convention and Directory emerged as the new aristocracy of the Napoleonic Empire. But Napoleon had from beginning to end a profound contempt for the opinions and aspirations of the common order of men. The great administrative and legislative achievement of the Consulate and Empire bears the unmistakable stamp of his passion for order and authority. He not only directed policy but gave painstaking attention to the details of new civil codes, local government and higher education [15*b*]. In Europe his despotic rule roused against him the very nationalism which his own armies had in earlier years done so much to promote and stimulate.

Defeated at Waterloo and exiled to St. Helena, Napoleon was anxious to justify his conduct before world opinion. In his soliloquies and discussions with the Count de Las Cases and other devoted supporters [15*c*], he presented himself not only as a lover of order and authority, but as a great peacemaker and a prophet of European nationalism and union. This image of the Emperor passed into the "Napoleonic legend" of the nineteenth century and profoundly influenced the ideas and political career of his nephew, the future Napoleon III.

16. THE SETTLEMENT OF EUROPE

The new territorial settlement of Europe was made by the coalition of powers that had been formed in 1813 to defeat Napoleon and destroy the French domination of the continent. Though commonly associated only with the Congress of Vienna of 1815, it was the result of a number of treaties, reflecting the successive and conflicting hopes and aims of the victor powers. The Treaty of Chaumont signed in March 1814 followed Napoleon's defeat at Leipzig and his retreat to France; it bound the signatories — Austria, Prussia, Russia and the United Kingdom — to overthrow Napoleon and to remain in alliance for twenty years. When Napoleon abdicated a month later, it was agreed by the first Treaty of Paris (May 30, 1814) that France's boundaries should be fixed at those of 1792, that is, that she should give up Belgium and the left bank of the Rhine; but she was not to be disarmed or occupied or made to pay any reparations. It was already conceded that France, having once more become a legitimate monarchy, with Louis XVIII as king and the archtrimmer Talleyrand as foreign minister, should be represented at subsequent congresses to negotiate a more general settlement. Such plans were delayed by Napoleon's surprise return to

France from his first exile in Elba and the new military measures called for on the part of his opponents. But even before their final victory at Waterloo the five powers decided by the Treaty of Vienna of June 9, 1815 [16] on the main lines of the territorial resettlement of Europe; these were supplemented after Waterloo and Napoleon's dispatch to St. Helena by the second Treaty of Paris (November 20, 1815), which pushed France's frontiers back to where they had been in 1790 and subjected her to a three-year military occupation and to the payment of a large indemnity.

The purposes of the new settlement were to reward the victors and to punish and restrain the aggressors, to restore the old legitimist Europe that had been torn and toppled by the years of revolution, to re-establish something like the old balance of power, and by implication to hold in check the rising and dangerous forces of nationalism and democracy. It joined the former Austrian Netherlands (the later Belgium) and the duchy of Luxembourg with the kingdom of Holland to form a single buffer state against France in the North; gave the Rhineland to Prussia; created a confederation of thirty-nine states in Germany under the presidency of Austria; restored Lombardy to Austria and gave her Venetia and the over-lordship of Parma, Modena and Tuscany; while the Spanish Bourbons were restored to Naples and the Pope to his Papal States. Meanwhile the Duchy of Warsaw was returned to Russia; Norway was transferred from Denmark to Sweden and Finland from Sweden to Russia; and Great Britain gained a number of additional colonies from Holland and France and persuaded her allies to abolish the slave trade.

But the peacemakers of 1815, while concerned to restore the past, also looked to the future. By their Quadruple Alliance of November 1815 they bound themselves to a twenty-year agreement termed "the Concert of Europe," whereby they would hold periodic meetings "for the purpose of consulting upon their common interest and for the consideration of the measures most salutary for the maintenance of the peace of Europe." Thus, alongside their reactionary aims and undertakings — the "Holy Alliance" of Christian rulers and their short-lived attempt to reverse the course of historical progress — the Vienna signatories also bequeathed to coming centuries the germs of a new conception—that of a community of nations empowered to settle disputes without resort to war.

1

The Law of Nations

EMMERICH VATTEL (1714–67) was a Swiss lawyer, diplomat, and philosophe of the Enlightenment. His treatise The Law of Nations, or Principles of the Law of Nature, applied to the Conduct of the Affairs of Nations and Sovereigns, was written in French and was printed posthumously at Neufchâtel in 1773.

Emmerich Vattel on the Law of Nations (1773)

WE CALL THAT the *Necessary law of Nations* which consists in the application of the law of nature to *Nations*. It is *Necessary* because nations are *absolutely* bound to observe it. This law contains the precepts prescribed by the *law of nature* to *States*, on whom that law is not less obligatory than on individuals, since states are composed of men, their resolutions are taken by men, and the law of nature is binding on all men, under whatever relation they act. This is the law which Grotius, and those who follow him, call the *Internal law of Nations*, on account of its being obligatory on nations in point of *conscience*. Several writers term it the *Natural law of Nations*.

Since therefore the necessary law of nations consists in the application of the law of nature to states, — which law is immutable, as being founded on the nature of things, and particularly on the nature of man, — it follows, that the *Necessary* law of nations is *immutable*.

Whence, as this law is immutable, and the obligations that arise from it necessary and indispensable, nations can neither make any changes in it by their conventions, dispense with it in their own conduct, nor reciprocally release each other from the observance of it.

This is the principle by which we may distinguish *lawful* conventions or treaties from those that are not lawful, and innocent and rational customs from those that are unjust or censurable.

From Emmerich Vattel, THE LAW OF NATIONS, Joseph Chitty (ed.) (London, 1834), "Preliminaries," pp. lviii–lxvi.

There are things, *just in themselves,* and allowed by the necessary law of nations, on which states may mutually agree with each other, and which they may consecrate and enforce by their manners and customs. There are others of an *indifferent nature,* respecting which, it rests at the option of nations to make in their treaties whatever agreements they please, or to introduce whatever custom or practice they think proper. But every treaty, every custom, which contravenes the injunctions or prohibitions of the *Necessary* law of nations, is unlawful. It will appear, however, in the sequel, that it is only by the *Internal* law, by the law of *Conscience,* such conventions or treaties are always condemned as unlawful, and that, for reasons which shall be given in their proper place, they are nevertheless often valid by the external law. Nations being free and independent, though the conduct of one of them be illegal and condemnable by the laws of conscience, the others are bound to acquiesce in it, when it does not infringe upon *their* perfect rights. The liberty of that nation would not remain entire, if the others were to arrogate to themselves the right of inspecting and regulating *her* actions; an assumption on their part, that would be contrary to the law of nature, which declares every nation free and independent of all the others.

Man is so formed by nature, that he cannot supply all his own wants, but necessarily stands in need of the intercourse and assistance of his fellow-creatures, whether for his immediate preservation, or for the sake of perfecting his nature, and enjoying such a life as is suitable to a rational being. This is sufficiently proved by experience. We have instances of persons, who, having grown up to manhood among the bears of the forest, enjoyed not the use of speech or of reason, but were, like the brute beasts, possessed only of sensitive faculties. We see moreover that nature has refused to bestow on men the same strength and natural weapons of defence with which she has furnished other animals — having, in lieu of those advantages, endowed mankind with the faculties of speech and reason, or at least a capability of acquiring them by an intercourse with their fellow-creatures. Speech enables them to communicate with each other, to give each other mutual assistance, to perfect their reason and knowledge; and having thus become intelligent, they find a thousand methods of preserving themselves, and supplying their wants. Each individual, moreover, is intimately conscious that he can neither live happily nor improve his nature without the intercourse and assistance of others. Since, therefore, nature has thus formed mankind, it is a convincing proof of her intention that they should communicate with, and mutually aid and assist each other.

Hence is deduced the establishment of natural society among men. *The general law of that society is, that each individual should do for the others every thing which their necessities require, and which he can perform without neglecting the duty that he owes to himself:* a law which all men must observe in order to live in a manner consonant to their nature, and conformable to the views of their common creator, — a law which our own safety, our happiness, our dearest interests, ought to render sacred to every one of us. Such is the general obligation that binds us to the observance of our duties: let us fulfil them with care, if we would wisely endeavour to promote our own advantage.

It is easy to conceive what exalted felicity the world would enjoy, were all men willing to observe the rule that we have just laid down. On the contrary, if each man wholly and immediately directs all his thoughts to his own *interest,* if he does nothing for the sake of other men, the whole human race together will be immersed in the deepest wretchedness. Let us therefore endeavour to promote the general happiness of mankind: all mankind, in return, will endeavour to promote ours, and thus we shall establish our felicity on the most solid foundations.

The *universal society* of the human race being an institution of nature herself, that is to say, a necessary consequence of the nature of man, — all men, in whatever stations they are placed, *are bound to cultivate it, and to discharge its duties.* They cannot liberate themselves from the obligation by any convention, by any private association. When, therefore, they unite in civil society for the purpose of forming a separate state or nation, they may indeed enter into particular engagements towards those with whom they associate themselves; but they remain still bound to the performance of *their duties towards the rest of mankind.* All the difference consists in this, that having agreed to act in common, and having resigned their rights and submitted their will to the body of the society, in every thing that concerns their common welfare, it thenceforward belongs to that body, that state, and its rulers, to fulfil the duties of humanity towards strangers, in every thing that no longer depends on the liberty of individuals; and it is the state more particularly that is to perform those duties towards other states. We have already seen, that men united in society remain subject to the obligations imposed upon them by human nature. That society, considered as a moral person, since possessed of an understanding, volition, and strength peculiar to itself, *is therefore obliged to live on the same terms with other societies or states, as individual man was obliged, before those establishments, to live with other men,* that is to say, according to the laws of the natural society established among the human race, with the difference only of such exceptions as may arise from the different nature of the subjects.

Since the object of the natural society established between all mankind is — that they should lend each other mutual assistance, in order to attain perfection themselves, and to render their condition as perfect as possible, — and since nations, considered as so many free persons living together in a state of nature, are bound to cultivate human society with each other, — the object of the great society established by nature *between all nations* is also the interchange of *mutual assistance* for their own improvement and that of their condition.

The first general law that we discover in the very object of the society of nations, is that *each individual nation is bound to contribute every thing in her power to the happiness and perfection of all the others.*

But the duties that we owe to ourselves being unquestionably paramount to those we owe to others, — a nation owes herself in the first instance, and in preference to all other nations, to do every thing she can to promote her own happiness and perfection. (I say, every thing she *can,* not only in a *physical* but in a *moral* sense, — that is, every thing that she can do *lawfully, and consistently with justice and honour*). When, therefore, she cannot contribute to the welfare of another nation without doing an essential injury to herself, her obligation ceases on that particular occasion, and she is considered as lying under a disability to perform the office in question.

Nations being free and independent of each other, in the same manner as men are naturally free and independent, the *second* general law of their society is, *that each nation should be left in the peaceable enjoyment of that liberty which she inherits from nature.* The natural society of nations cannot subsist, unless the natural rights of each be duly respected. No nation is willing to renounce her liberty; she will rather break off all commerce with those states that should attempt to infringe upon it.

As a consequence of that liberty and independence, it exclusively belongs to each nation to form her own judgment of what her conscience prescribes to her, — of what she can or cannot do, — of what it is proper or improper for her to do: and of course it rests solely with her to examine and determine *whether she can perform any office for another nation without neglecting the duty which she owes to herself.* In all cases, therefore, in which a nation has the *right* of judging what her duty requires, no other nation can compel her to act in such or such particular manner: for any attempt at such compulsion would be an infringement on the liberty of nations. We have no right to use constraint against a free person except in those cases where such person is *bound to perform* some particular thing for us, and for some particular reason which does not depend on his judgment, — in those cases, in short, where we have a *perfect* right against him.

In order perfectly to understand this, it is necessary to observe, that the obligation, and the right which corresponds to or is derived from it, are distinguished into *external* and *internal*. The obligation is *internal,* as it binds the *conscience,* and is deduced from the rules of our duty: it is *external,* as it is considered relatively to other men, and produces some right between them. The internal obligation is always the same in its nature, though it varies in degree; but the external obligation is divided into *perfect* and *imperfect*; and the right that results from it is also *perfect* or *imperfect*. The *perfect right* is that which is accompanied by the *right of compelling* those who refuse to fulfil the correspondent obligation; the *imperfect* right is unaccompanied by that right of compulsion. The *perfect obligation* is that which gives to the opposite party the *right of compulsion*; the *imperfect* gives him only a right *to ask*.

It is now easy to conceive why the right is always imperfect, when the correspondent obligation depends on the judgment of the party in whose breast it exists; for if, in such a case, we had a right to compel him, he would no longer enjoy the freedom of determination respecting the conduct he is to pursue in order to obey the dictates of his own conscience. Our obligation is always imperfect with respect to other people, while we possess the liberty of judging how we are to act: and we retain that liberty on all occasions where we ought to be free.

Since men are naturally equal, and a perfect equality prevails in their rights and obligations, as equally proceeding from nature —

Nations composed of men, and considered as so many free persons living together in the state of nature, are naturally equal, and inherit from nature the same obligations and rights. Power or weakness does not in this respect produce any difference. A dwarf is as much a man as a giant; a small republic is no less a sovereign state than the most powerful kingdom.

By a necessary consequence of that equality, whatever is lawful for one nation, is equally lawful for any other; and whatever is unjustifiable in the one, is equally so in the other.

A nation then is mistress of her own actions so long as they do not affect the proper and perfect rights of any other nation — so long as she is only *internally* bound, and does not lie under any *external* and *perfect* obligation. If she makes an ill use of her liberty, she is guilty of a breach of duty; but other nations are bound to acquiesce in her conduct, since they have no right to dictate to her.

Since nations are *free, independent,* and *equal* — and since each possesses *the right of judging,* according to the dictates of her conscience, what conduct she is to pursue in order to fulfil her duties; the effect of the whole is, to produce, at least externally and in the eyes of mankind, a perfect equality of rights between nations, in the administration of their affairs and the pursuit of their pretensions, without regard to the intrinsic justice of their conduct, of which others have no right to form a definitive judgment; so that whatever may be done by any one nation, may be done by any other; and they ought, in human society, to be considered as possessing equal rights.

Each nation in fact maintains that she has justice on her side in every dispute that happens to arise; and it does not belong to either of the parties interested, or to other nations, to pronounce a judgment on the contested question. The party who is in the wrong is guilty of a crime against her own *conscience*; but as there exists a possibility that she may perhaps have justice on her side, we cannot accuse her of violating the laws of society.

It is therefore necessary, on many occasions, that nations should suffer certain things to be done, though in their own nature unjust and condemnable; because they cannot oppose them by open force, without violating the liberty of some particular state, and destroying the foundations of their natural society. And since they are bound to cultivate that society, it is of course presumed that all nations have consented to the principle we have just established. The rules that are deduced from it, constitute what Monsieur Wolf calls *"the volun-*

tary law of nations;" and there is no reason why we should not use the same term, although we thought it necessary to deviate from that great man in our manner of establishing the foundation of that law.

The laws of natural society are of such importance to the safety of all states, that, if the custom once prevailed of trampling them under foot, no nation could flatter herself with the hope of preserving her national existence, and enjoying domestic tranquillity, however attentive to pursue every measure dictated by the most consummate prudence, justice, and moderation. Now all men and all states have a perfect right to those things that are necessary for their preservation, since that right corresponds to an indispensable obligation. All nations have therefore a right to resort to forcible means for the purpose of repressing any one particular nation who openly violates the laws of the society which Nature has established between them, or who directly attacks the welfare and safety of that society.

But care must be taken not to extend that right to the prejudice of the liberty of nations. They are all free and independent, but bound to observe the laws of that society which Nature has established between them; and so far bound, that, when any of them violates those laws, the others have a right to repress her. The conduct of each nation, therefore, is no farther subject to the control of the others, than as the interests of natural society are concerned. The general and common right of nations over the conduct of any sovereign state is only commensurate to the object of that society which exists between them.

The several *engagements* into which nations may enter, produce a new kind of law of nations, called *Conventional*, or *of Treaties.* As it is evident that a *treaty* binds none but the contracting parties, the conventional law of nations is not a universal but a particular law. All that can be done on this subject in a treatise on the Law of *Nations,* is to lay down those general rules which nations are bound to observe with respect to their *treaties.* A minute detail of the various agreements made between particular nations; and of the rights and obligations thence resulting, is matter of fact, and belongs to the province of history.

Certain maxims and *customs,* consecrated by long use, and observed by nations in their mutual intercourse with each other as a kind of law, form the *Customary Law of Nations,* or the *Custom of Nations.* This law is founded on a *tacit* consent, or, if you please, on a tacit convention of the nations that observe it towards each other.

Whence it appears that it is not obligatory except on those nations who have adopted it, and that it is not universal, any more than the *conventional law.* The same remark, therefore, is equally applicable to this *customary law,* viz. that a minute detail of its particulars does not belong to a systematic treatise on the law of nations, but that we must content ourselves with giving a general theory of it; that is to say, the rules which are to be observed in it, as well with a view to its effects, as to its substance: and with respect to the latter, those rules will serve to distinguish lawful and innocent customs from those that are unjust and unlawful.

When a custom or usage is *generally* established, either between all the civilized nations in the world, or only between those of a certain continent, as of Europe, for example, or between those who have a more frequent intercourse with each other; if that custom is in its own nature indifferent, and much more, if it be useful and reasonable, it becomes obligatory on all the nations in question, who are considered as having given their consent to it, and are bound to observe it towards each other, as *long as they have not expressly* declared their resolution of not observing it in future. But if that custom contains any thing unjust or unlawful, it is not obligatory; on the contrary, every nation is bound to relinquish it, since nothing can oblige or authorize her to violate the law of nature.

These *three* kinds of law of nations, the *Voluntary,* the *Conventional,* and the *Customary,* together constitute the *Positive Law of Nations.* For they all proceed from the will of Nations; the *Voluntary* from their *presumed* consent, the *Conventional* from an *express* consent, and the *Customary* from *tacit* consent; and as there can be no other mode of deducing any law from the will of nations, there are only these three kinds of *Positive Law of Nations.*

We shall be careful to distinguish them from the *Natural* or *Necessary* law of nations, without, however, treating of them separately. But after having, under each individual head of our subject, established what the *necessary* law prescribes, we shall immediately add how and why the decisions of that law must be modified by the *Voluntary* law; or (which amounts to the same thing in other terms) we shall explain how, in consequence of the liberty of nations, and pursuant to the *rules* of their natural society, the *external* law which they are to observe towards each other, differs in certain instances from the maxims of the *Internal* law, which nevertheless remains always obligatory in point of conscience. As to the rights introduced by *Treaties* or by *Custom,* there is no room to apprehend that any one will confound them with the *Natural* law of nations. They form that species of law of nations which authors have distinguished by the name of *Arbitrary.*

To furnish the reader beforehand with a general direction respecting the distinction between the *Necessary* and the *Voluntary* law, let us here observe, that, as the *Necessary* law is always obligatory on the *conscience,* a nation ought never to lose sight of it in deliberating on the line of conduct she is to pursue in order to fulfil her duty; but when there is question of examining what she may demand of other states, she must consult the *Voluntary* law, whose maxims are devoted to the safety and advantage of the universal society of mankind.

2

Monarchy, Court, and Government

BOLINGBROKE (1678–1751), former Chief Minister under Queen Anne, had joined James Stuart, the "Old Pretender," in exile in 1715. Returning to England in 1722, he played a leading part in the parliamentary opposition to Sir Robert Walpole. After numerous defeats, he retired from active politics in 1736 to write his treatise The Idea of a Patriot King, the first edition of which appeared in 1738.

René-Louis, Marquis d'Argenson (1694–1757) was Foreign Minister under Louis XV from November 1744 to January 1747. The passage quoted from his journal was written a month after his dismissal from office.

Rousseau was among the French political theorists to whom members of the Polish Diet turned, shortly before the First Partition, to advise them on the best form of constitution for their country; he completed the work in April 1772.

William Richardson, whose Anecdotes were published in the form of letters, wrote his pen portrait of the Empress Catherine II while serving as secretary to the British Ambassador in St. Petersburg in 1768–72. He later became professor of Humanity at the University of Glasgow and a scholar of slavery.

The picture of the Ottoman Empire given by Hill does not entirely accord with that given a few years later by Lady Mary Wortley Montagu [3b], with which it might profitably be compared.

a Bolingbroke on the "Patriot King" (1738)

❧ TO ESPOUSE no party, but to govern like the common father of his people, is so essential to the character of a Patriot King, that he who does otherwise forfeits the title. It is the peculiar privilege and glory of this character, that princes who maintain it, and they alone, are so far from the necessity, that they are not exposed to the temptation, of *governing by a party*: which must always end in the government of a *faction*: the faction of the *prince*, if he has abil-

From Henry St. John, Viscount Bolingbroke, THE IDEA OF A PATRIOT KING (London, 1752), pp. 162–172.

ity; the faction of his *ministers,* if he has not; and, either one way or other, in the oppression of the people. For *faction* is to *party* what the *superlative* is to the *positive*: *party* is a political evil, and *faction* is the *worst* of all *parties.* The true image of a free people, governed by a Patriot King, is that of a patriarchal family, where the head and all the members are united by one common interest, and animated by one common spirit: and where, if any are perverse enough to have another, they will be soon borne down by the superiority of those who have the same; and, far from making a *division,* they will but confirm the *union* of the little state. That to approach as near as possible to these ideas of perfect government, and social happiness under it, is desirable in every state, no man will be absurd enough to deny. The sole question is, therefore, how near to them it is possible to attain? For, if this attempt be not absolutely impracticable, all the views of a Patriot King will be directed to make it succeed. Instead of abetting the divisions of his people, he will endeavour to unite them, and to be himself the centre of their union: instead of putting himself at the head of *one party* in order to govern *his people,* he will put himself at the head of *his people* in order to govern, or more properly to subdue, *all parties.* Now, to arrive at this desirable union, and to maintain it, will be found more difficult in some cases than in others, but absolutely impossible in none, to a wise and good prince.

If his people are *united* in their submission to him, and in their attachment to the established government, he must not only *espouse* but *create* a party, in order to govern by *one*: and what should tempt him to pursue so wild a measure? A prince, who aims at more power than the constitution gives him, may be so tempted; because he may hope to obtain in the disorders of the state what cannot be obtained in quiet times; and because contending parties will give what a nation will not. Parties, even before they degenerate into absolute factions, are still numbers of men associated together for certain purposes, and certain interests, which are not, or which are not allowed to be, those of the community by others. A more private or personal interest comes but too soon, and too often, to be superadded, and to grow predominant in them: and when it does so, whatever occasions or principles began to form them, the same logic prevails in them that prevails in every church. The interest of the state is supposed to be that of the party, as the interest of religion is supposed to be that of the church: and, with this pretence or prepossession, the interest of the state becomes, like that of religion, a remote consideration, is never pursued for it's own sake, and is often sacrificed to the other. A king, therefore, who has ill designs to carry on, must endeavour to divide an united people; and by blending or seeming to blend his interests with that of a party, he may succeed perhaps, and his party and he may share the spoils of a ruined nation: but such a party is then become a faction, such a king is a tyrant, and such a government is a conspiracy. A Patriot King must renounce his character, to have such designs; or act against his own designs, to pursue such methods. Both are too absurd to be supposed. It remains, therefore, that as all the good ends of government are most attainable in an united state, and as the divisions of a people can serve to bad purposes alone, the king we suppose here will deem the union of his subjects his greatest advantage, and will think himself happy to find that established, which he would have employed the whole labor of his life to bring about. This seems so plain, that I am ready to make excuses for having insisted at all upon it.

Let us turn ourselves to another supposition, to that of a *divided state*. This will fall in oftener with the ordinary course of things in free governments, and especially after iniquitous and weak administrations. Such a state may be better or worse, and the great and good purposes of a Patriot King more or less attainable in it, according to the different nature of those *divisions*: and, therefore, we will consider this state in different lights.

A people may be *united* in submission to the prince, and to the establishment, and yet be *divided* about *general principles,* or *particular measures* of government. In the first case, they will do by their constitution what has been frequently done by the Scripture, strain it to their own notions and prejudices; and, if they cannot strain it, alter it as much as is necessary to render it conformable to them. In the second, they will support or oppose particular acts of administrations, and defend or attack the persons employed in them: and both these ways a conflict of parties may arise, but no great difficulty to a prince who determines to pursue the union of his subjects, and the prosperity of his kingdoms independently of all parties.

When parties are divided by different notions and principles concerning some particular ecclesiastical or civil institutions, the constitution, which should be *their* rule, must be that of the prince. He may and he ought to shew his dislike or his favor, as he judges the constitution may be hurt or improved, by one side or the other. The

hurt he is never to suffer, not for his own sake; and therefore surely
not for the sake of any whimsical, factious, or ambitious set of men.
The improvement he must always desire; but as every new modifica-
tion in a scheme of government and of national policy is of great
importance, and requires more and deeper consideration than the
warmth, and hurry, and rashness of party-conduct admit, the duty of
a prince seems to require that he should render by his influence the
proceedings more *orderly* and more *deliberate,* even when he ap-
proves the end to which they are directed. All this may be done by
him without fomenting division; and, far from forming or espousing
a party, he will defeat party in defence of the constitution, on some
occasions; and lead men, from acting with a party-spirit, to act with
a national spirit, on others.

When the division is about *particular measures* of government,
and the conduct of the administration is alone concerned, a Patriot
King will stand in want of party as little as in any other case. Under
his reign, the opportunities of forming an opposition of this sort will
be rare, and the pretences generally weak. Nay, the motives to it will
lose much of their force, when a government is strong in reputation,
and men are kept in good humor by feeling the rod of a party on no
occasion, tho they feel the weight of the sceptre on some. Such opportunities, however, may happen; and there may be reason, as well
as pretences, sometimes for opposition even in such a reign: at least
we will suppose so, that we may include in this argument every
contingent case. Grievances then are complained of, mistakes and
abuses in government are pointed out, and ministers are prosecuted
by their enemies. Shall the prince on the throne form a party by
intrigue, and by secret and corrupt influence, to oppose the prosecution? When the prince and the ministers are *participes criminis,*
when every thing is to be defended, lest something should come out,
that may unravel the silly wicked scheme, and disclose to public
sight the whole turpitude of the administration; there is no help, this
must be done, and such a party must be formed, because such a party
alone will submit to a drudgery of this kind. But a prince, who is
not in these circumstances, will not have recourse to these means. He
has others more open, more noble, and more effectual in his power:
he knows that the views of his government are right, and that the
tenor of his administration is good; but he knows that neither he nor
his ministers are infallible, nor impeccable. There may be abuses in
his government, mistakes in his administration, and guilt in his min-

isters, which he has not observed: and he will be far from imputing the complaints, that gave him occasion to observe them, to a spirit of party; much less will he treat those who carry on such prosecutions in a legal manner, as incendiaries, and as enemies to his government. On the contrary, he will distinguish the voice of his people from the clamor of a faction, and will hearken to it. He will redress grievances, correct errors, and reform or punish ministers. This he will do as a good prince: and as a wise one, he will do it in such a manner that his dignity shall be maintained, and that his authority shall increase, with his reputation, by it.

b The Marquis d'Argenson on the Court of Louis XV (1747)

February 26, 1747] THE ROYAL FAMILY is beginning to conspire against Mme. de Pompadour; at the last hunt she was in the calèche of the dauphin, the dauphine, and Mesdames, who all agreed to say nothing to her, no matter what she said to them. She raged, she roared.

So here is the storm beginning to swell; they mean to take the king on the inconveniences of possessing a mistress of such low birth, and little by little bring him to disgust through shame: for this purpose the dauphin would not let the dauphine go to the private theatricals, and made her sham illness. The queen guides the family with certain advice which she has taken; M. de Maurepas whispers this system in her ear; and by this means she is getting some consideration at Court; whereas the king takes no counsel, and has confidence in no one, not even his mistress. In what danger I see him stand on all sides! I have endeavoured to be his friend; I did so through the purest truth, absolutely detached from ambition, and they told him I had not the "Court air;" he believed them, and dismissed me. I was the only one who would have guided him aright.

Three circles of the four antérieurs have joined the circle of Austria; that of Suabia alone resists; soon the decree of imperial security will pass the Diet at Ratisbon, and in two months they will

From Katharine Prescott Wormeley (trans.), JOURNAL AND MEMOIRS OF THE MARQUIS D'ARGENSON, 2 vols. (London, 1902), vol. ii, pp. 1–6. Reprinted by permission of William Heinemann Ltd.

have an army of forty thousand men on the Rhine; the Austrian hussars will camp among them and insult us incessantly in Alsace and Lorraine. The Prince de Conti will disdain the command of so small an army as ours; already he is siding with the malcontents, and I fear there are many combustible matters ready to give rise to troubles. The king may be as absolute as he will in fact and right, in character and practice, but we must have consistent counsels to direct affairs, otherwise the most absolute of kings will find difficulties that cannot be surmounted and will only increase.

The treaty with Sweden has failed; Russia opposed great obstacles and marched regiments into Finland; every one inveighed against our treaty; the Comte de Tessin dared not take the place of Comte Gyllemburg; the Russian ambassador at Stockholm was sustained; the King of Prussia dared not ally himself with us, and still less to seem to do so; the Swedish Diet is nearly over, and with it all hopes of that alliance; the whole thing fails because of the King of Prussia's lack of confidence in our ministry.

February 28] Persons who see clearly and who stand well at Court declare that Mme. de Pompadour will soon be dismissed; the cause being the king's shame at his fetters and at the love he has placed so low. The Prince de Conti, on leaving the Court made a furious assault upon the Pâris. It is the royal family who will be the instrument of this expulsion. The dauphin and Mesdames, under orders from the queen, have begun to attack the marquise by openly showing their contempt and barely speaking to her; they mean to propose to the king a system of amusement in his own family, of which he is very fond, and where he always finds pleasure; he will play cards and sup there; he likes the new dauphine very much; she enlivens him. The sure and secret trick by which to take the king is *le bon air,* good style, and there is plenty to attack in that respect in the mistress and the company she brings about him.

March 13] The dauphin increases in coarseness, in apathy, in hatred to his father's mistress; the moment he sees her his temper shows itself; the queen fans the flame. An angry affair has just happened about the command of the dauphin's regiment, vacant by the death of M. de Volvire. Mme. de Pompadour asked for it for one of her friends; she sent as usual for the minister of war (Comte d'Argenson). He explained to her that the dauphin had earnestly requested it for M. de Marbeuf, nephew of the Abbé de Marbeuf, his reader. Mme. de Pompadour was angry, and asked why the dauphin should meddle in the matter; wrangle, complaints, bitterness; finally the matter had to be yielded to the dauphin, but M. de Marbeuf was made to pay eighty thousand francs for the regiment.

Two new offices of ladies-in-waiting to Mesdames have just been created; this contributes to swell expenses. M. de Puysieux (secretary of State for Foreign Affairs) has had a pension of thirty thousand *livres* given him by way of consolation for his suffering in his recent illness; they have bestowed two thousand *livres* on each of the authors of the music and words of a bad ballet given in praise of Mme. de Pompadour; they have also given two thousand crowns to Deshayes, an Italian actor who arranges the ballets for the little comedies of the king at Versailles. There is an outcry against all this, and it must be owned that such expenses are not in proportion to the necessities of the present conjuncture.

The dauphin and Mesdames are becoming melancholy, and are giving way to their personal tastes without constraint; they dislike seeing any one, and never speak to others; their talk is of death and catafalques; they amuse themselves by playing quadrille in their dark antechamber by the light of one yellow wax candle and saying to one another with delight, "We are dead."[1]

M. de Maurepas increases in favour with the king, while I have been dismissed from my ministry because, showing with sincerity the necessity of peace (however made), I brought forward the means of doing so, while others retrograded. I formed for the king a strong party in Germany, both for the present moment and for that succeeding the peace; I smoothed his enemies, I preserved and inspired his friends; above all, I showed by my conduct that confidence could be placed in our sincerity.

M. de Maurepas is inexcusable in allowing our navy to run down; the parsimony of the late cardinal is no valid excuse; a zealous and intelligent man manages to do the little he has to do the best he can. Has he ever yet made a journey to any of the ports? He prefers an idle, intriguing life in Paris to all that urgent duty suggests for so essential a minister.

They tell an amusing tale in public of how the king dreamed the other night about cats; he saw four of them fighting: one thin, one fat, one blind of an eye, one blind in both eyes. A faithful valet explained to him his dream thus: "The thin cat is your people; the fat cat is the financiers; the one-eyed cat is your council; and the blind cat is your Majesty, who does not choose to see anything."

July 27] The different Court parties have united into two. At the head of one is the Prince de Conti and his mother (granddaughter of the Great Condé). M. de Maurepas is the soul of it at Court, but in the greatest secrecy. The least of his duties is that of the navy, which he does so ill; the true office he has taken upon himself, and which he performs with the ability of a genius and a great man, is that of governing the Court by embroiling it, of managing women, and turning the royal family against the king. He has excited the queen to jealousy, Madame Henriette to hate her father, the dauphin to declare war against his father's mistress. My brother has put himself into this miserable party, thinking that there was nothing so useful at Court as to be on the side of a prince of the blood. In the other party are the Pâris, Maréchal de Saxe, Mme. de Pompadour, and M. de Puysieux. The latter, however, is gentle and the friend of everybody. The bottom of his mind is hidden beneath a veil of delicacy and friendliness to all; the Pâris want only valets in the ministry; at the cost of a little work and a few successes they attain their end, which is to continue the war, make much money out of it, and so master the State.[2] I was not their man; they found that out in a very short time. I failed in compliance to their vile henchmen. Like Chavigny, I held out against them, and I brought the whole courtier crowd upon my back because I attached myself solely to the king and the State. There are some men at Court who belong to everybody, like Puysieux; and a few who belong to no one, like me.

My brother carries on his alliance with Maurepas with the utmost secrecy. He concurred in sacrificing me in order to gain merit with the irritated courtiers, and believed himself all the stronger for not having to support, externally, a brother he could not disavow, but who had become a burden to him. The Noailles are among the Court dandies; they decide nothing, they add only numbers without weight.

The great object, and the most culpable of all, has been to make the Maréchal de Saxe fail in this campaign, in order to force his retirement as Commander-in-chief, either by his own act or by violence. For this reason, they forced him to fight the battle of Lawfeldt, at which there was such slaughter. When he came to receive the thanks of his Majesty he said to him: "This is the result, sire, of forcing generals." After that he wrote as if disgusted and wishing to retire from the generaliship and the Court also; he makes no secret of his feelings. The object of the Court party is to give the command-in-chief to the Prince de Conti. Such are the horrors of a Court.

Which will carry the day? the Pâris or the party of the Prince de Conti? I think that Maréchal de Saxe's threat of leaving will act like a thunderbolt on the mind of the king; the maréchal has a way of speaking naturally to his Majesty which carries everything before it; I have seen that; and he is now supported by the strongest side.

TRANSLATOR'S NOTES

1. Louis XV had ten children, of whom one son, the dauphin, and six daughters, Mesdames, grew up. The daughters were as follows: the eldest, Louise-Élisabeth, married to Don Philip, Infant of Spain, became Duchess of Parma; the others (all unmarried) were: Madame Henriette (1727–1752); Madame Adélaïde (1732–1800); Madame Victoire (1733–1799); Madame Sophie (1734–1782); Madame Louise (1737–1787).
2. The Pâris, three brothers, financiers; one called Pâris-Duverney, another Pâris-Montmartel; formerly charged with examining the system of Law.

c *Frederick II on Prussia under Frederick William I, the "Sergeant King"*

🙚🙚 THE STATE UNDERWENT almost an entire change, as to its outward form, under Frederick-William in 1713. Numbers of courtiers were dismissed, and the great pensions were reduced. Many who had kept their coaches now walked on foot: which made people say, that the king had restored the lame to the use of their limbs. Under Frederick I Berlin was the Athens of the North; under Frederick-William it was become the Sparta. It was now a military government, the army was increased; and, in the heat of the first levies, some artisans were pressed into the service, which struck such a terror into a great many others, that they saved themselves by flight. This unforeseen accident did a vast deal of harm to our manufactures.

The king soon remedied these abuses, and applied himself with a particular attention to the re-establishment and progress of industry. He published a severe edict, prohibiting the exportation of our wool; and he built the Lagerhaus in 1714, which is a kind of warehouse,

From Frederick II, King of Prussia, MEMOIRS OF THE HOUSE OF BRANDEN-BURG, 2 vols. (London, 1758–68), vol. i, pp. 283–90; vol. ii, pp. 152–6.

from whence wool is delivered out to poor manufacturers, which they pay for after they have woven it. Our cloths found a sure sale from the consumption made by the army, which was new cloathed every year. This consumption extended afterwards to foreigners; for a Russian company was established in 1725, and our merchants furnished cloth for the whole Russian army. But the English sent their guineas into Muscovy, which were soon followed by their cloth; so there was an end of that trade. Our manufactures indeed suffered by this in the beginning, but we soon found other markets. The manufacturers had not wool enough of their own, and the people of Mecklenburg were permitted to sell us theirs. Thus, as early as 1733, our manufactures were in so flourishing a condition, that we exported 44,000 pieces of cloth, of 24 yards each.

Berlin was like the magazine of Mars. Every artist that can be employed in the service of an army was sure to thrive, and their ware was sought for all over Germany. At Berlin we set up powder-mills, at Spandaw sword-cutlers, at Potsdam gunsmiths; and at Neustadt tradesmen, who worked in iron and copper.

The king granted privileges and rewards to those who would undertake to build in any part of his dominions. He added the ward of Frederic-stadt to his capital, and filled that part with houses, which had been covered before with old ramparts. He founded, as it were, and peopled the town of Potsdam; and all this while he did not erect the least building for himself, but every thing for his subjects. The architecture of his reign is generally infected with the Dutch taste; and we could have wished, that the great sums which this prince laid out in buildings, had been directed by abler architects. He had the fate of all founders of cities, who are generally taken up with the solidity of their designs, and neglect what, with the same experience, might add to their embellishment.

After Berlin was inlarged, it was subjected to a new civil regulation in 1734, upon the same footing, very near, as that of Paris. Officers of the police were established almost in every ward of the town; hackney coaches were set up at the same time; the city was disincumbered of those lazy wretches, who get their bread by importunity; and those unhappy objects of our dislike and compassion, to whom nature has been a kind of step-mother, found an asylum in the public hospitals.

While all these changes were making, luxury, magnificence, and pleasures disappeared; the spirit of œconomy was introduced among people of all conditions, the rich as well as the poor. Under the preceding reigns a great many of the nobility sold their lands to buy laced cloaths, but now this abuse was put an end to. In most of the Prussian dominions, the gentlemen ought to be very good œconomists, to be able to maintain their families, because there is no such thing among them as the right of primogeniture. And as the fathers of families may have many children to settle in the world, economy alone can enable them to make a decent provision for those, who after their decease will divide their family into different branches.

This diminution of public expense did not hinder a great many artisans from perfecting themselves in their several trades. Our coaches, gold laces, velvets, and goldsmith's ware, were spread all over Germany.

But the mischief was, that while such useful and excellent regulations were making in the manufactures, there was a total decline in the academy of sciences, the universities, the liberal arts and commerce.

The places that became vacant in the academy were filled without any manner of judgment, and the public, through a singular depravation of taste, affected a contempt for a society of so illustrious an original, whose labours tended as much to the honour of the nation, as to the improvement of the human understanding. While this whole body was fallen into a lethargy, medicine and chymistry maintained their ground. Pott, Margraff, and Eller compounded and dissolved matter, improving the world with their discoveries; and the anatomists obtained a hall for their public dissections, which became an excellent school of chirurgery.

The professorships in the universities were filled by favour and intrigue. The bigots, who put their noses every where, obtained a share in the direction of the universities, where they raised a persecution against good sense, especially in philosophy. Wolfius was banished for giving an admirable chain of the proofs of the existence of a God. The young nobility, who were designed for the army, thought it a debasement to apply themselves to study; and as the human mind generally runs into extremes, they looked upon ignorance as a title of merit, and learning as ridiculous pedantry.

The same cause made the liberal arts decline. The academy of painting was no more. Pesne, who had been the director of it, left off history-painting to apply himself to portraits; joiners turned sculptors, and masons architects. A chymist, whose name was

Bottcher, went from Berlin to Dresden, and gave the king of Poland the secret for a kind of porcelane, which surpasses that of China, both for the elegance of the figures, and the fineness of the diapering.

Our commerce was not yet set on foot; the government checked it, by following principles directly opposite to its progress. But we must not conclude from thence, that the nation wanted a genius for trade. The Venetians and the Genoese were the first who applied themselves to it; the discovery of the compass transferred it to the Portuguese and Spaniards; it shifted afterwards to England and Holland; the French followed it the last, but soon recovered by their diligence what they had neglected through ignorance. If the inhabitants of Dantzick, Hamburg, and Lubeck, as well as the Danes and the Swedes, enrich themselves every day by navigation, why should not the Prussians do the same? . . .

People were less attentive at that time to the increase of commerce than to the reduction of useless expenses. Mournings had been formerly destructive to families. They used to give entertainments at burials; and even the funeral pomp was expensive. All those customs were abolished; neither houses nor chariots were hung with black, nor did they even so much as give black liveries; so that ever since that time people have died cheap.

This military government influenced the manners of the inhabitants, and even regulated their fashions. The public affected to assume a sour air; through all the Prussian territories no one had above three yards of cloth in his coat, or less than two yards of a sword hanging by his side. The women shunned the company of men, and the men took their revenge of them by drinking, smoking and buffoonry. In short, our manners had no longer any resemblance either to those of our ancestors, or of our neighbours; we were originals, and had the honour of being wretchedly copied by some of the petty princes of Germany. . . .

Frederick-William II (sic!) made an entire change in the form of government: he set bounds to the power of the ministers, who from masters, that they had been to his father, became his clerks. . . .

The king combined the war-office with the finances. Formerly the bare pleading of the causes before these colleges took up all the time of forty lawyers, who composed them; to the neglect of the public affairs it was their duty to superintend. Since the uniting of them, they attend one and all to the business of the state.

Under these principal departments, the king established, in every province, a college of justice and another of finances, both subordinate to the ministers. The ministers for foreign affairs, with those of justice and of the finances, made their report daily to the king, who decided every thing laid before him: during the whole of his reign, there did not appear the most trifling ordinance that was not of his signing; nor the most trifling instruction that was not of his drawing up. . . .

This great regularity in his affairs, his good œconomy, and the considerable improvements he made in his revenues, enabled him to keep up the formidable army, of which I have already treated.

d J.-J. Rousseau on the Constitution of Poland (1772)

🎗 THE LEGISLATION of Poland has been successively compounded of bits and pieces, like all others in Europe. As an abuse was discovered, so a law was passed to correct it. From this law other abuses sprang, which were corrected in turn. This manner of proceeding is endless and leads to the greatest abuse of all, which is to paralyse all laws by their endless multiplication.

In Poland, the progressive weakening of legislation has proceeded in a way all its own, which is perhaps unique: it has, in fact, lost all its vigour without ever having been subjugated by the executive power. Even today the legislative power retains all its authority: it is completely atrophied, but has no authority imposed over it. The Diet is as sovereign as it was at the time of its inception. But it is virtually powerless: no other authority commands it, yet it commands no obedience. This is a remarkable situation that is worthy of reflexion.

What has preserved the laws up till now? It is the continuous presence of the legislative body. It is the frequency of Diets and the frequent renewal of the representatives (*nonces*) that have maintained the Republic. England, while enjoying the former of these

From Jean-Jacques Rousseau, Considérations sur le Gouvernement de Pologne (1772), Chap. VIII, in C. E. Vaughan (ed.), THE POLITICAL WRITINGS OF JEAN JACQUES ROUSSEAU, 2 vols. (London, 1915), vol. i, pp. 446–50. Translation by the editor. Reprinted by permission of Basil Blackwell, Oxford.

advantages, has lost its liberties for having neglected the latter. The same Parliament lasts so long that the Court, which would exhaust its resources if it had to buy it every year, achieves its purpose by buying it for seven years and does not fail to do so. This is a first lesson for you to learn.

A second means whereby the legislative power has been preserved in Poland is, first, the division of the executive power, which has prevented its guardians from acting in concert in order to crush it; and, secondly, the frequent transference of this same executive power to new hands: a fact which has prevented any consistent system of usurpation. Every king, in the course of his reign, has taken a few steps towards arbitrary power. But the election of his successor has forced the latter to take a step back rather than pursue this course further; and every king has, at the beginning of his reign, been compelled by the *pacta conventa* to start from the same point. In this way, in spite of the constant downward slope towards despotism, there has never been any marked progress towards it.

The same has been the case with ministers and high officers of state. All, being independent of both the Senate and of one another, have enjoyed, within their respective departments, unlimited authority; yet not only did these offices mutually balance one another, but, not being engrossed by the same families, they have not been able to bring their incumbents any absolute power; and power, even when usurped, has continually reverted to its source. This would not have been the case, if the whole executive power had been vested in a single body like the Senate or, if the Crown were hereditary, in a family. This family or this body would, sooner or later, probably have crushed the legislative power and thus placed the Poles under the same yoke as other nations, from which they alone are still exempt; for I can no longer count the Swedes as being so. That is a second lesson.

Therein lies the advantage, a great one no doubt. But there is also a disadvantage, which is no less great. The executive power, being divided between several individuals, lacks any constituent harmony and is continually being pulled in different directions, which is incompatible with good order. Every custodian of a part of this power places himself, by virtue of this part, in every respect above the magistrates and the laws. In truth, he acknowledges the authority of the Diet; but, recognizing no other, when the Diet is dissolved, he acknowledges none at all; he scorns the tribunals and defies their judgments. They become so many petty despots who, without exactly usurping the sovereign authority, nevertheless subject the citizens to their petty oppressions and set a dangerous and persistent example of violating the rights and liberties of individuals without fear or scruple.

I believe that this is the first and principal cause of the anarchy that prevails in the state. To remove this cause I see but one means: ... it is to vest with full executive power a respected and permanent body, such as the Senate, which, by its stability and its authority, is capable of keeping along the path of duty those magistrates who may be tempted to stray from it. ...

For the administration to be strong and honest and to achieve its objectives, the whole executive power must rest in the same hands. But it is not enough for these hands to change; they must act only, if possible, in full view of the legislative body and it must be the latter that guides them. That is the true secret of how they may not usurp its authority.

As long as the Estates meet and the representatives change frequently, it will be difficult for the Senate or the King to crush or to usurp the legislative authority. It is remarkable that, up till now, kings should not have attempted to summon Diets less frequently, although they were not compelled, like the kings of England, to summon them frequently for fear of lacking money. It must be that either things have always been in a state of crisis, which has rendered the royal authority too weak to achieve such a measure, or that the kings have been assured, through their factions among the electors (Dietines), of always having the majority of the representatives at their disposal; or, again, that, by the operation of the *liberum veto,* they have been able to cut short any deliberations that displeased them and to dissolve the Diet at will. When each one of these factors has ceased to exist, it must be expected that the King or the Senate, or both together, will make great efforts to become rid of the Diet and make its meetings as infrequent as possible. That is the main danger to guard against and to avert. The means proposed provides the only remedy; it is simple and cannot fail to be effective. It is remarkable that no one should have thought of it before I first put it forward in the *Contrat Social.*

One of the great disadvantages of great states, and that most injurious to liberty, is that the legislative power cannot there be directly exercised and can only act by delegation. This has both its good and its bad sides, but it is the bad that prevails. The electors as a body are impossible to corrupt but are easy to mislead. Their representatives cannot easily be misled but they are easily corrupted. [He cites the example of England and Poland.]

I can see two ways of preventing this terrible evil of corruption from turning the organ of liberty into an instrument of servitude.

The first, as I have said, is the frequency of Diets; for the frequent change of representatives makes their corruption more costly and more difficult. In this respect your Constitution is better than that of Great Britain; and once you have removed or modified the *liberum veto,* I can see no reason for further changes, unless it be to place further obstacles in the way of electing the same representatives to two consecutive Diets and to prevent their frequent re-election.

The second way is to compel the representatives to follow their instructions to the letter and to render their constituents an exact account of their conduct in the Diet. On this point I cannot but be amazed by the carelessness and (dare I say?) stupidity of the English who, having armed their deputies with supreme power, set no limits to the use that they may put it to during the full seven years of their stewardship.

e *William Richardson's Portrait of the Empress Catherine II (1768)*

1. *Fairer Than Her Daughters*

August 19, 1768] The Empress of Russia is taller than the middle size, very comely, gracefully formed, but inclined to grow corpulent; and of a fair complexion, which, like every other female in this country, she endeavours to improve by the addition of rouge. She has a fine mouth and teeth; and blue eyes, expressive of scrutiny, something not so good as observation, and not so bad as suspicion. Her features are in general regular and pleasing. Indeed, with regard to her appearance altogether, it would be doing her an

From William Richardson, ANECDOTES OF THE RUSSIAN EMPIRE, in Peter Putnam (ed.), SEVEN BRITONS IN IMPERIAL RUSSIA 1698–1812 (Princeton, 1952), pp. 145–58. Reprinted by permission of the Princeton University Press and Oxford University Press, Inc.

injustice to say it was masculine, yet it would not be doing her justice to say, it was entirely feminine. As Milton intended to say of Eve, that she was fairer than any of her daughters, so this great Sovereign is certainly fairer than any of her subjects, whom I have seen. . . . Her demeanour to all around her seemed very smiling and courteous.

2. *An Imperial Day*

Nov. 7, 1768] Her Majesty . . . rises at five in the morning, and is engaged in business till near ten. She then breakfasts and goes to prayers: dines at two: withdraws to her own apartments soon after dinner: drinks tea at five: sees company, plays at cards, or attends public places, the play, opera, or masquerade, till supper: and goes to sleep at ten. By eleven every thing about the palace is as still as midnight. Whist is her favourite game at cards. She usually plays for five imperials (ten guineas) the rubber; and as she plays with great clearness and attention, she is often successful: she sometimes plays, too, at picquet and cribbage. . . . In the morning between prayers and dinner, she frequently takes an airing, according as the weather admits, in a coach or a sledge. On these occasions, she has sometimes no guards, and very few attendants; and does not chuse to be known or saluted as Empress. It is in this manner that she visits any great works that may be going on in the city, or in the neighbourhood. She is fond of having small parties of eight or ten persons with her at dinner. . . . When she retires to her palaces in the country, especially to Zarskocelo [Tsarskoe Selo] she lays aside all state, and lives with her ladies on the footing of an easy intimacy as possible. Any one of them who rises on her entering or going out of a room, is fined a ruble, and all forfeits of this sort are given to the poor. You will easily perceive, that by her regular and judicious distribution of time, she is able to transact a great deal of business; and that the affability of her manners renders her much beloved.

3. *Philanthropist or Peacock?*

I will not yet say anything very positive concerning her character and principles of action. For, she may be very social, and very affable and "smile and smile and" — you know the rest.

I may, however, very safely affirm, that a great number of her actions, so great indeed as to constitute a distinguishing feature in her character, proceed either from the desire of doing good, or the love of fame. If from the last, it must also be acknowledged, that the praise she is so desirous of obtaining, is, in many instances, the praise of humanity. Sometimes, indeed, there is a sort of whim or affectation of singularity, in the manner of conferring her favours, that looks as if the desire of being spoken of, fully as much as the desire of doing good, is the fountain from which they flow.

January 1769] I assure you, my dear Sir, I do not find it an easy matter to obtain information. . . . No intelligence of a political nature, but such as the court chuses to communicate; no views of men and manners, and no anecdotes of incidents in domestic life, can be collected from the news-papers. How unlike England! that land enlightened by the radiance of Chroniclers, Advertisers, and Gazetteers. The half of Russia may be destroyed, and the other half know nothing about the matter. . . .

I have to contend, too, with another difficulty. I perceive that the same objects are seen in very different lights by different persons. . . . I was lately present at a distribution of prizes to the students educated in the Academy of Arts and Sciences. . . . There were . . . present many ladies and gentlemen of the Court. Count Betskoy began the ceremony by addressing a speech to the Grand Duke, in which he recommended the seminary to his protection. To this His Imperial Highness replied: "As the welfare of Russia shall ever be the object nearest my heart; and as the proper education of youth is of so much consequence in every well-ordered state, it claims, and shall ever obtain, my most constant attention." . . .

I was told that the Empress was present among the ladies. . . .

Tell me now, would not a stranger, on witnessing such a scene, on seeing one of the most powerful Sovereigns on earth and the presumptive heir of this mighty empire so attentive to the welfare and improvement of their people, would he not feel rapture, approve, and applaud? Yet, when I expressed those sentiments, there were persons who shake their heads. . . . This Academy has subsisted for many years, but what have they done? It may be mentioned, with ostentatious pomp, in a news-paper, or by Voltaire, and nothing else is intended.

4. *Emancipator or Autocrat?*

November 1768] I was lately present at a meeting of the deputies summoned by the Empress from all the nations of her empire, and who have been assembled to assist Her Majesty in forming a system of legislation. There is something magnificent in this idea: and if she really intends what she professes, to give equitable laws to all her subjects and dependents, from the Baltic to the wall of China, and from Lapland to the Caspian, she deserves admiration. . . .

The meeting consists of about six hundred members. They meet in the palace, where they have one large hall for the whole assembly; and several adjoining rooms for committees. They consist of representatives of the nobility, the peasantry, and the inhabitants of towns or cities. . . . The chief officers in this assembly are a Marischal, who presides; and a Procureur General for the Crown. . . .

In transacting business, the following method is observed. The Procureur lays before the deputies some principle or subject of law proposed by the Empress, and concerning which they are to give an opinion. They then adjourn; and the committee to whom that subject particularly belongs, prepare it for the next general meeting. Then all the members are permitted to deliver their opinions in a written speech, and to determine the point before them, by the plurality of votes. But whatever their determinations may be, it remains with the Empress to ratify them or not, as she pleases. Two of the subjects lately discussed in this assembly were, "Whether any but the nobility had a right to buy lands?" and, "Whether any but the nobility had a right to buy slaves?"

I have heard that freedom of extemporaneous speaking was allowed in some of the first meetings of this assembly; but that that being likely to occasion too much disorder, it was discontinued. At present, it is expected that no person, unless his views be very well known, shall deliver a speech without previously consulting the Marischal; and if he disapproves of it, the orator, though he had the powers of a Cicero, must keep his speech in his pocket. Indeed, this assembly has no pretensions whatever to freedom of debate, and scarcely any tendency towards establishing political liberty. The members, in general, are chosen by the will of the sovereign: by her the subjects of debate are proposed: she keeps in her own hands the right of ratifying every determination: and the assembly, convoked by her sole authority, may be dismissed at her pleasure.

ʃ   Aaron Hill on the Grand Vizier of the Ottoman Empire (1709)

BY THE foregoing Chapters, the prodigious Power and unlimited Authority of the *Turkish Sultan* has been fully taught the Reader. But tho' his Rule is Arbitrary, and his Sway Despotick and Tyrannical, he submits the Management of his Large Dominions to the depending Government of a deputed *Viceroy;* and indeed it has ever been the Custom of the *Eastern* Emperors to Constitute some favour'd Subject in a Degree of Honour next themselves, a Custom by many Authors condemn'd, as owing its Institution to the slothful Disposition of some Inglorious Monarch, wholly given up to Ease and Luxury; but in my Opinion founded on the subtle Maxims of a deeper Policy; for by these means, the Emperours may not only, when they please, unbend their Minds from the fatiguing Cares of an intangled Government, but when the growing Anger of their injur'd Subjects provoke them to a Resentment of their oppressive Cruelties, they throw the odium of their own Injustice upon their Guiltless *Viceroy,* who skreening the Miscarriages of his Imprudent *Sultan* from the Revenge of a Rebellious Multitude, becomes himself the Object of their Hatred, and lays the Foundation of his Master's Safety, on the Peaceful Consequences of his own Destruction.

This Officer among the *Turks* is distinguish'd by the Title of *Vizier Azem,* or Councellour in Chief to the *Grand Signior,* from whom all Power is immediately deriv'd to him, and by whom he is Created without any other Ceremony than the delivery of a large Golden Seal, whereon is Engrav'd the Name and Age of the then Reigning *Sultan;* this Seal he always carries in his Bosum, and becomes thereby Invested with an Authority almost as Arbitrary and Unlimited as that of the Emperour himself.

Amurath the Third was the Institutor of this Office, at a time when breaking into *Europe,* he conferr'd the Dignity of General and Chief Chancellour on one *Lala Schabin* his Tutor, since which time his Successors have continued to appoint some favour'd Subject to the

From Aaron Hill, Gent., A FULL AND JUST ACCOUNT OF THE OTTOMAN EMPIRE IN ALL ITS BRANCHES (London, 1709), pp. 9–12.

Dignity of *Vizier Azem,* and honour those Officers with the Name of Tutor as often as they hold Conversation with them.

The *Vizier Azem,* as in Title, so in Power, is the Head and Mouth of the *Turkish* Law; to him Appeals are brought from all their Courts of Judicature, and by him the former Sentences of Inferiour Judges are frequently disannull'd, and the Cause decided in favour of the Party who before had lost it. There lies no Appeal beyond him, unless to the Person of the *Grand Signior;* and that so very difficult, that 'tis very rarely put in Practice. The manner of doing it is so odd and different from the European Customs, that the Reader will be inclin'd to pardon the Digression if I describe the Ceremony as briefly as is possible: At certain Hours of the Day, when the Gates of the *Seraglio* are set open for the Admittance of great Numbers of Citizens and Others, whose Business with the Officers of that Place require their daily Attendance there, the Persons who would complain of any grievous Injury they have suffer'd, and which the Injustice or Connivance of the *Grand Vizier* has refus'd to redress, enter hastily the Outward Court, and putting Pots of Fire upon their Heads run swiftly forward, nor dare the greatest Officer presume to stop them, till they arrive in the Presence of the *Grand Signior,* and humbling themselves at his Feet, declare the weighty Wrongs they labour under, and implore the gracious Mark of his unquestion'd Justice in a kind Redress of their Oppressive Injuries.

There is a private *Divan* or Court of Justice held in the Palace of the *Vizier Azem* every Wednesday and Thursday; on the other Days (excepting Friday, which is the *Turkish* Sabbaoth) the *Divan* is kept in an open Chamber of the *Seraglio,* whither the *Vizier* is magnificently attended by a great number of Pursuivants and Serjeants; at his Arrival he is saluted with the noisy Acclamations of the People, and guarded by a sort of Soldiers, maintain'd purposely for that Use, to his Place upon the Bench; where being seated with the *Cadeelescheer* or Lord Chief Justice, and Six *Viziers* of the Bench, who are Grave Men that have formerly born offices in the Government, and are skill'd in the Knowledge of their Law, but not permitted to give their Opinions on any Point unless demanded by him. He listens to the Judgment of the Lord Chief Justice, who hears and determines all Causes, unless the *Vizier* shall disapprove his Sentence, and Reverse it as he thinks is most agreeable to the Justice of the Cause, or his own private Inclinations.

Thus much may serve as to the Judicative Power of the *Grand Vizier,* but is far from expressing the utmost limits of his Authority, which extends its self so far beyond that of the other Great Officers of the Empire, that tho' he cannot by virtue of his own immediate Order take off their Heads, or recall them from their Governments, he has so great an Interest in the *Grand Signior,* that he can, without the smallest Difficulty obtain his Warrant for the Displacing or Beheading any Officer at Court or elsewhere, who has unfortunately disoblig'd him, or stands obnoxious to the danger of his Envy.

In time of War he has the Command in Chief of the Sultan's Armys, and leads them where he pleases, without the least necessity of waiting for his Master's Order. He gives Audience to the Embassadors of Foreign Princes, Receives and Answers the Contents of their Memorials, and is in short the only Master of the Executive Power over the *Grand Signior's* whole Dominions.

Answerable to the vast Authority of this great Officer is the pompous State in which he lives; his Court consisting frequently of Five and Twenty Hundred Servants, including the Officers about him; when he appears Abroad he is distinguish'd not only by the Splendour of his Equipage, but the bearing on the fore part of his Turbant two large Feathers, set on with a great Knot of Diamonds and other Jewels of inestimable Value, the peculiar Mark of his Degree, the *Bashaws* being permitted to wear but One, and the *Sultan* himself never appearing with more than Three. Three horsetails are carried before him on a lofty Staff, another distinguishing Mark of His Authority. Great Numbers of stately Horses adorn'd with trappings of Gold and Silver set thick with Precious Stones are led before him; his Stirrops held by the obsequious Hands of his surrounding Slaves, and his Garment kiss'd with the most profound Respect by endless Crowds of prostrate Officers, whose servile Souls encline their Actions to the basest Practice of a vile Subjection to Men by Fortune plac'd above them, while they basely Triumph over the miserable Wretches that are under their Command, with all the haughty Marks of an insulting Arrogance.

Prodigious and beyond Belief are the amazing Profits arising from this Post to the Coffers of its Possessors. For tho' the Revenues of the *Grand Vizier,* or his immediate Salary from the Crown does scarce exceed Five Thousand Pounds *per annum,* 'tis yet impossible to guess the vast Advantages it brings him; for besides the great Sums of Money he receives from the Numbers of his Petitioners, who, be their Business of what nature it will, dare never move it empty Handed, there are daily Rivolets of Plenty from all Parts of the Empire flowing to his Treasury. No Subject of the *Grand Signior* dares enter on a place of Power, till by the moving Rhetorick of some considerable Present he has brib'd the Favour of the *Grand Vizier;* without which he is always sensible his Head will surely pay the Forfeit of his Avarice. There are certain times of the Year, when all the Governours of Provinces are oblig'd to send presents to the *Sultan,* after the manner of our *New-Year's-Gifts,* and tho' there is no Obligation which compels them at that time to remember the *Vizier,* a fatal Experience of the Consequences of such a Neglect has often convinc'd them, that, 'tis highly Dangerous to forget him. The Rulers of the Remotest Branches of the *Turkish* Empire are Oblig'd to Court his Favourable Representation of their Services with the Perswasive Oratory of their Golden Messengers, and in short no Man who omits his Duty this way can reasonably hope a long Possession of his Honours or Preferments.

By these means a *Vizier* of a Covetous Disposition, who loses no Advantage he may Reap from his Authority, has such Incredible Opportunities of Encreasing his Wealth, that many at the Death which generally Attends their short liv'd Splendor, have been found Possessors of such Immense Heaps of Treasure as have equall'd if not exceeded that of the *Grand Signior* their Master. But those very Riches which still render this High Office desireable in the Emulative Breasts of the Turkish Candidates, are the very Poyson of its Pleasures, and to a Genius blest with a serious Contemplation on the Frailties of Humanity would open all the dangers of its Gawdy Glories and rather frighten him from their search than allure him to their Possession.

For few there are who long enjoy the Slippery Honours of this wish'd Preferment; the Sultan's policy forbids a long Permission of such unbounded Power, and urges him to frequent changes of such dangerous Officers, nor are there many, who survive the loss of this High Post, for having some time serv'd like a necessary Sponge to gather Riches for the *Sultan's* use, he Squeezes them at last into his own vast Treasure; and to free himself from all the fears of their Resentment, invents some Plausible pretence to take them off and put others in their Place, to grow up Gradually to the same Fate their Predecessors met with.

3

The People of Europe

WILLIAM COXE, the later Archdeacon Coxe and biographer of Sir Robert Walpole, visited Russia as a traveling tutor in 1778–9.

Lady Mary Wortley Montagu (1689–1762), an inveterate traveler and letter-writer, wrote this description of the tyranny of the Janissaries from Adrianople in April, 1717. Her account may be compared with that made ninety years later by Lord Broughton, who confirms that "they [the Janissaries] have several times disposed of the Turkish sceptre, and have been the origin of, and the actors in, a quick succession of bloody commotions, which, were it not for the sturdy example before our eyes, might be judged incompatible with the existence of any empire" (Travels in Albania and other Provinces of Turkey in 1809 and 1810 [London, 2 vols., 1855], Vol. II, pp. 368–369).

D'Argenson's concern for the conditions of the poor was remarkable for a French aristocrat of his day. His description (written in 1739) may be contrasted with the very different impression that a travel through France's eastern provinces made on Lady Mary Wortley Montagu in August of the same year: "The French are more changed than their roads: instead of pale, yellow faces, wrapped up in blankets, as we saw them, the villages are all filled with fresh-coloured lusty peasants, in good health and clean linen. It is incredible the air of plenty and content that is over the whole country" (Correspondence, Vol. II, p. 47). But D'Argenson is, of course, specifically concerned with the poorer, western provinces; besides, the portrayal of social conditions is not a strong point of Lady Mary's.

Daniel Defoe (1661?–1731), journalist and novelist, author of Robinson Crusoe and Moll Flanders, also wrote A Tour through the Whole Island of Great Britain, first published in 1724–1726.

a William Coxe on Social Classes in Russia (1778)

The Nobility

Emptiness of Titles] IN RUSSIA, as in the Oriental governments, there is scarcely any distinction of ranks among the nobility, excepting what is derived from the service of the sovereign.

From William Coxe, TRAVELS IN POLAND, RUSSIA, SWEDEN AND DENMARK, in Peter Putnam (ed.), SEVEN BRITONS IN IMPERIAL RUSSIA 1698–1812 (Princeton, 1952), pp. 268–73, 285–9. Reprinted by permission of the Princeton University Press and Oxford University Press, Inc.

Even the eldest sons of those persons, who have been raised to the most considerable honours and highest employments, excepting the advantages which they undoubtedly retain of facilitating their promotion by a ready access to court, do not derive any solid benefits from their birth, like those which the peers of England, the grandees of Spain, or the dukes, who are peers of France, enjoy from their hereditary descent. The importance of a noble family of large property and official honours, is almost annihilated on the death of the chief; because his property is equally divided among his sons; and because titles, although allowed to be hereditary, do not, independent of the sovereign's favour, contribute much to aggrandize the possessors: that of a prince, a count, or a baron, conveying in themselves little personal distinction, unless accompanied by a civil or military employment.

Military Precedence] Although the law of Peter I, which compelled each nobleman or gentleman, under pain of degradation, to serve in the army, was abolished by Peter III; yet the effects still subsist. No one under the rank of a major is permitted to drive more than two horses; under that of a brigadier, more than four: a nobleman of the highest fortune and distinction, who has never been in the army, is not allowed, excepting by the special permission of the crown, to use in the capital a carriage drawn by more than one horse; while a merchant may have two. There are various methods, however, of procuring military dignity, and the privileges annexed to it. Amongst others, a chamberlain, for instance, to the sovereign, *ranks* as a major-general; the office of a secretary, in the different departments of government, confers the *rank* of an officer; and the contributor of a certain sum to the foundling-hospital at Moscow, obtains the *rank* of a lieutenant. . . . But, however ridiculous those promotions may appear, yet they are founded on the principles of the soundest policy; for as, by a decree of Peter the Great, every officer is noble during his life, and the children of a staff-officer are classed among the nobility, any institution tending to increase the number of this order of men, who alone are entitled to possess land, cannot fail of being highly beneficial to society.

* * *

The Middle Class

Encouragements to Growth] Peter, who during his travels, perceived the utility of a third estate for the purposes of commerce, made many regulations with this view, which, though excellent in themselves, yet not being adapted to the state of property in Russia, did not answer the end proposed. Among these regulations, he endowed some free towns with certain privileges, which were afterwards augmented by Elizabeth. But these privileges were confined to Petersburgh, Moscow, Astracan, Tver, and a few other great provincial towns; and all the inhabitants, even merchants not excepted, were not distinguished from the peasants, in two instances, which are considered in this country as indelible marks of servitude: they were subject to the poll-tax, and to be draughted for the army and navy. Catherine has exempted the body of merchants from these two instances of servitude, has increased the number and immunities of the free towns, and permitted many of the crownpeasants, and all free men, to enroll themselves, under stipulated conditions, in the class of merchants or burghers.

The merchants are distributed into three classes. The first comprehends those who have a capital of 10,000 roubles; the second those who possess 5,000; and the third, those who are worth 500 . . . all persons who chuse to enter themselves in any of these classes are exempted from the poll-tax, on condition of paying annually one per cent. of their capital employed in trade to the crown. . . .

This alteration in the mode of assessing merchants is advantageous both to the crown and to the subjects; the former receives, and the latter cheerfully pay, one per cent. of their capital, because they are exempted from the poll-tax, and are entitled to additional immunities. It is also a just impost, as each merchant pays according to his fortune. . . . With respect to the general interests of the nation, it is a masterpiece of policy; it excites industry, by holding up to the people a principle of honour, as well as of interest, to be derived from the augmentation of their capital; and affords an additional security from arbitrary impositions, by pledging the good faith of government in the protection of their property. It is likewise productive of another essential public benefit, by creating, as it were, a third estate, which, as it increases in wealth, credit, and importance, must by degrees acquire additional privileges and gradually rise into consequence.

The burghers form the second division of this order: the term burgher is applied to all inhabitants of free towns, who declare that they possess a capital of less than £100. . . . They possess many privileges superior to the peasants; but are distinguished from the merchants by being still subject to the poll-tax, and to enrollment in the army or navy.

Under this third order must be included all the other free subjects
of the empire; namely, those slaves who have received liberty from
their masters; those who have obtained their dismission from the
army and navy; the members of the Academy of Arts, and of other
similar institutions . . . and, lastly, the children of all these freemen.
All these persons have permission to settle and trade in any part of
the empire, and may enroll themselves, according to their capital,
among the burghers or merchants. By these wise regulations, the
number of persons above slaves will gradually increase, and must in
time form a very considerable order of men, as soon as they shall
acquire the right of possessing land.

*   *   *

The Peasants

Of the Crown and of the Nobles] The peasants of Russia are generally serfs, or slaves, and may be divided into,

1] Peasants of the crown.
2] Peasants belonging to individuals.

1] The crown peasants inhabit the imperial demesnes; and probably comprehend, including those belonging to the church lands . . .
about the sixth part of the Russian peasants. They are immediately
under the jurisdiction of the imperial officers or bailiffs. Although
liable to great exactions, by the tenure of their subjection from these
petty tyrants, yet they are much more secure of their property; and
being under the protection of the sovereign, any flagrant instances
of oppression are more easily made known and redressed. Many of
these vassals, in particular districts, have been enfranchised, and permitted to enroll themselves among the merchants and burghers; and
the whole body will gradually receive more privileges, as the spirit
of humanity and policy penetrates further into these regions.

2] Peasants belonging to individuals are the private property of
the landholders, as much as implements of agriculture. . . . With
respect to his own demands on his peasants, the lord is restrained by
no law. He is absolute master of their time and labour. . . . Any
capital which they acquire by their industry, may be seized, and there
could be no redress; as, according to the old feudal law, which still
exists, a slave cannot institute a process against his master.

Technical Education and Legal Improvement] The mode adopted

by many landholders with their peasants, reminds me of the practice among the Romans. Atticus, we are told, caused many of his slaves to be instructed in the art of copying manuscripts, which he sold at a very high price, and raised a considerable fortune. On similar principles some of the Russian nobility send their vassals to Moscow or Petersburgh, for the purpose of learning various handicraft trades; they either employ them on their own estates, let them out for hire, sell them at an advanced price, or receive from them an annual compensation for the permission of exercising their trade for their own advantage.

In regard to the lord's authority over their persons, according to the antient laws, he might try them in his own courts of justice, or punish them without any process, he could inflict every species of penalty excepting the knoot, order them to be whipped, or confined in dungeons; he might send them to houses of correction, or banish them into Siberia; or, in short, take cognizance of every misdemeanour which was not a public offence. . . . By the new regulations, this enormous power is reduced by restrictions more consonant to the humane principles which distinguish all the regulations of the empress, and the right of inflicting punishment is lodged, where it ever ought to be, in the hands of the public magistrate. Abuses, however, still subsist; but must, in time, yield to the influence of such salutary institutions. . . .

Although the sovereign cannot alter the fundamental state of property, by conferring on the peasants, as individuals, privileges which might infringe those of the nobles; yet she has alleviated their condition by issuing several laws in their favour. By allowing free peasants to settle in any part of her dominions, and enroll themselves among the burghers or merchants, according to their respective capital. She has given a stability to their freedom, and afforded the strongest incitements for the exertions of industry. She has repealed those oppressive laws, which forbade, in certain districts, all peasants to marry without the consent of the governor of the province, or the wayvode of the town, who usually exacted a present from the parties.

The Bar to Civilization] I am far from asserting, that inhumanity is the general characteristic of the Russian nobility; or that many persons do not treat their vassals with the utmost benevolence. I am also well aware, that several peasants are in such a flourishing condition as to have accumulated very considerable capitals without dread of exaction; and that some even possess landed estates under their masters' names. But if we consider the unhappy pleasure which too many feel in tyrannizing over their inferiors, we have every reason to conclude, that the generality of boors must be still cruelly oppressed. How then can a country be said to be civilized, in which domestic slavery still exists?

The vassals who work for their masters, generally receiving their maintenance, or being accommodated with a small portion of land, always enjoy in sufficient abundance the common necessaries of life; and usually spend their earnings in clothes or spirituous liquors. Those who, in contradiction of this general rule, save the profits of their labour, or trade, conceal as much as possible an acquisition of fortune. . . . The practice of hiding money is common in all countries of the East, where property is not well secured; and where the people, through dread of exactions cannot even venture to use the riches which they have acquired. . . .

From this general review of the various inhabitants in Russia, it may be perceived, that, though proceeding towards civilization, they are still far removed from that state; that a general improvement cannot take place while the greater part continue in absolute vassalage; nor can any effectual change be introduced in the national manners until the people enjoy full security in their persons and property.

b Joseph Townsend on Feudalism in Catalonia (1786)

BUT THAT, which contributes most to the wealth and prosperity of Catalonia, is the power which gentlemen of landed property have over their estates, to grant a particular species of lease called *Establishment by Emfiteutic Contracts*. To that circumstance Count Campomanes pays particular attention, when he would account for the superior cultivation and improvement of this industrious province; nor is he singular in his opinion. He not only observes, respecting Catalonia, *El usu del derecho emfiteutico mantiene alli al labrador sobre sustierras y produce un sobrante de gentes para los oficios;* but to form the contrast he remarks; that Andalusia, although more fertile than either Catalonia or Galicia, yet is destitute of industry,

From Joseph Townsend, A.M., Rector of Pewsey, Wiltshire, A JOURNEY THROUGH SPAIN IN THE YEARS 1786 AND 1787, 3 vols. (London, 1792), vol. iii, pp. 328–33.

because the land being occupied by few proprietors, the bulk of the people are day labourers, who only find occasional employment. Hence, clothed in rags and wretchedness, they crowd into cities, where they obtain a precarious livelihood through the bounty of rich ecclesiastics. . . .

Not merely in Andalusia, but in other provinces, the great estates being strictly entailed, and administered on the proprietor's account, little land is to be rented by the farmer, less can be purchased by the monied man, and, for want of floating property, industry is left to languish. In Catalonia it is totally the reverse of this.

By the *emfiteutic contract,* the great proprietor, inheriting more land than he can cultivate to profit, has power to grant any given quantity for a term of years, either absolute or conditional, either for lives, or in perpetuity, always reserving a quit-rent, like our copy-holds, with a relief on every succession, a fine on the alienation of the land, and other seignioral rights dependant on the custom of the district, such as tithes, mills, public-houses, the obligation to plough his land, to furnish him with teams, and to pay hearth-money, with other contributions, by way of commutation for ancient stipulated services.

One species of grant for uncultivated land, to be planted with vines, admitted formerly of much dispute. The tenant holding his land as long as the first planted vines should continue to bear fruit; in order to prolong this term, he was accustomed to train layers from the original stocks, and, by metaphysical distinctions between identity and diversity, to plead, that the first planted vines were not exhausted; claiming thus the inheritance in perpetuity. After various litigations and inconsistent decisions of the judges, it was finally determined, that this species of grant should convey a right to the possession for fifty years, unless the plantation itself should previously fail.

The lord of this allodial property may appoint any one as judge, with the assistance of an attorney, to hold court for him, provided he has previously obtained permission from the provincial court, or, supposing the district to be a barony, from the baron or his ordinary judge. Having constituted the tribunal, the lord, even whilst a cause is pending, may at pleasure remove the judge, and name another in his place, and the tenant has, at any period of the trial, a right to his challenge, without assigning reasons, other than his own suspicions. Each party may equally reject three advocates appointed for assessors.

The reserved rent is paid commonly in money; but often the agreement is for oil, wine, corn, or poultry.

Should the property thus granted in fee pass into mortmain, the lord of the soil may insist on its being sold, or he may increase the reserved rent in proportion to the value of the usual fine.

The tenant, whenever summoned, must produce in court his title, which he is bound to trace upward, till it arrives ultimately at the royal grant; and when his term expires, on quitting, he must be paid for his improvements, before he can be legally ejected: but at the same time he may be compelled to indemnify his lord for all damages sustained by his neglect.

Should the tenant be desirous of quitting before the expiration of his term, he is at liberty to do it; but in that case he is precluded from all claims for his improvements.

The tenure in Catalonia is evidently feodal. All property in land is traced up to the king, and is held by knights service from the crown, subject to relief, to fines, and to escheat. Under the royal grant, the great lords claim, not merely tithes of all lands not being freehold, with quit rents and fines, mills, and public houses, as we have remarked above, but the right of appointing magistrates and receiving tolls on the passage of cattle over their estates.

To the power retained by them of making emfiteutic contracts, has with reason been attributed the cultivation of such waste lands as are most susceptible of tillage, and the consequent increase of population. Industry has been promoted, new families have been called into existence, and many, rescued from poverty and wretchedness, are now maintained in comfortable affluence. In the year 1738, one James Vilaplana purchased at a public auction, for two hundred livres Catalan, a tract of waste land, on which, in 1778, were found twenty families established, although he had reserved one third of this possession for himself; and the whole being planted with vines, for which the soil was best adapted, what had been originally purchased for two hundred livres became, in the space of forty years, worth many thousands.

Yet advantageous as this kind of establishment has been, both to individuals and to the community at large, some great proprietors are so inattentive, both to the general good and to their private benefit, that they leave their lands uncultivated. Even in Catalonia, according to the government returns, more than three hundred villages have been deserted.

c Lady Mary Wortley Montagu on Tyranny of the Janissaries in Turkey (*1717*)

Adrianople, April 1, O.S. [1717]

... THE JOURNEY we have made from Belgrade hither by land, cannot possibly be passed by any out of a public character. The desert woods of Servia are the common refuge of thieves, who rob, fifty in a company, [so] that we had need of all our guards to secure us; and the villages so poor, that only force could extort from them necessary provisions. Indeed the janissaries had no mercy on their poverty, killing all the poultry and sheep they could find, without asking whom they belonged to; while the wretched owners durst not put in their claim, for fear of being beaten. Lambs just fallen, geese and turkies big with egg, all massacred without distinction! I fancied I heard the complaints of Meliboeus for the hope of his flock. When the pashas travel, it is yet worse. Those oppressors are not content with eating all that is to be eaten belonging to the peasants; after they have crammed themselves and their numerous retinue, they have [the] impudence to exact what they call *teeth-money,* a contribution for the use of their teeth, worn with doing them the honour of devouring their meat. This is a literal known truth, however extravagant it seems; and such is the natural corruption of a military government, their religion not allowing of this barbarity no more than ours does.

I had the advantage of lodging three weeks at Belgrade with a principal effendi, that is to say, a scholar. This set of men are equally capable of preferments in the law or the church, those two sciences being cast into one, a lawyer and a priest being the same word. They are the only men really considerable in the empire; all the profitable employments and church revenues are in their hands. The Grand Signior, though general heir to his people, never presumes to touch their lands or money, which go, in an uninterrupted succession, to their children. It is true, they lose this privilege by accepting a place

From Lord Wharncliffe (ed.), THE LETTERS AND WORKS OF LADY MARY WORTLEY MONTAGU, 2 vols. (London, 1908), vol. ii, pp. 164–5, 170–3. Reprinted by permission of George Bell and Sons.

at court, or the title of pasha; but there are few examples of such fools among them. You may easily judge the power of these men, who have engrossed all the learning, and almost all the wealth, of the empire. 'Tis they that are the real authors, though the soldiers are the actors, of revolutions. They deposed the late Sultan Mustapha; and their power is so well known, it is the Emperor's interest to flatter them.

* * *

The government here is entirely in the hands of the army; and the Grand Signior, with all his absolute power, as much a slave as any of his subjects, and trembles at a janissary's frown. Here is, indeed, a much greater appearance of subjection than among us: a minister of state is not spoken to, but upon the knee; should a reflection on his conduct be dropped in a coffee-house (for they have spies everywhere), the house would be rased to the ground, and perhaps the whole company put to the torture. No huzzaing mobs, senseless pamphlets, and tavern disputes about politics:

> "A consequential ill that freedom draws;
> A bad effect, — but from a noble cause."

None of our harmless calling names! but when a minister here displeases the people, in three hours' time he is dragged even from his master's arms. They cut off his hands, head, and feet, and throw them before the palace gate, with all the respect in the world; while that Sultan (to whom they all profess an unlimited adoration) sits trembling in his apartment, and dare neither defend nor revenge his favourite. This is the blessed condition of the most absolute monarch upon earth, who owns no *law* but his *will*.

I cannot help wishing, in the loyalty of my heart, that the parliament would send hither a ship-load of your passive-obedient men, that they might see arbitrary government in its clearest strongest light, where it is hard to judge whether the prince, people, or ministers, are most miserable. I could make many reflections on this subject; but I know, madam, your own good sense has already furnished you with better than I am capable of.

I went yesterday with the French embassadress to see the Grand Signior in his passage to the mosque. He was preceded by a numerous guard of janissaries, with vast white feathers on their heads, *spahis* and *bostangees* (these are foot and horse guard), and the royal gardeners, which are a very considerable body of men, dressed in different habits of fine lively colours, that, at a distance, they appeared like a parterre of tulips. After them the aga of the janissaries, in a robe of purple velvet, lined with silver tissue, his horse led by two slaves richly dressed. Next him the *kyzlár-aga* (your ladyship knows this is the chief guardian of the seraglio ladies) in a deep yellow cloth (which suited very well to his black face) lined with sables, and last his Sublimity himself, in green lined with the fur of a black Muscovite fox, which is supposed worth a thousand pounds sterling, mounted on a fine horse, with furniture embroidered with jewels. Six more horses richly furnished were led after him; and two of his principal courtiers bore, one his gold, and the other his silver coffee-pot, on a staff; another carried a silver stool on his head for him to sit on.

It would be too tedious to tell your ladyship the various dresses and turbans by which their rank is distinguished; but they were all extremely rich and gay, to the number of some thousands; [so] that, perhaps, there cannot be seen a more beautiful procession. The Sultan appeared to us a handsome man of about forty, with a very graceful air, but something severe in his countenance, his eyes very full and black. He happened to stop under the window where we stood, and (I suppose being told who we were) looked upon us very attentively, [so] that we had full leisure to consider him, and the French embassadress agreed with me as to his good mien: I see that lady very often; she is young, and her conversation would be a great relief to me, if I could persuade her to live without those forms and ceremonies that make life formal and tiresome. But she is so delighted with her guards, her four-and-twenty footmen, gentlemen ushers, &c., that she would rather die than make me a visit without them: not to reckon a coachful of attending damsels yclep'd maids of honour. What vexes me is, that as long as she will visit with a troublesome equipage, I am obliged to do the same: however, our mutual interest makes us much together.

I went with her the other day all round the town, in an open gilt chariot, with our joint train of attendants, preceded by our guards, who might have summoned the people to see what they had never seen, nor ever would see again — two young Christian embassadresses never yet having been in this country at the same time, nor I believe ever will again. Your ladyship may easily imagine that we drew a vast crowd of spectators, but all silent as death. If any of them had taken the liberties of our mob upon any strange sight, our janissaries had made no scruple of falling on them with their scimitars, without danger for so doing, being above law. Yet these people have some good qualities; they are very zealous and faithful where they serve, and look upon it as their business to fight for you upon all occasions. Of this I had a very pleasant instance in a village on this side Philipopolis, where we were met by our domestic guard. I happened to bespeak pigeons for my supper, upon which one of my janissaries went immediately to the cadi (the chief civil officer of the town), and ordered him to send in some dozens. The poor man answered, that he had already sent about, but could get none. My janissary, in the height of his zeal for my service, immediately locked him up prisoner in his room, telling him he deserved death for his impudence, in offering to excuse his not obeying my command; but, out of respect to me, he would not punish him but by my order, and accordingly, came very gravely to me, to ask what should be done to him; adding, by way of compliment, that if I pleased he would bring me his head.— This may give you some idea of the unlimited power of these fellows, who are all sworn brothers, and bound to revenge the injuries done to one another, whether at Cairo, Aleppo, or any part of the world; and this inviolable league makes them so powerful, the greatest man at the court never speaks to them but in a flattering tone; and in Asia, any man that is rich is forced to enrol himself a janissary, to secure his estate. . . .

d The Marquis d'Argenson on the Condition of France in 1739

THE REAL EVIL, which is sapping the strength of the kingdom and must inevitably lead to its ruin, is the failure to realize the decay of our provinces. The reports that come from them are treated as mere exaggeration, and no one that I know of has yet

From MÉMOIRES DU MARQUIS D'ARGENSON, MINISTRE SOUS LOUIS XV (Paris, 1825), pp. 322–8. Translation by the editor.

taken the trouble to seek the origins of this state of affairs. In my lifetime I have observed the gradual decrease in the wealth and population of France, and every disinterested observer agrees with me that the sudden depreciation of the currency effected by the Duke (of Orleans) produced its first symptoms. But the situation is far worse now than it was then. We now have the conviction that poverty has, generally speaking, reached an unheard of level. At the moment that I write, in the midst of peace and with the prospects of a harvest which, if not abundant, is at least tolerably satisfactory, men are dying all around us like flies, from sheer poverty and from being reduced to eating grass. The provinces of Maine, Angoumois, Touraine, Upper Poitou, Périgord, Orléanais, and Berry are the worst affected; and scarcity is approaching the neighbourhood of Versailles. The fact is beginning to be recognized, although it has as yet made but a momentary impression.

For long I have realized the danger, and I was perhaps the first to give the alarm when I returned, nearly two years ago, from a journey that I made to my estates. I said then, and I still think, that this state of affairs is not the product of passing circumstances, and that though a bad year may have made the evil more apparent, its roots lie deeper than is popularly imagined. Elsewhere, I have proposed means for restoring activity to our countryside and for freeing it from the financial tyranny that is paralysing it; but the moment is not favourable for innovations.

The Cardinal's (Fleury's) intimates have persuaded him that these are tales spread abroad by the Chauvelin party to discredit his ministry. M. Orry only lends credence to the reports of the financiers who, naturally, are interested in hiding the truth from him. He treats those intendants that speak to him with greater frankness exactly as he would *curés* or charitable ladies who, from misplaced compassion, exaggerate the picture of poverty. So all the intendants have become discouraged; no voice is raised between the people and the throne: the kingdom is treated like enemy territory that has to be squeezed for taxes. The only thought is to have the tax paid in for the current year, without any thought for what the tax-payer will be able to pay the year after.

It is true that all our theorists are at fault: there has been nowhere any complete failure of the harvest; at most, there have been half-years of scarcity in certain provinces with moderate harvests in others.

But everywhere there is a shortage of money, the lack of *means* to buy food. Midst this poverty wheat and provisions rise in price, and men are not given work. Meanwhile, taxes are rigorously exacted, and the *taille* is levied at an exorbitant rate. The Comptroller General has won the praises of the Cardinal by being able to show him a comfortable surplus in his receipts.

At last a few voices have been raised from among the chief magistrates; even among the most politically-minded of them: M. Turgot, for example, whose opposition does him credit; M. de Harlay who has suspended the repair of roads by forced labour (*corvée*). The dowager Duchess of Rochechouart wrote a moving letter to the Cardinal; and M. de la Rochefoucauld on returning from Angoumois did the same. The Bishop of Le Mans hastened from his diocese to Versailles for the single purpose of reporting that everything there was dying away. The *bailli* of Froulay, who is widely received at court, came from Maine to confirm this testimony. These reports have caused a few moments' anxiety, but then they have been forgotten. One of my colleagues on the Council of State, whom I often have occasion to converse with, said to me the other day: "Sir, all this is the fault of Chancellor d'Aguesseau. Since he severely limited the competence of the provosts of the *maréchaussée* (constabulary) it has become impossible to arrest these beggars. There has been too long a delay in resorting to this measure, that is why they have reached such a number."

It is certain that the present poverty of our provinces is doing greater damage to this kingdom than the wretched Turkish war has done to the House of Austria, however great may be the secret satisfaction that we derive from their defeats.

Even a magnificent province like Normandy is succumbing beneath the burden of its taxes and the vexations of its tax-farmers; the farmers are ruined and no more are to be found. I know people who have been reduced to turn over excellent estates to be exploited by their servants.

The Duke of Orleans recently brought to the Council a piece of bread baked from fern that we had procured for him. At the opening of the session he placed it on the King's table, saying: *Sire, that is how your subjects are being fed.*

Meanwhile, M. Orry is boasting of the prosperity of the kingdom, the regularity of tax-payments, and the abundance of money in Paris which, he says, is the guarantee of the royal credit. He basks in the affection of the financiers, and there is no doubt that the greater the number of the poor, the wealthier those people become. They are received, and treated with deference everywhere, and yet they contribute nothing to the public exchequer.

The Bishop of Chartres expressed himself in a singularly bold manner at the King's *lever* and at the Queen's dinner. When the King asked him about the state of his diocese, he replied that it was ravaged by famine and mortality; that men were eating grass like sheep; and that soon the plague would follow, and that would spare no one (the court included, he meant). The Queen having offered him a hundred *louis* for the poor, the good Bishop replied: "Madam, keep your money; when the King's finances, and mine, are exhausted, Your Majesty will be able to assist my poor diocesans, if anything remains to you." The answer given to all these tales is that the season is good and that the harvest promises to be plentiful. But I wonder what the harvest will yield to the poor? Is the wheat theirs? The harvest belongs to the rich farmers who, even they, as soon as they gather it in, are pestered with demands by their landlords, their creditors and the collectors of the royal revenues, who have only suspended their prosecutions in order to resume them with even greater severity when the moment comes.

M. de Chauvelin has been criticized for giving alms to a large number of poor at Bourges and for having with him a clever surgeon to dress their wounds. It has been said that it was done from ostentation, for the fashionable view among the Cardinal's supporters is that the present distress is nothing, and that its extent is being exaggerated by the Chauvelinites. Of course, if M. de Chauvelin had given no alms, he would have been blamed for being hard-hearted.

Last Sunday (September 1739), as the King journeyed via Issy to Choisy to visit the Cardinal, he passed through the Faubourg St. Victor. This became known, and the people gathered and cried, not Long live the King!, but *hunger, famine, bread*! The King was mortified and, arriving at Choisy, he dismissed the workmen working on his gardens; he did this from goodness of heart, being scandalized by expenditure on luxuries while such poverty prevailed. He wrote the same evening to the Cardinal to tell him what had happened and of the orders he had given. The Cardinal replied immediately, praising his goodness of heart, but urging him to re-engage his workmen,

74

or he would deprive them of all means of subsistence. Since that moment the King has been in a pitiable state of sadness and dejection.

The same Councillor of State of whom I spoke earlier, and who has just returned from a two months' stay on his estates in the Perche country, tells me that he saw there nothing but a band of rascals who refuse to work, and that it is a waste of money to give them alms. He has, in all seriousness, persuaded the ministry that it is slothful habits that are corrupting the manner of living of the provinces. In much the same manner, I have heard people accusing poor children being operated on by a surgeon of being too noisy.

Following his advice, they have put men to work on the roads, not on forced labour but for wages; so our ministers and governors derive some benefit by having fine avenues constructed, leading to their *châteaux*. They say that this is *to sow in order to reap*; for, at the same time, they will press forward with the collection of the *taille,* so that they may take back with one hand what they give with the other. Such are the men in charge of our affairs: hard, tyrannical, self-satisfied, and judging their neighbour's fate by their own; like execution-judges, accustomed to watch cold-bloodedly as the limbs of their tortured victims are broken.

All poverty arises from idleness, and the present level of taxation is not high enough. These brutal ministers think that they will give a spur to industry and reform manners by forcing people to pay fatter contributions. For a long time now I have heard this cruel maxim expounded, which is based on the belief that there is idleness in a few districts that have been exempt from taxation (merely because it was too easy to make false returns there), whereas there is hard work done in districts subject to the heaviest taxes. They do not realize that this goad has already exceeded its limits and has become a saw or a cutlass, and that labour is discouraged as soon as the increase in taxation far exceeds the increase that it may yield in profit. In truth, it would be better to pursue a course that is exactly contrary to the one that is apparently being adopted: to fix each parish's quota by agreement and to declare, once and for all, that this quota may subsequently be reduced, but never increased; and that it is permissible to work, to multiply, and to settle one's affairs without fear of punishment.

e Daniel Defoe on the Wealthy Trading Class in England (1726)

AS TO THE wealth of the nation, that undoubtedly lies chiefly among the trading part of the people; and tho' there are a great many families rais'd within few years, in the late war by great employments, and by great actions abroad, to the honour of the *English* gentry; yet how many more families among the tradesmen have been rais'd to immense estates, even during the same time, by the attending circumstances of the war? such as the cloathing, the paying, the victualling and furnishing, &c. both army and navy? And by whom have the prodigious taxes been paid, the loans supplied, and money advanced upon all occasions? By whom are the Banks and Companies carried on? And on whom are the Customs and Excises levied? Has not the trade and tradesmen born the burthen of the war? And do they not still pay four millions a year interest for the publick debts? On whom are the funds levied, and by whom the publick credit supported? Is not trade the inexhausted fund of all funds, and upon which all the rest depend?

As is the trade, so in proportion are the tradesmen; and how wealthy are tradesmen in almost all the several parts of *England,* as well as in *London?* How ordinary is it to see a tradesman go off of the stage, even but from mere shop-keeping, with, from ten to forty thousand pounds estate, to divide among his family? when, on the contrary, take the gentry in *England* from one end to the other, except a few here and there, what with excessive high living, which is of late grown so much into a disease, and the other ordinary circumstances of families, we find few families of the lower gentry, that is to say, from six or seven hundred a year downwards, but they are in debt and in necessitous circumstances, and a great many of greater estates also.

On the other hand, let any one who is acquainted with *England,* look but abroad into the several counties, especially near *London,* or within fifty miles of it: How are the antient families worn out by

From Daniel Defoe, THE COMPLETE ENGLISH TRADESMAN (1726), in ENGLISH HISTORICAL DOCUMENTS (London, 1957), vol. x (1714–1783), pp. 524–7. Reprinted by permission of Eyre and Spottiswoode and Oxford University Press, Inc.

time and family misfortunes, and the estates possess'd by a new race of tradesmen, grown up into families of gentry, and establish'd by the immense wealth, gain'd, as I may say, behind the counter; that is, in the shop, the warehouse, and the compting-house? How are the sons of tradesmen rank'd among the prime of the gentry? How are the daughters of tradesmen at this time adorn'd with the ducal coronets, and seen riding in the coaches of the best of our nobility? Nay, many of our trading gentlemen at this time refuse to be Ennobled, scorn being knighted, and content themselves with being known to be rated among the richest Commoners in the nation: And it must be acknowledg'd, that whatever they be as to court-breeding, and to manners, they, generally speaking, come behind none of the gentry in knowledge of the world.

At this very day we see the son of Sir *Thomas Scawen* match'd into the ducal family of *Bedford,* and the son of Sir *James Bateman* into the princely house of *Marlborough,* both whose ancestors, within the memory of the writers of these sheets, were tradesmen in *London*; the first Sir *William Scawen's* apprentice, and the latter's grandfather a *P——* upon, or near, *London-Bridge.*

How many noble seats, superior to the palaces of sovereign Princes (in some countries) do we see erected within few miles of this city by tradesmen, or the sons of tradesmen, while the seats and castles of the antient gentry, like their families, look *worn out,* and fallen into *decay*; witness the noble house of Sir *John Eyles,* himself a Merchant, at *Giddy-hall* near *Rumford*; Sir *Gregory Page* on *Black-heath,* the son of a *Brewer*; Sir *Nathanael Mead* near *Weal-green,* his father a *Linen-Draper,* with many others, too long to repeat; and to crown all, the Lord *Castlemain's* at *Wanstead,* his father Sir *Josiah Child* originally a Tradesman.

It was a smart, but just repartee of a *London* tradesman, when a gentleman, *who had a good estate too,* rudely reproach'd him in company, and bad him hold his tongue, for he was no Gentleman; *No, Sir,* says he, *but I can buy a Gentleman,* and therefore I claim a liberty to speak among Gentlemen.

Again, in how superior a port or figure (as we now call it) do our tradesmen live, to what the middling gentry either do or can support? An ordinary tradesman now, not in the city only, but in the country, shall spend more money by the year, than a gentleman of four or five hundred pounds a year can do; and shall encrease and lay up every year too; whereas the gentleman shall at the best stand stock still, just where he began, nay, perhaps decline; and as for the lower gentry, from an hundred pounds a year to three hundred, or thereabouts, *though they are often as proud and high in their appearance as the other*; as to them, I say, a *Shoemaker* in *London* shall keep a better house, spend more money, cloath his family better, and yet grow rich too: It is evident where the difference lies, *an Estate's a pond*, but *a Trade's a spring*; The first, if it keeps full, and the water wholesom, by the ordinary supplies and dreins from the neighbouring grounds, 'tis well, and 'tis all that is expected; but the other is an inexhausted current, which not only fills the pond, and keeps it full, but is continually running over, and fills all the lower ponds and places about it.

This being the case in *England*, and our trade being so vastly great, it is no wonder that the tradesmen in *England* fill the lists of our nobility and gentry; no wonder that the gentlemen of the best families marry tradesmen's daughters, and put their younger sons apprentices to tradesmen; and how often do these younger sons come to buy the elder sons' estates, and restore the family, when the elder, and head of the house, proving rakish and extravagant, has wasted his patrimony, and is obliged to make out the blessing of *Israel's* family, where the younger son bought the birth-right, and the elder was doom'd to serve him?

Trade is so far *here* from being inconsistent with a Gentleman, that *in short* trade in *England* makes Gentlemen, and has peopled this nation with Gentlemen; for after a generation or two the tradesmen's children, or at least their grand-children, come to be as good Gentlemen, Statesmen, Parliament-men, Privy-Counsellors, Judges, Bishops and Noblemen, as those of the highest birth and the most antient families; and nothing too high for them: Thus the late Earl of *Haversham* was originally a Merchant, the late Secretary *Craggs* was the son of a *Barber*; the present Lord *Castlemain's* father was a Tradesman; the great grandfather of the present Duke of *Bedford* the same, and so of several others: Nor do we find any defect either in the genius or capacities of the posterity of tradesmen, arising from any remains of mechanick blood, which 'tis pretended should influence them; but all the gallantry of spirit, greatness of soul, and all the generous principles, that can be found in any of the antient families, whose blood is the most untainted, as they call it, with the low mixtures of a mechanick race, are found in these; and, as is said before, they generally go beyond them in knowledge of the world, which is the best education.

We see the tradesmen of *England,* as they grow wealthy, coming every day to the Herald's office, to search for the Coats of Arms of their ancestors, in order to paint them upon their coaches, and engrave them upon their plate, embroider them upon their furniture, or carve them upon the pediments of their new houses; and how often do we see them trace the registers of their families up to the prime nobility, or the most antient gentry of the kingdom?

In this search we find them often qualified to raise new families, if they do not descend from old; as was said of a certain tradesman of *London,* that if he could not find the antient race of Gentlemen, from which he came, he would begin a new race, who should be as good Gentlemen as any that went before them: They tell us a story of the old Lord *Craven,* who was afterwards created Earl of *Craven* by King *Charles* II, that being unbraided with his being of an upstart nobility, by the famous *Aubery,* Earl of *Oxford,* who was himself of the very antient family of the *Veres,* Earls of *Oxford,* the Lord *Craven* told him, he (*Craven*) would Cap pedigrees with him (*Oxford*) for a wager; the Earl of *Oxford* laugh'd at the challenge, and began, reckoning up his famous ancestors, who had been Earls of *Oxford* for an hundred years past, and Knights for some hundreds of years more; but when my Lord *Craven* began, he read over his family thus; I am *William* Lord *Craven,* my father was *Lord* Mayor of *London,* and my grandfather was *the Lord knows who*; wherefore I think my pedigree as good as yours, my Lord, (meaning the Earl of *Oxford*:) The story was merry enough, but is to my purpose exactly; for let the grandfather be who he would, his father Sir *William Craven,* who was Lord-Mayor of *London,* was a Wholesale-Grocer, and rais'd the family by trade, and yet no body doubts but that the family of *Craven* is at this day, as truly noble in all the beauties which adorn noble birth and blood, as can be desir'd of any family, however antient, or antiently noble.

4

Economic Changes

THE CHANGES taking place in agriculture and the possibilities of further improvements in soil cultivation are illustrated by two extracts from the writings of Arthur Young (1741–1820), the great advocate of enclosure and land reclamation. In the first Young points out that the high cost of enclosure by Act of Parliament in England frequently made it far less profitable than was generally supposed. In the second he describes the fertility of the soil of France.

The description by John Aiken illustrates the progress made by the "Industrial Revolution" in England before the close of the century. As a sign of the times, it is perhaps of interest to note how lyrical the author becomes when he describes the dexterity of young children in handling cotton pieces!

a Arthur Young on the "Agricultural Revolution"

Enclosures in England (1770)

LASTLY, let me offer some remarks on the great improvement carrying on of inclosures; but this will require a more diffusive examination. There is scarcely any point in rural œconomics more generally acknowledged, than the great benefits of inclosing open lands: some authors, it is true, have attacked them as suppositious, and asserted them to be a national disadvantage, of trivial use to the proprietors, but very mischievous to the poor. My residence in this part of *Yorkshire* brought (at first accidentally) to my knowledge some particulars respecting the merits of inclosing, and the means commonly pursued in the execution, which are not to be found in the *face* of any *acts* whatever; but which are certainly of importance in weighing and deciding the advantages of the measure. To give you

From Arthur Young, A SIX MONTHS' TOUR THROUGH THE NORTH OF ENGLAND (1770), in ENGLISH HISTORICAL DOCUMENTS (London, 1957), vol. x (1714–1783), pp. 435–9. Reprinted by permission of Eyre and Spottiswoode.

a tolerable idea of these circumstances, it will be necessary to sketch the progress of an inclosure, as it generally is conducted, without any eye to legal forms, or the letter of the act.

First, The proprietors of large estates generally agree upon the measure, adjust the principal points among themselves, and fix upon their attorney before they appoint any general meeting of *all* the proprietors. The small proprietor, whose property in the township is perhaps his all, has little or no weight in regulating the clauses of the Act of Parliament, has seldom if ever an opportunity of putting a single one in the bill favourable to his rights, and has as little influence in the choice of commissioners; and of consequence, they have seldom any great inducement to be attentive to his interest; some recent instances of which I have heard of.

II] Any proprietor possessing a fifth of the manor, parish, lord-ship, &c. to be inclosed, has the right of a negative upon the meas-ure, consequently the poorer proprietors are often obliged to assent to unreasonable clauses, rather than give up all the advantages they hope from the inclosure.

III] The attorney delivers his bill to the commissioners, who pay him and themselves without producing any account, and in what manner they please. Is it therefore any wonder, that the expences previous to the actual inclosing the ground are very frequently (un-less where the township is very small) from 1800*l.* to 2000*l.* all which is levied and expended by the commissioners absolutely, and without controul? To this extravagant expence add, that attending the inclosure itself, the making the ditches; the posts and railing; buying and setting the quickwood, &c. this, added to the former expence, must surely run away with great part of the profits expected from the inclosure, even if it was absolutely unavoidable. But what must we think of the indolence of the proprietors, who will thus unnecessarily neglect the great improvement of their estates to ad-vance the private interests of the commissioners, &c.

IV] The division and distribution of the lands are totally in their breasts, and as the quality of the soil as well as the number of acres is considered, the business is extremely intricate, and requires uncom-mon attention; but on the contrary is often executed in an inaccurate and blundering manner. Nor is there any appeal but to the commis-sioners themselves, from their allotments, however carelessly or par-tially made. Thus is the property of the proprietors, and especially the poor ones, entirely at their mercy; every passion of resentment, prejudice, &c. may be gratified without controul; for they are vested with a despotic power known in no other branch of business in this free country.

V] Justice as well as common sense requires that after the *survey* and *division*, the *award* of the commissioners should be directly published, it being the record which proves the respective properties: and likewise that their accounts should, upon the conclusion of the business, be regularly arranged under each distinct head attended by every corresponding voucher, and made public to the inspection of every proprietor, but unfortunately this is far from being the case, the time of publishing the award, is greatly procrastinated, and as to accounts they seldom show any, all the particulars of that sort remain for ever a profound secret, save the particular sum demanded from each proprietor. That indeed if they chuse it, they may communicate to each other and be able to form some judgment of the inequality of particular assessments, but as there lies no appeal from the award they are generally induced to sit down quietly, though the disproportion of the allotments and assessments should be glaringly conspicuous. . . .

VII] There is no remedy against the impositions or blunders of the commissioners, but that which, perhaps, is as bad as the disease, *viz.* filing a bill in chancery; a remedy, which in all probability, one or two persons must support for the good of *the whole,* but without the assistance of *half.*

VIII] And if I am not greatly mistaken, even this means of redress is more limited than in most other cases: it may compel the commissioners to deliver in their accounts, but how can it rectify any unjust management of the land? It lies in the breast of the commissioners when to make their award, and I do not imagine, that till they have signed it, it would be prudent to file the bill against them. It might possibly be two or three years before a decree could be obtained, and when any proprietor has been at the expence of inclosing his share, cultivating the ground, and raising the fences, how is it possible that even the power of the court of chancery, extensive as it is, can in this case redress the injury, whether it arises from the particular situation of the allotment, the quantity, or the quality of the soil. Need I say any thing further, to point out the real necessity of the proprietors of land exerting themselves to retrench this enormous power, vested in the commissioners. The advantages resulting from inclosures, are not to be looked upon as merely beneficial to the individual, they are of the most extensive national advantage. The improvements in agriculture, that source of all our power, must be trifling without them; surely therefore, every measure that can promote them should be adopted, every difficulty attending them *smoothed,* and every injury redressed.

It appears clearly from the above circumstances that the proprietors of a lordship to be inclosed, give to the commissioners for executing the act, an unlimited power of taxing their estates, and including that unheard of power of being party, judge, and jury in the whole affair of paying themselves. If a proprietor is offended at their proceedings, and refuses to pay the sums levied on him, they are entrusted by the act, with powers immediately to distrain. Such immense confidence in the commissioners, might be attended with few inconveniences, if they were universally men of considerable property, and known integrity; but when the hacknied sons of *business* are employed (which is the case nine times out of ten), the proprietors have just reason to tremble at the situation of their purses. It is very natural to conclude, that such causes must be attended with a very striking effect, and this accordingly is the case; for impositions, and the inaccuracy of commissioners have arose to such a height, that many proprietors who were eager for inclosures, on a sanguine prospect of benefit, have found the measure highly injurious and totally owing to the immense expences. There is a very false idea current, that rents are doubled by inclosing; a measure may be vastly advantageous without possessing such uncommon merit. This notion hurries numbers to inclosing, who afterwards find the expences to run away with great part of the profit. But even where the expences do not exceed the profit, it is very often the case, that the proprietor is not repaid in six or seven years, perhaps more; and when it is considered, how little able some proprietors, even in good circumstances, are to wait so long before they are reimbursed their expences; how often they are disabled (by advancing their proportions necessary for an inclosure) to provide for the settlement of their children in the world, how often they are prevented cultivating their new inclosure to any advantage, by being drained of their ready money — I think it will incontestibly appear, that the advantages resulting from this extravagant method, are trivial to the majority of proprietors in comparison to what they might reasonably have expected, from a more equal management.

You will not think this surprizing, when you are informed the immediate rise of rent in many inclosures in this neighbourhood, has not amounted to above five or six shillings an acre, and in some to no more than eighteen pence and two shillings an acre. In strong rich lands where they have some meadow lands, the rise is higher. But indeed the smallness of the rise is, in some measure, owing to their want of better husbandry; for with very few meadows, they know scarce any thing of clover and ray-grass or turnips; consequently the value of an inclosure is comparatively small to them.

But whatever cause the fact is owing to, it remains equally surprizing that the proprietors should not be more attentive to their interest, a rise of rent sufficient to pay the expences of the inclosure under the management of honest, able, and careful conductors, *may* vanish into nothing upon the mention of those who have neither integrity, abilities, or attention; and it must be strange supineness indeed, that can suffer the gentlemen of a county to be duped in so flagrant a manner, as to allow even in idea, the trains of imposition which are now common in the business of inclosures. It is wonderful they do not exert themselves to introduce common sense and honesty, in an affair hitherto under the cognizance of ignorance, knavery, and self-interest.

For this purpose, it seems requisite, that the following clauses should be added to the acts for inclosure.

I] That the small proprietors should have a share in the nomination of commissioners; either by a union of votes or otherwise, as might be determined.

II] That the attorney and commissioners should, before the passing the act, agree upon their several rewards, and on no account whatever be suffered to pay themselves one shilling.

III] That the commissioners proceed immediately to the survey, distribution, and assignment, and the building or forming public works.

IV] That in case any man thinks himself injured, he may be at liberty (but totally at his own expence, in case he is in the wrong) to summons a jury immediately, to view and decide the affair.

V] That as soon as the abovementioned business is concluded, the commissioners do give in their account of all sums received and expended, in the most regular manner, and with all the vouchers for payment; and that they immediately publish their award.

VI] That an action at common law be had against the commissioners for false, or unvouched accounts, *&c. &c.*

By means of these or other clauses better imagined, but of the same intention, this undoubtedly beneficial measure of inclosing would be infinitely extended, and the interests of the community, as well as individuals, greatly secured.

The Fertility of the Soil in France (1789)

In respect to the geoponic [agricultural] division of the soils of the kingdom, the rich calcareous plain of the north-eastern quarter first calls for our attention. I crossed this in several directions, and from the observations I made, the following are the limits I would assign to it. On the coast it may be said to extend from Carentan in Normandy, for the northern promontory of that province, which projects into the sea at Cherbourg, is of a different soil. From Carentan to Coutances the land is chiefly poor and stony, and holds, with many variations, quite to Brest. In a line a little to the south of the coast, before Caen, is seen the first considerable change of soil from Calais; it there becomes a red *stone brash*; this rich tract is here, therefore, narrow. On re-entering Normandy on the side of Alençon, from Anjou and Maine, I first met with the rich loams on a calcareous bottom at Beaumont; at Alençon there is a noble soil, which I then lost no more in advancing northwards. In another line I entered this rich district about 10 miles to the south of Tours. The hills on the Loire, though all calcareous that I noticed, are not all rich, though on some the soil is deep and good. Directly to the south of Orléans there begins the miserable Sologne, which, though on a calcareous bottom of marl, is too poor to be included in the present district. From Orléans to Paris, and also Fontainebleau, no exceptions are to be made, but in the small space of poor sandstone in the royal forest of the latter town. In a fourth direction this district is entered, a few miles to the south of Nemours. At Croisière the first chalk is visible to the traveller. Advancing to the north-east, very good land is found near Nangis, and then bearing north, I entered the fertile plain of Brie. Some of the vales through which the Marne flows are rich, but the hills are poor. The plain of Reims may be classed in the present district, but at Soissons and thence due north all is ex-

From Constantia Maxwell (ed.), TRAVELS IN FRANCE DURING THE YEARS 1787, 1788, & 1789 (London, 1950), pp. 269–74. Reprinted by permission of the Cambridge University Press.

cellent. These limits enclose one of the finest territories that I suppose is to be found in Europe. From Dunkirk to Nemours is not less
than 180 miles in a right line. From Soissons to Carentan is another
right line of about 200 miles. From Eu, on the Norman coast, to
Chartres is 100 miles, and though the breadth of this rich district at
Caen, Bayeux, etc. is not considerable, yet the whole will be found
to contain not a trifling proportion of the whole kingdom. This
noble territory includes the deep, level, and fertile plain of Flanders,
and part of Artois, than which a richer soil can hardly be desired to
repay the industry of mankind. Every step of the way from the very
gate of Paris to near Soissons, and thence to Cambrai, is a sandy
loam of an admirable texture. About Meaux it is to be ranked among
the finest in the world. The line through Picardy is inferior, yet for
the most part excellent. But all the arable part of Normandy, which
is within these limits, is of the same rich friable sandy loam; that
from Bernay to Elbeuf can scarcely be exceeded. As to the pastures
of the same province, we have, I believe, nothing either in England
or Ireland equal to them. The famous Pays de Beauce, which I
crossed between Arpajon and Orléans, resembles the vales of Meaux
and Senlis; it is not, however, in general, so deep as the former.

The limits I have traced are those of great fertility; but the calcareous district, and even [the] chalk, is much more extensive. To
the east it reaches across Champagne; a strong change, not having
occurred to me till about Ste Menehould. From Metz to Nancy all
is calcareous, but not chalk. Limestone land I found plentifully in
the southern parts of Alsace, and from Belfort across Franche Comté
to Dôle all the stones I tried were calcareous. Immense districts in
Dauphiné and Provence are the same. I remarked the chalk country
to extend east to about Ste Menehould and south to Nemours and
Montargis in one line. In another, all that of the Angoumois which
I saw is the same; much in Poitou, and through Touraine to the
Loire. Most of the course of the Loire is, I believe, chalk, and the
whole of it calcareous. Hence it appears that the chalk country of
France is of very considerable extent, and comprises by far the richest
and most fertile provinces of the kingdom.

The next considerable district, for fertility, is the plain of the
Garonne. Passing to the south from Limousin, it is entered about
Cressensac, with the province of Quercy, and improves all the way
to Montauban and Toulouse, where it is one of the finest levels of

fertile soil that can anywhere be seen. It continues, but not equally fruitful, to the foot of the Pyrenees, by St Gaudens etc., very even to the eye, when viewed from the promenade at Montauban, which commands one of the richest, as well as magnificent, prospects to be met with in France. This plain I found, however, to be much indented and irregular; for to the west of Auch, and all beyond it to Bayonne, is too inferior to be admitted; and to the east Mirepoix, Pamiers and Carcassonne are among the hills, and all the way from Agen to Bordeaux, though the river flows through one of the richest valleys that is to be seen in the world, yet the breadth appeared to be everywhere inconsiderable.

In travelling from Narbonne to Béziers, Pézenas, Montpellier and Nîmes, everyone I conversed with represented that vale as the most fruitful in France. Olives and mulberries, as well as vines, render it very productive, but in point of soil much the greater part of it is inferior to all I have named. The Bas Poitou, as I was informed by a person who resides in it, is of a fertility that deserves to be classed with the richest soils of France; 100,000 arpents of rich marshes have been drained there. The narrow plain of Alsace must [also] be classed among the richest soils of France. It resembles Flanders a good deal, though inferior to that fine province. It consists of a deep rich sandy loam, equal to the large production of all sorts of crops. A more celebrated district is the Limagne of Auvergne, a flat and chiefly a calcareous vale, surrounded by great ranges of volcanic mountains. It is certainly one of the finest soils in the world. I have now noticed all the districts of France, which, to my knowledge, are of any remarkable fertility; they amount to above 28 millions of English acres.

Of the other provinces, Bretagne is generally gravel, or gravelly sand, commonly deep, and on a gravelly bottom, of an inferior and barren nature. All that I saw in the two provinces of Anjou and Maine are gravel, sand, or stone. Immense tracks in both these provinces are waste, under ling, fern, furze, etc. Touraine is better, but considerable tracks in the northern part of the province are no better than Anjou and Maine. Sologne is one of the poorest and most unimproved provinces of the kingdom. It is flat consisting of a poor sand or gravel, everywhere on a clay or marl bottom, retentive of water to such a degree, that every ditch and hole was full of it. Berry is much better, though both sandy and gravelly. La Marche and

Limousin consist of friable sandy loams. There are tracts in these provinces that are very fertile, and I saw none that should be esteemed sterile. Poitou consists of two divisions, the upper and the lower; the last of which has the reputation of being a much richer country, especially the grass lands on the coast. All I saw of Angoumois is chalk, and much of it thin and poor. Those parts of Guienne and Gascoign not included in the rich vale of the Garonne must be considered in respect of soil as poor. The *landes* (heaths) of Bordeaux, though neither unproductive nor unimprovable, are in their present state to be classed amongst the worst soils of France. The roots of the Pyrenees are covered with immense wastes, which demand much industry to render profitable. Roussillon is in general calcareous, much of it flat and very stony, as well as dry and barren; but the irrigated vales are of a most exuberant fertility.

The vast province of Languedoc, in productions one of the richest in the kingdom, does not rank high in the scale of soil; it is by far too stony. I take seven-eighths of it to be mountainous. The productive vale from Narbonne to Nîmes is generally but a few miles in breadth, and considerable wastes are seen in most parts of it. Many of the mountains are productive from irrigation. Some parts of the vale are very rich, and there are few finer soils in France than what I saw near the canal in going from Béziers to Carcassonne. Provence and Dauphiné are mountainous countries, with the variation of some lovely plains and valleys, which bear a very inconsiderable proportion to the whole. Of these two provinces the former is certainly the driest, in point of soil, in the kingdom. Rock with sandy gravels abound there, and the course of the Durance is so ruined by sand and shingle, that on a moderate calculation, above 130,000 acres have been destroyed, which would have been the finest soil in the country if it had not been for that river. All I saw in both provinces is calcareous; and I was informed that the greater part of the mountains of Provence are so. These, towards Barcelonnette, and in all the higher parts of the province, are covered with good grass, that feeds a million of emigrating sheep, besides wast herds of cattle. The vales which I saw are in general fine. The county of Venaissin, or district of Avignon, is one of the richest in the kingdom. Its admirable irrigation is, of itself, sufficient to make it appear so, but I found the soil to consist of deep rich loam, with white and calcareous clays. The whole coast of Provence is a poor stony soil, with exceptions of very small spaces under happier circumstances. This province contains one of the most singular districts in the kingdom, namely that of the Crau, which is a stony plain to the south-east of Arles not containing less than 350 square miles. It is absolutely covered with round stones of all sizes, some of which are as large as a man's head. Vegetation is extremely thin.

The Lyonnais is mountainous, and what I saw of it, is poor, stony and rough, with much waste land. Auvergne, though chiefly mountainous, is not a poor province; the soil for a hilly country is in general above mediocrity, and the highest mountains feed vast herds of cattle, which are exported to a considerable amount. The Bourbonnais and the Nivernais form one vast plain, through which the Loire and the Allier pass; the predominant soil is gravel. The whole in its present cultivation must be reckoned amongst the most unproductive provinces of the kingdom. Burgundy is exceedingly diversified; some good vales, some mountains, and some poor granite soils. The subdivision of the province, called Bresse, is a miserable country, where the ponds alone amount to not much less than 250,000 acres. Franche Comté abounds with red ferruginous loams, schistus, gravel, with limestone in the mountains very common. The whole province is very improvable. Lorraine is poor in soil. The predominant feature of Champagne is chalk; in great tracks it is thin and poor. The southern part has from its poverty acquired the name of *pouilleux,* or lousy.

I have now made the tour of all the French provinces, and shall in general observe, that I think the kingdom is superior to England in the circumstance of soil. The proportion of poor land in England, to the total of the kingdom, is greater than the similar proportion in France; nor have they anywhere such tracks of wretched blowing sand as are to be met with in Norfolk and Suffolk. Their heaths, moors, and wastes not mountainous, what they term *landes,* and which are so frequent in Brittany, Anjou, Maine and Guienne, are infinitely better than our northern moors; and the mountains of Scotland and Wales cannot be compared, in point of soil, with those of the Pyrenees, Auvergne, Dauphiné, Provence and Languedoc. Another advantage almost inestimable is, that their tenacious loams do not take the character of clays, which in some parts of England are so stubborn and harsh, that the expense of culture is almost equal to a moderate produce. Such clays as I have seen in Sussex, I never met with in France.

b John Aikin on the "Industrial Revolution" in England (*1795*)

SPINNING MACHINES ... were first used by the country people on a confined scale, twelve spindles being thought a great matter; while the awkward posture required to spin on them was discouraging to grown up people, who saw with surprize children from nine to twelve years of age manage them with dexterity, whereby plenty was brought into families formerly overburthened with children, and the poor weavers were delivered from the bondage in which they had lain from the insolence of spinners. The following state of the case will explain this matter. From the time that the original system in the fustian branch, of buying pieces in the grey from the weaver, was changed, by delivering them out work, the custom of giving them out weft in the cops, which obtained for a while, grew into disuse, as there was no detecting the knavery of spinners till a piece came in woven; so that the practice was altered, and wool given with warps, the weaver answering for the spinning. And the weavers in a scarcity of spinning have sometimes been paid less for the weft than they gave the spinners, but durst not complain, much less abate the spinner, lest their looms should be unemployed. But when spinning-jennies were introduced, and children could work upon them, the case was reversed.

The plenty of weft produced by this means gave uneasiness to the country people, and the weavers were afraid lest the manufacturers should demand finer weft woven at the former prices, which occasioned some risings, and the demolition of jennies in some places by the uninformed populace. At length Dorning Rasbotham, Esq., a worthy magistrate near Bolton, wrote and printed a sensible address to the weavers, in order to convince them of their own interest in encouraging these engines, which happily produced a general acquiescence in their use to a certain number of spindles. These were soon multiplied to three or four times the number; nor did the invention of mechanics rest here, for the demand for twist for warps was greater as weft grew more plentiful, whence engines were soon constructed for this purpose.

From John Aikin, A DESCRIPTION OF THE COUNTRY FROM THIRTY TO FIFTY MILES ROUND MANCHESTER (London, 1795), pp. 167–81.

The improvements kept increasing, till the capital engines for twist were perfected, by which thousands of spindles are put in motion by a water wheel, and managed mostly by children, without confusion and with less waste of cotton than by the former methods. But the carding and slubbing preparatory to twisting required a greater range of invention. The first attempts were in carding engines, which are very curious, and now brought a great degree of perfection; and an engine has been contrived for converting the carded wool to slubbing, by drawing it to about the thickness of candlewick preparatory to throwing it into twist. When these larger machines that moved by water were first set to work, they produced such excellent twist for warps, that they soon out-rivalled the warps made on the larger jennies, which had yielded good profits to the owners. In consequence of this, according to the usual short-sighted policy of narrow-minded and interested men, the country was excited against the water-machines, and some of them were demolished before protection could be obtained. Yet a little reflection would have shown the country people that, if some warps were made, there would be a greater demand for weft from their jennies, and a better price for it. This has since been fully experienced in the introduction of muslins; for no contrivance in the other machines can make the thread hold when it is so slack thrown as to suit for weft; nor can it be supposed that the attempt would be made, as the demand for twist for warps will fully employ them. For when cotton bears a reasonable price, the warps made of this twist will be as cheap as those made with yarn, and keep the money at home which used to be sent abroad for that article; there being no comparison between yarn and cotton warps in goodness. In fact, cotton warps have lately been introduced to a great extent, where yarn had before been used. As these machines are now to be seen by the curious, and specifications of their construction may be had at the Patent Office, no delicacy is necessary in laying descriptions of them fully before the public. We shall, therefore, attempt to give such an idea of them as can be communicated by words, beginning with the machine for carding cotton.

The spinners had begun to pick the husks of cotton seeds from their wool, and pass it through a lather of soap, preparatory to carding, before carding engines were invented; and upon their introduction, the full operation was to pick and soap the wool, wring it out well from the lather, dry it, then spread a given quantity upon the feeder of a carding engine. This feeder was a coarse cloth, sewed together at the ends, and strained upon small rollers; upon the cotton served by this feeder, a roller faced with tin punched through like a common grater, made a slow revolution, pinching up the cotton; and the feeder, answering its motion, kept delivering more, while the vacant part of the cloth coming up was served with more cotton. Thus the cotton was delivered to sets of cylinders with cards nailed upon them; as many of these as had a revolution onward from the feeder, were governed by one strap, from the first mover, fixed on several pullies or whorles upon the spindles passing through the centres of those cylinders. Other cylinders had a contrary motion, to strip the cotton from those of the first description, delivering it to the next, in the direct motion onward to the largest cylinder of all, which received the cotton thoroughly carded by the inverse and direct revolutions of these intermediate cylinders.

An invention was necessary at the end of the motion, to take off the cardings, which was first attempted by a fluted roller put in motion by a strap from the inverse system of cylinders, which pressing upon the card teeth of the large cylinders, rubbed off the cardings, which fell into a receptacle below; but these cardings were rubbed too close in the operation, and hence not so open for the purpose of spinning as could be wished. A most curious contrivance produced the remedy desired; this was effected by casting a wormlike or spiral fluxion at the centre of the great wheel, which was fixed upon the cylinder to be divested of the cardings; this spiral worm worked a small wheel upon a spindle which governed a tumbler by a crank, and threw a cross plate of metal garnished with small teeth against the cards at intervals, and took off the carding as open as could be wished.

This contrivance Mr. Arkwright claimed as his own invention till a verdict in the King's-Bench set aside his claim. This gentleman, knighted in the present reign for his ingenuity, is worthy of being celebrated for his industry in the early observations which he made of new inventions in carding and spinning, and his capacity in forming them into a perfect system in the twist machine, for which he obtained a patent. But finding several improvements not in his first specification, he got it extended, and specified in particular the above invention to take off the cardings. Before this time he had sued several cotton spinners for an invasion of his patent. They joined issue with him, and in the event he was non-suited. On the extension of his patent, care being taken to specify the additional improvements, he instituted another suit for invasion of his patent, and obtained a verdict in the court of Common Pleas. This occasioned a great alarm among many who had at a great expense erected machines for cotton spinning, of whom an acknowledgement of so much a spindle was demanded under the threat of immediate suit. The persons concerned got the matter removed into the court of King's-Bench, where, upon trial, it was proved that the apparatus above described for taking off the cardings was a prior invention of an ingenious merchant, Mr. Heys by name, in consequence of which a verdict was given against Mr. Arkwright. In fact, the roller upon which Mr. Heys's spindle-strings ran was immediately adapted after his public exhibition of it; his contrivance also of slipping his handle from a square to a round, which checked the operation of spinning and pushing on to an interior contrivance to wind up the spin thread, is adopted in the machines for spinning of twist, which process we shall now describe.

The cotton for this purpose is of the first staple, but not too long grained; being beaten out to open the grain, it is picked very carefully, and the usual process pursued to the carding, with this difference that, instead of several cylinders, there is one only to take cotton wool from the pincher, and deliver it to a very large one, whence it is received by another, and stript by the tumbler, and carried to the server of others in rotation, till it rises from the last in a fine well-corded sheet. This is kept from returning to the cylinder by the attendants; and being gently closed together, is conducted over a pulley high enough to make it fall by its own weight, as it is continually detached from the cards. A deep tin-can is set under, into which the carded wool coils itself, much resembling the wool drawn from Jersey combs: many of these tin-cans are in readiness to replace the filled ones, which are removed to serve a machine for roving, as the first operation of spinning is called; where the cardings of three cans put together are passed through rollers moved by clock-work, which also puts in motion small circular brushes to clear the loose flying hairs of cotton from the rollers; those deliver every three fleeces of carded cotton so connected that when a can is emptied and another is supplied, care is taken that two whole fleeces preserve the continuity of the preparation for twisting, which passes from the rollers to spindles furnished with a curious apparatus to give it a very slight throw and wind it on bobbins in rovings. These undergo several courses of drawing by rollers and throwing, till it is wound upon bobbins in an open and even state, for the final operation of spinning by the machines for making twist.

These machines exhibit in their construction an aggregate of clock-maker's work and machinery most wonderful to behold. The cotton to be spun is introduced through three sets of rollers, so governed by the clock-work, that the set which first receives the cotton makes so many more revolutions than the next in order, and these more than the last which feed the spindles, that it is drawn out considerably in passing through the rollers; being lastly received by spindles, which have every one on the bobbin a fly like that of a flax wheel; both the flyers and the bobbin in like manner are loose on the spindle, which are whirled with amazing rapidity; but every bobbin, resting upon a board, is checked in its course, and only can wind up what twist is spun; and to avoid the inconvenience of winding it in ridges, as in flax-spinning, the board upon which they rest has an alternate motion, which raises and depresses the bobbins, so that the twist winds to and fro, the whole length of each bobbin. A considerable number of spindles may be wrought in one twisting frame, but they are connected in systems of four to each system, so that, when a thread breaks, those four of the system to which they belong may be stopped, while the others are twisting. This advantage is obtained by lifting that system from the square part of a spindle, which by a whorl from the machinery governed the four, to a round part above, which moves without giving motion to the system, till the thread is again connected with the prepared cotton, by pinching off what was unspun, and clapping it to the last roller, where it lays hold of the untwisted cotton, when that set of four is dropped again upon the square of the spindles, and the twisting goes on. Children are soon very dexterous at connecting broken ends with prepared cotton at the rollers, their small fingers being more active and endued with a quicker sensibility of feeling than those of grown persons; and it is wonderful to see with what dispatch they can raise a system, connect threads, and drop it again into work almost instantaneously.

Upon these machines twist is made of any fineness proper for warps; but as it is drawn length way of the staple, it was not so proper for weft; wherefore on the introduction of fine callicoes and muslins, mules were invented, having a name expressive of their species, being a mixed machinery between jennies and the machines for twisting, and adapted to spin weft as fine as could be desired, by adding to the jennies such rollers, governed by clock-maker's work, as were described above, only with this difference that when the threads are drawn out, the motion of the rollers is suspended by an ingenious contrivance, till the weft is hardened and wound up; in which operation the spindles are alternately drawn from and returned to the feeding rollers, being fixed on a moveable frame like those of the billies to make cardings into what are called rovings for the common jennies.

These mules carry often to a hundred and fifty spindles, and can be set to draw weft to an exact fineness up to 150 hanks in the pound, of which muslin has been made, which for a while had a prompt sale; but the flimsiest of its fabric has brought the finer sorts into discredit, and a stagnation of trade damped the sale of the rest.

The worsted and woolen manufactories are alike benefited by improvements in carding and spinning, taken from the cotton machines, and adapted to their particular branches, which improvements make the work people uneasy till they experience that an increased sale of goods in proportion to improvements finds them employment, and that children, who had nothing to do before, earn wages by employment at the machines, whether employed in spinning woollen yarn, Jersey or cotton. Flax is now attempted by the same machinery, but the length of its staple in fine dressed flax may render it difficult to draw; yet the short hards dressed out of it may be spun this way evener and more compact than by the flax wheel, and what was too short for making yarn before may now be wrought up, which will be good economy and lessen the imports.

The new-invented steam engines by a single cylinder closed above, pushing over water to an overshot-wheel, which returns to the reservoir, suppose a common pump-spring, were a great improvement, and employed to advantage as the application of machinery to several branches of business was extended. For by this means, there is less occasion for horses, and any power may be applied by enlarging the diameter of the cylinders, as one of twenty-four inches will force over more than sixty gallons at a stroke. This improvement, which is as simple as ingenious, was the invention of a common pump-maker, Wrigley by name, of this town, who never applied for a patent, but imparted freely what he invented to those who thought proper to employ him.

Some attempts have been made to work a number of looms together by machinery. The first was upon the introduction of swivel-looms, above thirty years since, by Mr. Gartside, with a capital water-wheel at his factory near Garret-hall, now a very large one for cotton spinning by water. Mr. Whitehead, the chief projector, and a partner, has there fixed a steam engine to return the water occasionally, and another fixed in a case of brick on the principle of those to quench fire; upon the least alarm of fire he can screw on his pipe, set the engine to work by the great wheel, and no deficiency of water can occur, the engine forcing up water from the mill-race, so that a single person can send a continued stream of water to any part of the factory or over it; a contrivance worthy to be adopted in all cotton spinning factories, where there is a powerful wheel and plenty of water, which is the case here: for Mr. Gartside spared no cost in his scheme of working swivel-looms by water, and continued to employ them for a considerable time to very little advantage; for one weaver was necessary to take care of a loom, and if the division where the shuttle ranges in any piece was clogged with knots in the warp or broken ends, the whole of a piece or a great part of it was liable to be cut down before a loom could be thrown out of gear; but weavers who work a swivel-loom by the hand themselves have a facility acquired by habit of checking the motion in such cases, returning back the shuttles from a half-shoot to prevent any misfortune.

Mr. Grimshaw of Gorton attempted the construction of machinery to weave piece goods, in a capital factory at Knott-mill, which was burnt down before any judgement could be formed how it would have succeeded.

The prodigious extension of the several branches of the Manchester manufactures has likewise greatly increased the business of several trades and manufactures connected with or dependent upon them. The making of paper at mills in the vicinity has been brought to great perfection, and now includes all kinds, from the strongest parcelling paper to the finest writing sorts, and that on which banker's bills are printed. To the ironmongers' shops, which are greatly increased of late, are generally annexed smithies, where many articles are made, even to nails. A considerable iron foundry is established in Salford, in which are cast most of the articles wanted in Manchester and its neighbourhood, consisting chiefly of large cast wheels for the cotton machines; cylinders, boilers, and pipes for steam engines; cast ovens, and grates of all sizes. This work belongs to Bateman and Sharrard, gentlemen every way qualified for so great an undertaking. Mr. Sharrard is a very ingenious and able engineer, who has improved upon and brought the steam engine to great perfection. Most of those that are used and set up in and about Manchester are of their make and setting up. They are in general of a small size, very compact, stand in a small space, work smooth and easy, and are scarcely heard in the building where erected. They are now used in cotton mills, and for every purpose of the water wheel, where a stream is not to be got, and for winding up coals from a great depth in the coal pits, which is performed with a quickness and ease not to be conceived. . . .

We shall conclude this account of the trade of Manchester with some facts to show the rapid increase and prodigious amount of the cotton manufactures of this island, extracted from a pamphlet published in 1788, entitled, "An Important Crisis in the Callico and Muslin Manufactory in Great Britain explained"; the purpose of which was to warn the nation of the bad consequences which would result from the rivalry of the East India cotton goods which then began to be poured into the markets in increased quantities, and at diminished prices.

The author asserts that, not above twenty years before the time of his writing, the whole cotton trade of Great Britain did not return £200,000 to the country for the raw materials, combined with the labour of the people; and at that period, before the introduction of the water machinery and hand engines, the power of the single wheel could not exceed 50,000 spindles employed in spinning the cotton wool into yarn; but at the present moment, the power of spindles thus employed amounts to two millions; and the gross return for the raw materials and labour exceeds seven millions sterling. It was about the year 1784 that the expiration of Sir Richard Arkwright's patent caused the erection of water machines for the spinning of warps in all parts of the country, with which the hand engines for the spinning of weft kept proportion. At the time he wrote he estimates the number of

Water mills, or machines, at	143
Mule jennies or machines, consisting of 90 spindles each	550
Hand jennies of 80 spindles each	20,070

Of the water mills, 123 are in England, and nineteen in Scotland. Of those in England, Lancashire has 41. . . .

These establishments, when in full work, are estimated to give employment to about 26,000 men, 31,000 women, and 53,000 children, in spinning alone; and in all the subsequent stages of manufacture, the number of persons employed is estimated at 133,000 men, 59,000 women, and 48,000 children; making an aggregate of 159,000 men, 90,000 women, and 101,000 children, in all, 350,000 persons employed in the cotton manufacture.

5

Mercantilism and Free Trade

ADAM SMITH (1723–90), the friend of Hume and Turgot and professor
of Moral Philosophy in the University of Glasgow, published his Wealth
of Nations in London in 1776. In it he strongly argued the case for free
trade and criticized the prevailing system of mercantilism. "The mercantile system," he believed, restricted the volume of trade by promoting
monopoly, and failed to benefit the nation at large by favoring the interest of the producer at the expense of the consumer. In this passage he
expresses the view that the benefits accruing to European nations from
the "engrossing" of their colonial trade have proved largely illusory.

Adam Smith on the Wealth of Nations

THE DISCOVERY of America, and that of a passage to the East
Indies by the Cape of Good Hope, are the two greatest and
most important events recorded in the history of mankind. Their
consequences have already been very great: but, in the short period
of between two and three centuries which has elapsed since these
discoveries were made, it is impossible that the whole extent of their
consequences can have been seen. What benefits or what misfortunes
to mankind may hereafter result from those great events, no human
wisdom can foresee. By uniting, in some measure, the most distant
parts of the world, by enabling them to relieve one another's wants,
to increase one another's enjoyments, and to encourage one another's
industry, their general tendency would seem to be beneficial. To the
natives, however, both of the East and West Indies, all the commercial benefits which can have resulted from those events have been
sunk and lost in the dreadful misfortunes which they have occasioned.
These misfortunes, however, seem to have arisen rather from accident
than from anything in the nature of those events themselves. At the
particular time when these discoveries were made, the superiority of

From Adam Smith, THE WEALTH OF NATIONS, edited by James E. Thorold
Rogers, 2 vols. (Oxford, 1880), vol. ii, pp. 208–17.

force happened to be so great on the side of the Europeans, that they were enabled to commit with impunity every sort of injustice in those remote countries. Hereafter, perhaps, the natives of those countries may grow stronger, or those of Europe may grow weaker, and the inhabitants of all the different quarters of the world may arrive at that equality of courage and force which, by inspiring mutual fear, can alone overawe the injustice of independent nations into some sort of respect for the rights of one another. But nothing seems more likely to establish this equality of force than that mutual communication of knowledge and of all sorts of improvements which an extensive commerce from all countries to all countries naturally, or rather necessarily, carries along with it.

In the meantime, one of the principal effects of those discoveries has been to raise the merchant system to a degree of splendour and glory which it could never otherwise have attained to. It is the object of that system to enrich a great nation rather by trade and manufactures than by the improvement and cultivation of land, rather by the industry of the towns than by that of the country. But, in consequence of those discoveries, the commercial towns of Europe, instead of being the manufacturers and carriers for but a very small part of the world (that part of Europe which is washed by the Atlantic Ocean, and the countries which lie round the Baltic and Mediterranean Seas), have now become the manufacturers for the numerous and thriving cultivators of America, and the carriers, and in some respects the manufacturers too, for almost all the different nations of Asia, Africa, and America. Two new worlds have been opened to their industry, each of them much greater and more extensive than the old one, and the market of one of them is growing still greater and greater every day.

The countries which possess the colonies of America, and which trade directly to the East Indies, enjoy, indeed, the whole show and splendour of this great commerce. Other countries, however, notwithstanding all the invidious restraints by which it is meant to exclude them, frequently enjoy a greater share of the real benefit of it. The colonies of Spain and Portugal, for example, give more real encouragement to the industry of other countries than to that of Spain and Portugal. In the single article of linen alone the consumption of those colonies amounts, it is said, but I do not pretend to warrant the quantity, to more than three millions sterling a year. But this great consumption is almost entirely supplied by France, Flanders, Holland,

and Germany. Spain and Portugal furnish but a small part of it. The capital which supplies the colonies with this great quantity of linen is annually distributed among and furnishes a revenue to the inhabitants of those other countries. The profits of it only are spent in Spain and Portugal, where they help to support the sumptuous profusion of the merchants of Cadiz and Lisbon.

Even the regulations by which each nation endeavours to secure to itself the exclusive trade of its own colonies, are frequently more hurtful to the countries in favour of which they are established than to those against which they are established. The unjust oppression of the industry of other countries falls back, if I may say so, upon the heads of the oppressors, and crushes their industry more than it does that of those other countries. By those regulations, for example, the merchant of Hamburg must send the linen which he destines for the American market to London, and he must bring back from thence the tobacco which he destines for the German market; because he can neither send the one directly to America, nor bring back the other directly from thence. By this restraint he is probably obliged to sell the one somewhat cheaper, and to buy the other somewhat dearer than he otherwise might have done; and his profits are probably somewhat abridged by means of it. In this trade, however, between Hamburg and London, he certainly receives the returns of his capital much more quickly than he could possibly have done in the direct trade to America, even though we should suppose, what is by no means the case, that the payments of America were as punctual as those of London. In the trade, therefore, to which those regulations confine the merchant of Hamburg, his capital can keep in constant employment a much greater quantity of German industry than it possibly could have done in the trade from which he is excluded. Though the one employment, therefore, may to him perhaps be less profitable than the other, it cannot be less advantageous to his country. It is quite otherwise with the employment into which the monopoly naturally attracts, if I may say so, the capital of the London merchant. That employment may, perhaps, be more profitable to him than the greater part of other employments, but, on account of the slowness of the returns, it cannot be more advantageous to his country.

After all the unjust attempts, therefore, of every country in Europe to engross to itself the whole advantage of the trade of its own colonies, no country has yet been able to engross to itself anything but the expense of supporting in time of peace and of defending in time of war the oppressive authority which it assumes over them. The inconveniences resulting from the possession of its colonies, every country has engrossed to itself completely. The advantages resulting from their trade it has been obliged to share with many other countries.

At first sight, no doubt, the monopoly of the great commerce of America naturally seems to be an acquisition of the highest value. To the undiscerning eye of giddy ambition, it naturally presents itself amidst the confused scramble of politics and war as a very dazzling object to fight for. The dazzling splendour of the object, however, the immense greatness of the commerce, is the very quality which renders the monopoly of it hurtful, or which makes one employment, in its own nature necessarily less advantageous to the country than the greater part of other employments, absorb a much greater proportion of the capital of the country than what would otherwise have gone to it.

The mercantile stock of every country, it has been shown in the Second Book, naturally seeks, if one may say so, the employment most advantageous to that country. If it is employed in the carrying trade, the country to which it belongs becomes the emporium of the goods of all the countries whose trade that stock carries on. But the owner of that stock necessarily wishes to dispose of as great a part of those goods as he can at home. He thereby saves himself the trouble, risk, and expense of exportation, and he will upon that account be glad to sell them at home, not only for a much smaller price, but with somewhat a smaller profit than he might expect to make by sending them abroad. He naturally, therefore, endeavours as much as he can to turn his carrying trade into a foreign trade of consumption. If his stock again is employed in a foreign trade of consumption, he will, for the same reason, be glad to dispose of at home as great a part as he can of the home goods, which he collects in order to export to some foreign market, and he will thus endeavour, as much as he can, to turn his foreign trade of consumption into a home trade. The mercantile stock of every country naturally courts in this manner the near, and shuns the distant employment; naturally courts the employment in which the returns are frequent, and shuns that in which they are distant and slow; naturally courts the employment in which it can maintain the greatest quantity of productive labour in the country to which it belongs, or in which its owner resides, and shuns that in which it can maintain there the smallest quantity. It naturally courts the employment which in ordinary cases is most advantageous, and shuns that which in ordinary cases is least advantageous to that country.

But if in any of those distant employments, which in ordinary cases are less advantageous to the country, the profit should happen to rise somewhat higher than what is sufficient to balance the natural preference which is given to nearer employments, this superiority of profit will draw stock from those nearer employments, till the profits of all return to their proper level. This superiority of profit, however, is a proof that in the actual circumstances of the society, those distant employments are somewhat understocked in proportion to other employments, and that the stock of the society is not distributed in the properest manner among all the different employments carried on in it. It is a proof that something is either bought cheaper or sold dearer than it ought to be, and that some particular class of citizens is more or less oppressed either by paying more or by getting less than what is suitable to that equality, which ought to take place, and which naturally does take place, among all the different classes of them. Though the same capital never will maintain the same quantity of productive labour in a distant as in a near employment, yet a distant employment may be as necessary for the welfare of the society as a near one; the goods which the distant employment deals in being necessary, perhaps, for carrying on many of the nearer employments. But if the profits of those who deal in such goods are above their proper level, those goods will be sold dearer than they ought to be, or somewhat above their natural price, and all those engaged in the nearer employments will be more or less oppressed by this high price. Their interest, therefore, in this case requires that some stock should be withdrawn from those nearer employments, and turned towards that distant one, in order to reduce its profits to their proper level, and the price of the goods which it deals in to their natural price. In this extraordinary case, the public interest requires that some stock should be withdrawn from those employments which in ordinary cases are more advantageous, and turned towards one which in ordinary cases is less advantageous to the public; and in this extraordinary case, the natural interests and inclinations of men coincide as exactly with the public interest as in all other ordinary cases, and lead them to withdraw stock from the near, and to turn it towards the distant employment.

It is thus that the private interests and passions of individuals naturally dispose them to turn their stock towards the employments which in ordinary cases are most advantageous to the society. But if from this natural preference they should turn too much of it towards those employments, the fall of profit in them and the rise of it in all others immediately dispose them to alter this faulty distribution. Without any intervention of law, therefore, the private interests and passions of men naturally lead them to divide and distribute the stock of every society, among all the different employments carried on in it, as nearly as possible in the proportion which is most agreeable to the interest of the whole society.

All the different regulations of the mercantile system necessarily derange more or less this natural and most advantageous distribution of stock. But those which concern the trade to America and the East Indies derange it, perhaps, more than any other; because the trade to those two great continents absorbs a greater quantity of stock than any two other branches of trade. The regulations, however, by which this derangement is effected in those two different branches of trade are not altogether the same. Monopoly is the great engine of both; but it is a different sort of monopoly. Monopoly of one kind or another, indeed, seems to be the sole engine of the mercantile system.

In the trade to America, every nation endeavours to engross as much as possible the whole market of its own colonies, by fairly excluding all other nations from any direct trade to them. During the greater part of the sixteenth century, the Portuguese endeavoured to manage the trade to the East Indies in the same manner, by claiming the sole right of sailing in the Indian seas, on account of the merit of having first found out the road to them. The Dutch still continue to exclude all other European nations from any direct trade to their spice islands. Monopolies of this kind are evidently established against all other European nations, who are thereby not only excluded from a trade to which it might be convenient for them to turn some part of their stock, but are obliged to buy the goods which that trade deals in somewhat dearer, than if they could import them themselves directly from the countries which produce them.

But since the fall of the power of Portugal, no European nation has claimed the exclusive right of sailing in the Indian seas, of which the principal ports are now open to the ships of all European nations. Except in Portugal, however, and within these few years in France, the trade to the East Indies has in every European country been subjected to an exclusive company. Monopolies of this kind are properly established against the very nation which erects them. The greater part of that nation are thereby not only excluded from a trade to which it might be convenient for them to turn some part of their stock, but are obliged to buy the goods which that trade deals in, somewhat dearer than if it was open and free to all their country-men. Since the establishment of the English East India Company, for example, the other inhabitants of England, over and above being excluded from the trade, must have paid in the price of the East India goods which they have consumed, not only for all the extraordinary profits which the Company may have made upon those goods in consequence of their monopoly, but for all the extraordinary waste which the fraud and abuse, inseparable from the management of the affairs of so great a Company, must necessarily have occasioned. The absurdity of this second kind of monopoly, therefore, is much more manifest than that of the first.

Both these kinds of monopolies derange more or less the natural distribution of the stock of the society; but they do not always derange it in the same way.

Monopolies of the first kind always attract to the particular trade in which they are established a greater proportion of the stock of the society than what would go to that trade of its own accord.

Monopolies of the second kind may sometimes attract stock towards the particular trade in which they are established, and sometimes repel it from that trade according to different circum-stances. In poor countries, they naturally attract towards that trade more stock than would otherwise go to it. In rich countries, they naturally repel from it a good deal of stock which would otherwise go to it.

Such poor countries as Sweden and Denmark, for example, would probably have never sent a single ship to the East Indies, had not the trade been subjected to an exclusive company. The establish-ment of such a company necessarily encourages adventurers. Their monopoly secures them against all competitors in the home market, and they have the same chance for foreign markets with the traders of other nations. Their monopoly shows them the certainty of a great profit upon a considerable quantity of goods, and the chance of a considerable profit upon a great quantity. Without such extraor-dinary encouragement, the poor traders of such poor countries would probably never have thought of hazarding their small capitals in so very distant and uncertain an adventure as the trade to the East Indies must naturally have appeared to them.

Such a rich country as Holland, on the contrary, would probably, in the case of a free trade, send many more ships to the East Indies than it actually does. The limited stock of the Dutch East India Company probably repels from that trade many great mercantile capitals which would otherwise go to it. The mercantile capital of Holland is so great that it is, as it were, continually overflowing, sometimes into the public funds of foreign countries, sometimes into loans to private traders and adventurers of foreign countries, sometimes into the most round-about foreign trades of consumption, and sometimes into the carrying trade. All near employments being completely filled up, all the capital which can be placed in them with any tolerable profit being already placed in them, the capital of Holland necessarily flows towards the most distant employments.[1] The trade to the East Indies, if it was altogether free, would probably absorb the greater part of this redundant capital. The East Indies offer a market both for the manufacturers of Europe and for the gold and silver as well as for several other productions of America, greater and more extensive than both Europe and America put together.

Every derangement of the natural distribution of stock is necessarily hurtful to the society in which it takes place; whether it be by repelling from a particular trade the stock which would otherwise go to it, or by attracting towards a particular trade that which would not otherwise come to it. If, without any exclusive company, the trade of Holland to the East Indies would be greater than it actually is, that country must suffer a considerable loss by part of its capital being excluded from the employment most convenient for that part. And in the same manner, if, without an exclusive company, the trade of Sweden and Denmark to the East Indies would be less than it actually is, or, what perhaps is more probable, would not exist at all, those two countries must likewise suffer a considerable loss by part of their capital being drawn into an employment which must be more or less unsuitable to their present circumstances. Better for them, perhaps, in their present circumstances, to buy East India goods of other nations, even though they should pay somewhat dearer, than to turn so great a part of their small capital to so very distant a trade, in which the returns are so very slow, in which that capital can maintain so small a quantity of productive labour at home, where productive labour is so much wanted, where so little is done, and where so much is to do.

Though without an exclusive company, therefore, a particular country should not be able to carry on any direct trade to the East Indies, it will not from thence follow that such a company ought to be established there, but only that such a country ought not in these circumstances to trade directly to the East Indies. That such companies are not in general necessary for carrying on the East India trade, is sufficiently demonstrated by the experience of the Portuguese, who enjoyed almost the whole of it for more than a century together without any exclusive company.

ORIGINAL NOTE

1. This passage contains the germ of the theory subsequently developed by Mr. Mill, as to the tendency of profits to a minimum, and the necessity that there exists, under such circumstances, that fresh channels should be dug for capital at home, by the discovery of improvements in production, and in the employment of other capital in foreign advances. In point of fact, the emigration of superfluous capital is as advantageous as the emigration of superfluous labour. The misfortune is, that there is no harmony in their respective movements, but that the emigration of men is wasteful, and that of capital inconsiderate or timid.

6

The Colonial System

THE QUOTATION from Fayer Hall's pamphlet The Importance of the
British Plantations in America to this Kingdom (1731) illustrates the economic advantages that it was claimed Britain derived from the possession
of the West Indian Islands under the old colonial system.

The second passage illustrates the concessions made to Britain's newly
acquired French Canadian subjects by the Quebec Act of 1774.

a Fayer Hall on the Value to Britain of the West Indian Islands (1731)

... HENCE MAY be perceived the Excellence of our Oeconomy
and Government, that in Climes less temperate and kind, [than
the Spanish Indies] on Lands less luxurious and fruitful, unacquainted
with Mines of Gold or Silver, our own People enjoy Happiness and
Pleasures, are comparatively more wealthy, are justly esteemed
more considerable, their Productions from their Labour infinitely
more valuable, and their Trade more beneficial to their Native Kingdom, as well as themselves.

In pursuance of my Design, I shall consider the Advantages we
receive from our Sugar Islands: and first I shall begin with *Barbadoes*.

Of what Consequence the Island of *Barbadoes* is to this Kingdom,
might in a great measure be estimated from the Amount of the 4½
per cent on their Sugars only, which Sum hath amounted many
Years to upwards of 10,000£ a Year, as I have been informed.
And the vast Advantage it is of to this Kingdom will farther appear,
when we consider the numbers of People which are constantly employed for the supplying of that Island with almost all sorts of our
own Manufactures: And if it be farther considered and allowed that

From ENGLISH HISTORICAL DOCUMENTS (London, 1957), vol. x (1714–
1783), pp. 764–8. Reprinted by permission of Eyre and Spottiswoode.

not less than 1000 of our own Seamen are constantly employed, on account of that Island only; at a Time too when 200 Tons of Craft, or Shipping, do not require above 20 Men; so that there is not less than 10,000 Tons of Shipping constantly employ'd: which Shipping, or at least three fourths of the whole, if not built in *England* are always repaired, refitted, victualled and constantly paid here; and it never yet was suggested that one Penny of Money or Bullion was ever carried there from *England*.

Upon this Head we may also allow (what is near the Truth) that what we call the Outsett of every Ship clear for Sea for this Voyage, stands the Owners in 10*l*. per Ton, and then the Value of the Shipping employed in this Trade will be 100,000*l*. Now if after all Charges of Insurance, foreign Port Charges, and the Allowance made for the Wear of the Ship, there is gained but 10 *per Cent.* and supposing (what also may be near the Truth) that upon our own Accounts, we send of our own Manufactures and *East India* Goods, to the Value of 200,000*l. per Ann.* and that we gain thereby but 10 *per Cent.* then, upon these two Articles, we gain 30,000*l. per Ann.*

But these are not the only Ways we gain from that Island. A Governor there will find Ways to remit to *England* at the rate of 5,000*l. per Ann.* and if the Factors there remit but half their Commissions on the above Sum of 200,000*l.* that will be 10,000*l. per Ann.* Those Gentlemen in Publick Offices, and others there, who expect to return Home, we will only say remit 5,000*l. per Ann.* and we will suppose that there constantly are here in *England* at least a hundred Gentlemen of that Island, some for their Pleasure, and others for Education, who do not live at less Expence than 200*l. per Ann.* each, which is clear Gain to us 20,000*l. per Ann.* And if it be allowed that they are in Debt to us the Sum of 100,000*l.* for which they pay eight *per Cent. per Ann.* Interest, that is clear Gain of 8,000*l.* more; and if we reckon what we reasonably may, *viz.* The Freight of all Sugars which are again exported, and which are the Produce of this Island only, this will be 7,000*l.* more. The whole will amount to 95,000*l. per Ann.* A prodigious Sum to be gained annually from an Island but very little bigger than the Isle of *Wight*. But these are not the only Advantages; which will appear when we treat of the Trade of the Northern Colonies. And if we consider the *African* Trade, much more might be brought to Account of this Island, but as I design to keep within bounds in all my Computations,

I will leave it as above at 95,000*l*. Sterling *per Annum,* over and above the Employment of so many Sailors and Shipping, and the vast number of all sorts of Artificers employed at Home in fitting, repairing and building those Ships, &c. besides those for the Manufactures.

If the Island of *Tobago* belongs to this Kingdom, as I have been credibly informed it does, it will appear as surprizing as any ill Management we have been hitherto guilty of, that it hath not been settled by us. An Island which, tho' not quite so large as *Barbadoes,* yet for good Roads, convenient Rivers, and Richness of Soil, is superior to it; and if the Settlement were once accomplished, there is no doubt but the Advantage arising from that small Island for many Years to come, would be very near, if not quite, as considerable to us as the Island of *Barbadoes* now is; because as it is fresh and strong Land, one Acre would produce much more than is now produced by two of old, worn out, poor Land, such as some (and indeed no small Part) of *Barbadoes* now is; and it is allowed by all, that upon good new Land the Labour of fifty Slaves will produce as much Sugar as a hundred will, or can, in *Barbadoes*; tho' the Sugar perhaps will not be so fine.

This Island is in the Latitude of 11^d 5^m North, and lies from *Barbadoes* South by West half West, near forty Leagues: Nor is it the worse to be esteemed for lying within twelve Leagues of *Trinidado,* a *Spanish* Island. . . .

The *Leeward Islands* (so called with Respect to *Barbadoes,* which is the Easternmost and Windwardmost of all the *West-India* Islands) are numerous, and inhabited by *English, French, Dutch,* and *Danes.* The most considerable of these are *Antegoa, St. Christophers, Nevis* and *Montserat,* all settled by the *English.* And tho' these four Islands, with Regard to their Bigness and Extent, are equal to three such Islands as *Barbadoes*; And tho' it is well known these Lands in general turn out better Crops than those of *Barbadoes* do, yet because I would not be thought to exaggerate, I shall consider them all, with the Islands of *Burbuda, Anguilla, Tortola* and *Spanish Town,* which are all settled by the *English,* to be all together only of equal Consequence to this Kingdom at present, as the Island of *Barbadoes,* tho' they are capable of vast Improvements. . . .

About thirty Leagues to the Westward of this delightful Island, [Hispaniola] lies the Island of *Jamaica,* in Length a Hundred and fifty Miles, in Breadth about fifty Miles. We shall be able to form some Judgment of the Importance of this Island, by the Quantity of its own Produce annually shipped off to us; namely, in Sugar 10000 Tons, in Cotton, Indigo, Ginger, Piemento, Rum, Lime-juice, Cocoa, Mahogony Wood, &c. 2000 more. By this it will appear, that there is not less than 12000 Tons of our own Shipping constantly employed in that Service only, over and above what is employed between that Island and the Northern Plantations; all which, excepting that they do not fit and repair here, are of the same Benefit and Advantage to this Kingdom in all other Respects. But of this more particularly, when I treat of the Northern Colonies. And because I would not be suspected of favouring or flattering my self in my Design, which is to shew the great Benefit and Advantage arising to this Kingdom from our own Plantations, I will only consider this Island, as a Sugar Plantation, to be of the same Advantage to us as *Barbadoes,* tho' very capable of being improved to ten, if not twenty Times that Value. . . .

The *Bahama* Islands, which are very numerous, and capable of producing all things necessary for Life, are all owned by the *English,* and some few of them are inhabited, *viz. Providence, Illethera, Harbour-Island,* and *Green Turtle Key.* The most considerable for Extent and Richness of Soil is the Island of *Abaco;* but it hath not yet been settled, nor indeed do I apprehend that any great Advantages could accrue to this Kingdom by those Islands were they all inhabited; yet I think it not improper to keep up the Government already there, only as it prevents their becoming a Nest of Pyrates.

Those Islands produce Brazilletta Wood, Lignum Vitae, Cortex Winteriana, Salt, and on the Shores have been frequently found the Sperma-Ceti Whales and Ambergris; which last I have been credibly informed is the Excrement of that Whale: A whole Sloop's Company agreed in the Relation of that Fact to me in South Carolina, where they brought many Barrels of Sperma-Ceti (I saw at least thirty) and above five hundred Pounds of Amber-gris, all which they assured me came from one Whale. The Sperma-Ceti undoubtedly did, the Amber-gris they had Reason to think did so too, because they found it near the Place where they found the Whale, and they all agreed that the Excrement of that very Whale, which was found in the Gut near the *Anus,* was really Amber-gris, tho' not quite so good as that which was found on the Shore and floating in the Water. This I believed when I was told it, for I saw no Interest or Pleasure they had or proposed in deceiving me, or many others, which I often heard them tell it to. Here too are found the prettiest and greatest variety of Shells that any Part of the World produces. Upon the whole, except for keeping out of Pyrates, I don't think these Islands worth inhabiting, while we have so much of as fine a Countrey as any in the World uninhabited, I mean the Province of South Carolina. . . .

Bermudas, though a small Island, or rather a great many small Islands, lies in the Latitude of 32^d 30^m North; Longitude from *London* 64^d West; and about two hundred Leagues distant from the Continent of America. In Queen *Ann's* War there was upwards of a hundred Sail of Brigantines and Sloops belonging to this Island; but at present I am assured that there is not above half that Number. This Island, which was formerly one of the most fruitful, is now near worn out: And such is and will be the Fate of all small Islands, where People increase so fast, and so constantly keep their Lands tilled. Such in part is the Case of the Island of *Barbadoes* already, yet the Planters there are not willing to remove to Places where twice the Quantity of Sugars may be made by the same Labour as there. The People of *Bermudas* too are not easily to be persuaded to remove to a better Country, where the same Degree of Industry and Frugality, which these People are remarkable for, would soon enrich them. These People are extremely civil and kind to Strangers; and when they have a good Governor, as it is universally allowed they had by Governor *Bennet,* no People are more happy. They have very few Priests, very few Physicians, and fewer Lawyers. All the Necessaries which they want, such as Apparel and Household Goods, they are furnished with from hence; for which they send us Money, and fine Plait for making Womens Hats, &c. together with whatever they can spare, of any Commodities which bear a Price here. The *Bermudians* in general are excellent Hands on board of Sloops, and the best Fishermen that I ever knew. They navigate their Vessels at less Expence than any other People, and consequently can get by Smaller Freights.

To conclude, I am of Opinion that this Kingdom gains clear Profit by our *American* Colonies yearly, the Sum of one million Sterling, exclusive of what we get by any Trades for Negroes or dry Goods by the Spaniards; and that in and by our Colonies only we maintain and employ at least eighteen thousand Seamen and Fishermen.

b The Quebec Act (1774)

An Act for Making More Effectual Provision for the Government of the Province of Quebec in North America

WHEREAS HIS *Majesty, by his royal proclamation, bearing date the seventh day of* October, *in the third year of his reign, thought fit to declare the provisions which had been made in respect to certain countries, territories, and islands in* America, *ceded to his Majesty by the definitive treaty of peace, concluded at* Paris *on the tenth day of* February, *one thousand seven hundred and sixty-three; and whereas, by the arrangements made by the said royal proclamation, a very large extent of country, within which there were several colonies and settlements of the subjects of* France, *who claimed to remain therein under the faith of the said treaty, was left, without any provision being made for the administration of civil government therein; and certain parts of the territory of* Canada, *where sedentary fisheries had been established and carried on by the subjects of* France, *inhabitants of the said province of* Canada, *under grants and concessions from the government thereof, were annexed to the government of* Newfoundland, *and thereby subjected to regulations inconsistent with the nature of such fisheries:* may it therefore please your most excellent Majesty that it may be enacted; and be it enacted by the King's most excellent Majesty, by and with the advice and consent of the lords spiritual and temporal, and commons, in this present parliament assembled, and by the authority of the same, That all the territories, islands, and countries in *North America,* belonging to the crown of *Great Britain,* bounded on the south by a line from the bay of *Chaleurs,* along the high lands which divide the rivers that empty themselves into the river *Saint Lawrence* from those which fall into the sea, to a point in forty-five degrees of northern latitude, on the eastern bank of the river *Connecticut,* keeping the same latitude directly west, through the lake *Champlain,* until, in the same latitude, it meets the river *Saint Lawrence*; from thence up the eastern bank of the said river to the lake *Ontario*; thence through the lake *Ontario,* and the river commonly called

From ENGLISH HISTORICAL DOCUMENTS (London, 1957), vol. x (1714–1783), pp. 787–91. Reprinted by permission of Eyre and Spottiswoode.

Niagara; and thence along by the eastern and southeastern bank of lake *Erie,* following the said bank, until the same shall be intersected by the northern boundary, granted by the charter of the province of *Pensylvania,* in case the same shall be so intersected; and from thence along the said northern and western boundaries of the said province, until the said western boundary strike the *Ohio*; but in case the said bank of the said lake shall not be found to be so intersected, then following the said bank until it shall arrive at that point of the said bank which shall be nearest to the north-western angle of the said province of *Pensylvania,* and thence by a right line, to the said north-western angle of the said province; and thence along the western boundary of the said province, until it strike the river *Ohio*; and along the bank of the said river, westward, to the banks of the *Mississippi,* and northward to the southern boundary of the territory granted to the merchants adventurers of *England,* trading to *Hudson's Bay*; and also all such territories, islands, and countries, which have, since the tenth of *February,* one thousand seven hundred and sixty-three, been made part of the government of *Newfoundland,* be, and they are hereby, during his Majesty's pleasure, annexed to, and made part and parcel of, the province of *Quebec,* as created and established by the said royal proclamation of the seventh of *October,* one thousand seven hundred and sixty-three.

II] Provided always, That nothing herein contained, relative to the boundary of the province of *Quebec,* shall in anywise affect the boundaries of any other colony.

III] Provided always, and be it enacted, That nothing in this act contained shall extend, or be construed to extend, to make void, or to vary or alter any right, title or possession, derived under any grant, conveyance, or otherwise howsoever, of or to any lands within the said province, or the provinces thereto adjoining; but that the same shall remain and be in force, and have effect, as if this act had never been made.

IV] *And whereas the provisions, made by the said proclamation, in respect to the civil government of the said province of* Quebec, *and the powers and authorities given to the governor and other civil officers of the said province, by the grants and commissions issued in consequence thereof, have been found, upon experience, to be inapplicable to the state and circumstances of the said province, the inhabitants whereof amounted, at the conquest, to above sixty-five thousand persons professing the religion of the church of* Rome, *and*

*enjoying an established form of constitution and system of laws, by
which their persons and property had been protected, governed, and
ordered, for a long series of years, from the first establishment of the
said province of* Canada; be it therefore further enacted by the authority aforesaid, That the said proclamation, so far as the same
relates to the said province of *Quebec,* and the commission under the
authority whereof the government of the said province is at present
administered, and all and every the ordinance and ordinances made
by the governor and council of *Quebec* for the time being, relative
to the civil government and administration of justice in the said
province, and all commissions to judges and other officers thereof,
be, and the same are hereby revoked, annulled, and made void, from
and after the first day of *May,* one thousand seven hundred and
seventy-five.

V] *And, for the more perfect security and ease of the minds of
the inhabitants of the said province,* it is hereby declared, That his
Majesty's subjects, professing the religion of the church of *Rome* of
and in the said province of *Quebec,* may have, hold, and enjoy, the
free exercise of the religion of the church of *Rome,* subject to the
King's supremacy, declared and established by an act, made in
the first year of the reign of Queen *Elizabeth,* over all the dominions
and countries which then did, or thereafter should belong, to the
imperial crown of this realm; and that the clergy of the said church,
may hold, receive, and enjoy, their accustomed dues and rights, with
respect to such persons only as shall profess the said religion.

VI] Provided nevertheless, That it shall be lawful for his Majesty,
his heirs or successors, to make such provision out of the rest of the
said accustomed dues and rights, for the encouragement of the protestant religion, and for the maintenance and support of a protestant
clergy within the said province, as he or they shall, from time to
time, think necessary and expedient.

VII] Provided always, and be it enacted, That no person, professing the religion of the church of *Rome,* and residing in the said
province, shall be obliged to take the oath required by the said statute
passed in the first year of the reign of Queen *Elizabeth,* or any other
oaths substituted by any other act in the place thereof; but that every
such person who, by the said statute, is required to take the oath
therein mentioned, shall be obliged, and is hereby required, to take
and subscribe the following oath before the governor, or such other

person in such court of record as his Majesty shall appoint, who are hereby authorised to administer the same; *videlicet,*

I A.B. *do sincerely promise and swear, That I will be faithful, and bear true allegiance to his majesty King George, and him will defend to the utmost of my power, against all traitorous conspiracies, and attempts whatsoever, which shall be made against his person, crown, and dignity; and I will do my utmost endeavour to disclose and make known to his majesty, his heirs and successors, all treasons, and traitorous conspiracies, and attempts, which I shall know to be against him, or any of them; and all this I do swear without any equivocation, mental evasion, or secret reservation, and renouncing all pardons and dispensations from any power or person whomsoever to the contrary.*

So help me GOD.

And every such person, who shall neglect or refuse to take the said oath before mentioned, shall incur and be liable to the same penalties, forfeitures, disabilities, and incapacities, as he would have incurred and been liable to for neglecting or refusing to take the oath required by the said statute passed in the first year of the reign of Queen *Elizabeth.*

VIII] And be it further enacted by the authority aforesaid, That all his Majesty's *Canadian* subjects within the province of *Quebec,* the religious orders and communities only excepted, may also hold and enjoy their property and possessions, together with all customs and usages relative thereto, and all other their civil rights, in as large, ample, and beneficial manner, as if the said proclamation, commissions, ordinances, and other acts and instruments, had not been made, and as may consist with their allegiance to his Majesty, and subjection to the crown and parliament of *Great Britain*; and that in all matters of controversy, relative to property and civil rights, resort shall be had to the laws of *Canada,* as the rule for the decision of the same; and all causes that shall hereafter be instituted in any of the courts of justice, to be appointed within and for the said province by his Majesty, his heirs and successors, shall, with respect to such property and rights, be determined agreeably to the said laws and customs of *Canada,* until they shall be varied or altered by any ordinances that shall, from time to time, be passed in the said province by the governor, lieutenant governor, or commander in chief,

for the time being, by and with the advice and consent of the legislative council of the same, to be appointed in manner herein-after
mentioned.

IX] Provided always, That nothing in this act contained shall
extend, or be construed to extend, to any lands that have been
granted by his Majesty, or shall hereafter be granted by his Majesty,
his heirs and successors, to be holden in free and common soccage.

X] Provided also, That it shall and may be lawful to and for
every person that is owner of any lands, goods, or credits, in the said
province, and that has a right to alienate the said lands, goods, or
credits, in his or her life-time, by deed of sale, gift, or otherwise, to
devise or bequeath the same at his or her death, by his or her last
will and testament; any law, usage, or custom, heretofore or now
prevailing in the province, to the contrary hereof in any-wise notwithstanding; such will being executed either according to the laws
of *Canada,* or according to the forms prescribed by the laws of
England.

XI] *And whereas the certainty and lenity of the criminal law of*
England, *and the benefits and advantages resulting from the use of
it, have been sensibly felt by the inhabitants, from an experience
of more than nine years, during which it has been uniformly administered;* be it therefore further enacted by the authority aforesaid,
That the same shall continue to be administered, and shall be observed as law in the province of *Quebec,* as well in the description
and quality of the offence as in the method of prosecution and trial;
and the punishments and forfeitures thereby inflicted to the exclusion
of every other rule of criminal law, or mode of proceeding thereon,
which did or might prevail in the said province before the year of
our Lord one thousand seven hundred and sixty-four; any thing in
this act to the contrary thereof in any respect notwithstanding; subject nevertheless to such alterations and amendments as the governor,
lieutenant-governor, or commander in chief for the time being, by
and with the advice and consent of the legislative council of the said
province, hereafter to be appointed, shall, from time to time, cause
to be made therein, in manner herein-after directed.

XII] *And whereas it may be necessary to ordain many regulations
for the future welfare and good government of the province of*
Quebec, *the occasions of which cannot now be foreseen, nor, without much delay and inconvenience, be provided for, without intrust-
ing that authority, for a certain time, and under proper restrictions,*

*to persons resident there: and whereas it is at present inexpedient
to call an assembly;* be it therefore enacted by the authority aforesaid, That it shall and may be lawful for his Majesty, his heirs and
successors, by warrant under his or their signet or sign manual, and
with the advice of the privy council, to constitute and appoint a council for the affairs of the province of *Quebec,* to consist of such persons
resident there, not exceeding twenty-three, nor less than seventeen,
as his Majesty, his heirs and successors, shall be pleased to appoint;
and, upon the death, removal, or absence of any of the members of
the said council, in like manner to constitute and appoint such and
so many other person or persons as shall be necessary to supply the
vacancy or vacancies; which council, so appointed and nominated,
or the major part thereof, shall have power and authority to make
ordinances for the peace, welfare, and good government of the said
province, with the consent of his Majesty's governor, or, in his absence, of the lieutenant-governor, or commander in chief for the time
being.

XIII] Provided always, That nothing in this act contained shall
extend to authorise or impower the said legislative council to lay
taxes or duties within the said province, such rates and taxes only
excepted as the inhabitants of any town or district within the said
province may be authorised by the said council to assess, levy, and
apply, within the said town or district, for the purpose of making
roads, erecting and repairing publick buildings, or for any other purpose respecting the local convenience and oeconomy of such town or
district.

XIV] Provided also, and be it enacted by the authority aforesaid,
That every ordinance so to be made, shall, within six months, be
transmitted by the governor, or, in his absence, by the lieutenant-
governor, or commander in chief for the time being, and laid before
his Majesty for his royal approbation; and if his Majesty shall think
fit to disallow thereof, the same shall cease and be void from the
time that his Majesty's order in council thereupon shall be promulgated at *Quebec.*

XV] Provided also, That no ordinance touching religion, or by
which any punishment may be inflicted greater than fine or imprison-
ment for three months, shall be of any force or effect, until the same
shall have received his Majesty's approbation.

XVI] Provided also, That no ordinance shall be passed at any
meeting of the council where less than a majority of the whole coun-

118

cil is present, or at any time except between the first day of *January* and the first day of *May,* unless upon some urgent occasion, in which case every member thereof resident at *Quebec,* or within fifty miles thereof, shall be personally summoned by the governor, or, in his absence, by the lieutenant-governor, or commander in chief for the time being, to attend the same.

XVII] And be it further enacted by the authority aforesaid, That nothing herein contained shall extend, or be construed to extend, to prevent or hinder his Majesty, his heirs and successors, by his or their letters patent under the great seal of *Great Britain,* from erecting, constituting, and appointing, such courts of criminal, civil, and ecclesiastical jurisdiction within and for the said province of *Quebec,* and appointing, from time to time, the judges and officers thereof, as his Majesty, his heirs and successors, shall think necessary and proper for the circumstances of the said province.

XVIII] Provided always, and it is hereby enacted, That nothing in this act contained shall extend, or be construed to extend, to repeal or make void, within the said province of *Quebec,* any act or acts of the parliament of *Great Britain* heretofore made, for prohibiting, restraining, or regulating, the trade or commerce of his Majesty's colonies and plantations in *America*; but that all and every the said acts, and also all acts of parliament heretofore made concerning or respecting the said colonies and plantations, shall be, and are hereby declared to be, in force, within the said province of *Quebec,* and every part thereof.

7

The Methodists

John Wesley (1703-91) described the aims and organization of the early Methodist Societies in his pamphlet A Plain Account of the People Called Methodists.

John Wesley on the Methodist Societies (1749)

🦋 . . . I, 1] ABOVE TEN YEARS ago, my Brother and I were desired, to preach in many Parts of *London*. We had no View therein, but so far as we were able (and we knew GOD *cou'd* work by whomsoever it pleased Him) To *convince* those who wou'd hear, What True Christianity was, and to *persuade* them to embrace it.

2] The Points we chiefly insisted upon were Four: First, That *Orthodoxy* or *Right Opinions* is, at best, but a very slender *Part* of Religion, if it can be allowed to be any Part of it at all: That neither does Religion consist in *Negatives,* in bare Harmlessness of any Kind; nor merely in *Externals,* in doing Good or using the Means of Grace, in Works of Piety (so called) or of Charity: That it is nothing short of or different from *The Mind that was in* CHRIST, The *Image of* GOD stampt upon the Heart, Inward *Righteousness,* attended with the *Peace* of GOD, and *Joy in the Holy Ghost.* Secondly, That the only Way under Heaven to this Religion, is To *repent and believe the Gospel,* or (as the Apostle words it) *Repentance towards* GOD, *and Faith in our* LORD JESUS CHRIST: Thirdly, That by this Faith, *He that worketh not, but believeth on Him that justifieth the Ungodly,* is justified *freely by his Grace, thro' the Redemption which is in* JESUS CHRIST: And Lastly, That *being justified by Faith,* we taste of the Heaven to which we are going: We are Holy and Happy: We tread down Sin and Fear, and *sit in Heavenly Places with* CHRIST JESUS.

From ENGLISH HISTORICAL DOCUMENTS (London, 1957), vol. x (1714-1783), pp. 380-7. Reprinted by permission of Eyre and Spottiswoode.

3] Many of those who heard this, began to cry out, That we brought *Strange Things to their Ears*: That this was Doctrine which they never heard before, or, at least, never regarded. They *searched the Scriptures, whether these Things were so,* and acknowledge *the Truth as it is in* JESUS. Their Hearts also were influenced as well as their Understandings, and they determined to follow JESUS CHRIST *and Him crucified.*

4] Immediately they were surrounded with Difficulties: All the World rose up against them: Neighbours, Strangers, Acquaintance, Relations, Friends, began to cry out amain: *"Be not righteous over-much: Why shouldst thou destroy thyself? Let* not *much Religion make thee mad."*

5] One and another and another came to Us, asking, What they should do? Being distress'd on every Side, as every one strove to weaken, and none to strengthen their Hands in GOD. We advised them, "Strengthen you one another. Talk together as often as you can. And pray earnestly, with and for one another, That you may *endure to the End and be saved."* Against this Advice we presumed there could be no Objection; as being grounded on the plainest Reason, and on so many Scriptures, both of the Old Testament and the New, that it wou'd be tedious to recite them.

6] They said, "But we want *You* likewise to talk with us often, to direct and quicken us in our Way, to give us the Advices which you well know we need, and to pray with us, as well as for us." I ask'd, Which of you desires this? Let me know your Names and Places of Abode. They did so. But I soon found, they were too many for me to talk with severally so often as they wanted it. So I told them, "If you will all of you come together, every *Thursday,* in the Evening, I will gladly spend some Time with you in Prayer, and give you the best Advice I can."

7] Thus arose, without any previous Design on either Side, what was afterwards called *A Society*: A very Innocent Name, and very Common in *London,* for any Number of People, *associating* themselves together. The Thing proposed in their associating themselves together, was obvious to every one. They wanted to *flee from the Wrath to come,* and to assist each other in so doing. They therefore united themselves "in order to pray together, to receive the Word of Exhortation, and to watch over one another in Love, that they might help each other to work out their Salvation."

8] "There is One only Condition previously required, in those who desire Admission into this Society, *A Desire to flee from the Wrath to come, and to be saved from their Sins.* But wherever this Desire is fixt in the Soul, it will be shewn by its Fruits. It is therefore expected of all who continue therein, that they should continue to evidence their Desire of Salvation.

"First, By doing no Harm, by avoiding Evil in every kind; especially that which is most generally practised.

("Such as, The taking the Name of GOD in vain; The profaning the Day of the LORD; Drunkenness; Fighting, Quarrelling, Brawling; The Buying or Selling *uncustom'd* Goods; The doing to others as we would not they should do unto us; Uncharitable or Unprofitable Conversation, particularly, Speaking evil of Magistrates or Ministers:)

"Secondly, By doing Good, by being in every kind merciful after their Power; As they have Opportunity, doing Good of every possible Sort, and as far as it is possible to all Men:

"By all possible *Diligence* and *Frugality,* that the Gospel be not blamed:

"By submitting to bear the Reproach of CHRIST to be as *the Filth and Off-scouring* of the World, and looking that Men should *say all manner of Evil of them falsely* for their LORD's Sake:

"Thirdly, By attending upon all the Ordinances of GOD:

"Such as, The Publick Worship of GOD, The Supper of the LORD, Private Prayer, Searching the Scriptures, and Fasting or Abstinence."

They now likewise agreed, That as many of them as had Opportunity, wou'd meet together every *Friday,* and spend the Dinner Hour in crying to GOD, both for each other and for all Mankind.

9] It quickly appear'd, That their thus uniting together, answer'd the End proposed therein. In a few Months the far greater Part of those who had begun to *fear* GOD *and work Righteousness,* but were not united together, grew faint in their Minds, and fell back into what they were before. Mean while the far greater Part of those, who were thus united together continued *striving to enter in at the strait Gate,* and to *lay hold on Eternal Life.* . . .

II, 1] But as much as we endeavour'd to watch over each other, we soon found some who did not *live the Gospel.* I do not know, that any Hypocrites were crept in; for indeed there was no Temptation. But several grew cold, and gave Way to the Sins which had long easily beset them. We quickly perceiv'd, there were many ill Consequences of suffering these to remain among us. It was dangerous to others; inasmuch as all Sin is of an infectious Nature. It brought such a Scandal on their Brethren, as exposed them to what was not properly The Reproach of CHRIST. It laid a Stumbling-block in the Way of Others, and caused the Truth to be evil-spoken of.

2] We groaned under these Inconveniences long, before a Remedy could be found. The People were scattered so wide in all Part of the Town, from *Wapping* to *Westminster,* that I cou'd not easily see, what the Behaviour of each Person in his own Neighbourhood was. So that several disorderly Walkers did much Hurt, before I was apprized of it.

3] At Length, while we were thinking of quite another Thing, we struck upon a Method for which we have Cause to bless GOD ever since. I was talking with several of the Society in *Bristol,* concerning the Means of paying the Debts there; when one stood up and said, "Let every Member of the Society give a *Penny* a Week 'till all are paid." Another answered, "But many of them are poor, and cannot afford to do it." "Then said he, Put Eleven of the Poorest with me, and if they can give any Thing, well. I will call on them weekly, and if they can give Nothing, I will give for them as well as for myself. And each of you, call on Eleven of your Neighbours weekly: Receive what they give, and make up what is wanting." It was done. In a While some of these inform'd me, "They found, such and such an one did not live as he ought." It struck me immediately. "This is the Thing: The very Thing we have wanted so long." I call'd together all the *Leaders* of the *Classes,* (so we used to term them and their Companies) and desired That each wou'd make a particular Enquiry, into the Behaviour of those whom he saw weekly. They did so. Many disorderly Walkers were detected. Some turned from the Evil of their Ways. Some were put away from us. Many saw it with Fear, and rejoiced unto GOD with Reverence.

4] As soon as possible the same Method was used in *London* and all other Places. Evil Men were detected, and reproved. They were borne with for a Season. If they forsook their Sins, we receiv'd them gladly: If they obstinately persisted therein, it was openly declared, That they were not of us. The rest mourn'd and pray'd for them, and yet rejoiced, That as far as in us lay, the Scandal was roll'd away from the Society.

5] It is the Business of a Leader.

I] To see each Person in his Class, once a Week at the least: In order,

To enquire how their Souls prosper?

To advise, reprove, comfort or exhort, as Occasion may require;

To receive what they are willing to give, toward the Relief of the Poor.

II] To meet the Minister and the Stewards of the Society, in order

To inform the Minister of any that are Sick, or of any that are disorderly and will not be reproved;

To pay to the Stewards what they have receiv'd of their several Classes in the Week preceding.

6] At first they visited each Person at his own House: But this was soon found not so expedient. And that on many Accounts.

1] It took up more Time, than most of the Leaders had to spare.

2] Many Persons lived with Masters, Mistresses or Relations, who would not suffer them to be thus visited.

3] At the Houses of those who were not so averse, they had often no Opportunity of speaking to them but in Company. And this did not at all answer the End proposed, of exhorting, comforting or reproving.

4] It frequently happen'd, That one affirm'd what another denied. And this cou'd not be clear'd, without seeing them both together:

5] Little Misunderstandings and Quarrels of various Kinds, frequently arose among Relations or Neighbours: Effectually to remove which it was needful to see them all Face to Face. Upon all these Considerations it was agreed, That those of each Class should meet all together. And by this Means, a more full Enquiry was made, into the Behaviour of every Person. Those who cou'd not be visited at Home, or no otherwise than in Company, had the same Advantage with others. Advice or Reproof was given as need required; Quarrels made up, Misunderstandings removed. And after an Hour or two spent in this Labour of Love, they concluded with Prayer and Thanksgiving.

7] It can scarce be conceiv'd, what Advantages have been reap'd from this little Prudential Regulation. . . .

III, 1] About this Time, I was inform'd, That several Persons in *Kingswood,* frequently met together at the School, and (when they cou'd spare the Time) spent the greater Part of the Night, in Prayer and Praise and Thanksgiving. Some advised me to put an End to this: But upon weighing the Thing throughly, and comparing it with the Practice of the Antient Christians, I could see no Cause to forbid it. Rather, I believ'd, it might be made of more General Use. So I sent them Word, "I design'd to watch with them, on the *Friday* nearest the Full-Moon, that we might have Light thither and back again." I gave publick Notice of this, the *Sunday* before, and withall, That I intended to preach: Desiring, They and they only would meet me there, who could do it without Prejudice to their Business or Families. On *Friday* abundance of People came. I began Preaching between *Eight* and *Nine*; and we continued 'till a little beyond the Noon of Night, Singing Praying and Praising GOD.

2] This we have continued to do once a Month ever since, in *Bristol, London* and *Newcastle* as well as *Kingswood*. And exceeding great are the Blessings we have found therein: It has generally been an extremely Solemn Season; when the Word of GOD sunk deep into the Heart, even of those who 'till then knew Him not. If it be said, "This was only owing to the Novelty of the Thing, (the Circumstance which still draws such Multitudes together at those Seasons) or perhaps to the awful Silence of the Night," I am not careful to answer in this Matter. Be it so: However, the Impression then made on many Souls, has never since been effaced. Now allowing, that GOD did make Use either of the Novelty or any other indifferent Circumstance, in order to bring Sinners to Repentance, yet they are brought. And herein let us rejoice together.

3] Nay, May I not put the Case farther yet? If I can probably conjecture, That either by the Novelty of this *Antient* Custom, or by any other indifferent Circumstance, it is in my Power to *save a Soul from Death, and hide a Multitude of Sins*: Am I clear before GOD if I do it not? If I do not snatch that Brand out of the Burning?

IV, 1] As the Society increased, I found it requir'd still greater Care, to separate the precious from the vile. In order to this, I determin'd, at least once in three Months, to talk with every Member myself, and to inquire at their own Mouths, as well as of their Leaders and Neighbours, Whether they grew in Grace and in the Knowledge of our LORD JESUS CHRIST? At these Seasons I likewise particularly enquire, Whether there be any Mis-understandings or Differences among them? That every Hindrance of Peace and brotherly Love, may be taken out of the Way.

2] To each of those, of whose Seriousness and Good Conversation, I found no Reason to Doubt, I gave a Testimony under my own Hand, by writing their Name on a *Ticket* prepared for that Purpose: Every Ticket implying as strong a Recommendation of the Person to whom it was given, as if I had wrote at length, "I believe the Bearer hereof to be one that fears GOD and works Righteousness."

3] Those who bore these Tickets (these Σύμβολα or *Tesserae,* as the Antients term'd them; being of just the same Force with the ἐπιστολαὶ συστατικαὶ, *Commendatory Letters* mention'd by the Apostle) where-ever they came, were acknowledg'd by their Brethren, and received with all Chearfulness. These were likewise of Use in other Respects. By these it was easily distinguish'd when the Society were to meet a-part, who were Members of it and who not. These also supplied us with a quiet and inoffensive Method, of removing any Disorderly Member. He has no New Ticket, at the Quarterly Visitation; (for so often the Tickets are changed) and hereby it is immediately known, That he is no longer of this Community.

V] The Thing which I was greatly afraid of all this Time, and which I resolved to use every possible Method of preventing, was, A Narrowness of Spirit, a Party-Zeal, a being straiten'd in our own Bowels; That miserable Bigotry, which makes many so unready to believe, That there is any Work of GOD but among themselves. I thought it might be a Help against this, frequently to read, to all who were willing to hear, The Accounts I receiv'd from Time to Time, of the Work which GOD is carrying on in the Earth, both in our own and other Countries, not among us alone, but among those of various Opinions and Denominations. For this I allotted One Evening in every Month. And I find no Cause to repent my Labour. It is generally a Time of strong Consolation to those who love GOD, and all Mankind for his Sake: As well as of breaking down the Partition Walls, which either the Craft of the Devil, or the Folly of Men has built up: And of encouraging every Child of GOD to say, (O when shall it once be?) *Whosoever doth the Will of my Father which is in Heaven, the same is my Brother and Sister and Mother.*

VI, 1] By the Blessing of GOD upon their Endeavours to help one another, many found the Pearl of great Price. Being justified by Faith, they had *Peace with* GOD, *thro' our* LORD JESUS CHRIST. These felt a more tender Affection than before, to those who were Partakers of like precious Faith: And hence arose such a Confidence in each other, that they pour'd out their Souls into each other's Bosom. Indeed they had great Need so to do: For the War was not over, as they had supposed. But they had still to wrestle both with Flesh and Blood, and with Principalities and Powers: So that Temptations were on every Side: And often Temptations of such a Kind, as they knew not how to speak in a Class; in which Persons of every Sort, young and old, Men and Women met together.

2] These therefore wanted some Means of closer Union: They wanted to pour out their Hearts without Reserve; particularly with Regard to the Sin which did still *easily beset* them, and the Temptations which were most apt to prevail over them. And they were the more desirous of this, when they observ'd, it was the Express Advice of an inspired Writer, *Confess your Faults one to another, and pray one for another that ye may be healed.*

3] In Compliance with their Desire, I divided them into smaller Companies; putting Married or Single Men, and Married or Single Women together. The chief Rules of these *Bands,* (*i.e.* Little Companies; so that Old *English* Word signifies) run thus:

In order to *confess our Faults one to another and* pray one for another that we may be healed, we intend,

"1] To meet once a Week, at the least;
2] To come punctually at the Hour appointed;
3] To begin with Singing or Prayer;
4] To speak each of us in Order, freely and plainly, the true State of our Soul, with the Faults we have committed in Thought, Word or Deed, and the Temptations we have felt since our last Meeting:
5] To desire some Person among us (thence called a *Leader*) to speak *his* own State first, and then to ask the rest in order, as many and as searching Questions as may be, concerning their State, Sins and Temptations."

4] That their Design in meeting might be the more effectually answered, I desired all the Men-*Bands* to meet me together every *Wednesday* Evening, and the Women on *Sunday*; That they might receive such Particular Instructions, and such Exhortations, as from Time to Time, might appear to be most needful for them: That such Prayers might be offer'd up to GOD, as their Necessities should require: And Praise return'd to the Giver of every Good Gift, for whatever Mercies they had receiv'd.

5] In order to increase in them a grateful Sense of all his Mercies,

I desired that One Evening in a Quarter, all the Men; on a Second, all the Women wou'd meet; and on a Third, both Men and Women together; That we might together *eat Bread* (as the Antient Christians did) *with Gladness and Singleness of Heart.* At these *Love-Feasts* (so we term'd them, retaining the Name, as well as the Thing, which was in Use from the Beginning) our Food is only a little plain Cake and Water. But we seldom return from them, without being fed not only with *the Meat which perisheth,* but with *that which endureth to everlasting Life.*

6] Great and many are the Advantages which have ever since flow'd, from this closer Union of the Believers with each other. They pray'd for one another, That they might be healed of the Faults they had confest: And it was so. The Chains were broken: The Bands were burst in sunder, and Sin had no more Dominion over them. Many were deliver'd from the Temptations, out of which 'till then they found no Way to escape. They were built up in our most holy Faith. They rejoiced in the LORD more abundantly. They were strengthen'd in Love, and more effectually provoked to abound in every Good Work.

7] But it was soon objected to the *Bands* (as to the *Classes* before) "These were not at first. There is no Scripture for them. These are Man's Works, Man's Building, Man's Invention." I reply, as before, these are also Prudential Helps, grounded on Reason and Experience, in order to apply the General Rules given in Scripture, according to Particular Circumstances.

8] An Objection much more boldly and frequently urged, is That "all these Bands are mere *Popery.*" I hope, I need not pass a harder Censure on those, (most of them at least) who affirm this, than that they talk of they know not what, that they betray in themselves the most gross and shameful Ignorance. Do not they yet know, That the only *Popish* Confession is, the Confession made by a single Person to a Priest? (And this itself is in no wise condemn'd by our Church; nay, she recommends it in some Cases) whereas that *we* practise is, The Confession of several Persons conjointly, not to a Priest, but to each other. Consequently, it has no Analogy at all to *Popish* Confession. But the Truth is, This is a stale Objection, which many People make against any Thing they do not like. It is all *Popery* out of Hand. . . .

IX, 1] This is the Plainest and Clearest Account I can give of The *People,* commonly call'd *Methodists.* It remains only, to give you a short Account, of those who *serve* their Brethren in Love. There are *Leaders* of Classes and Bands (spoken of before) *Assistants, Stewards, Visitors* of the Sick, and *School-masters.*

2] In the Third Part of the *Appeal,* I have mention'd, How we are led to accept of *Lay-Assistants.* Their Office is, in the Absence of the Minister,

1] To expound every Morning and Evening:

2] To meet the United Society, the Bands, the Select Society, and the Penitents once a Week.

3] To visit the Classes (*London* and *Bristol excepted*) once a Month:

4] To hear and decide all Differences:

5] To put the Disorderly back on Trial, and to receive on Trial for the Bands or Society:

6] To see that the Stewards, the Leaders, and the School-masters faithfully discharge their several Offices:

7] To meet the Leaders of the Bands and Classes weekly, and the Stewards, and to over-look their Accounts.

3] I think, he must be no Fool, who has *Gifts* sufficient for these Things: As neither can he be void of the *Grace* of GOD, who is able to observe the Rules of an Assistant, which are these that follow:

"1] Be diligent. Never be unemploy'd a Moment. Never be triflingly employ'd. Never *while away* Time. Neither spend any more Time at any Place than is strictly necessary.

2] Be Serious. Let your Motto be, Holiness to the LORD. Avoid all Lightness, as you wou'd avoid Hell-fire.

3] Believe Evil of no one. If you *see* it done, well: Else take Heed how you credit it. Put the best Construction on every Thing. You know, the Judge is always supposed to be on the Prisoner's Side.

4] Speak Evil of no one. Else *your* Word especially wou'd eat as doth a Canker. Keep your Thoughts within your own Breast, 'till you come to the Person concern'd.

5] Tell every one what you think wrong in him and that plainly and as soon as may be. Else it will fester in your Heart. Make all Haste to cast the Fire out of your Bosom.

6] Do nothing as a Gentleman. You have no more to do with

this Character than with that of a Dancing-master. You are the Servant of all. Therefore

7] Be ashamed of nothing but Sin; Not of hewing Wood, if Time permit, or drawing Water.

8] Take no Money of any one. If they give you Food when you are hungry, or Cloaths when you need them, it is Good: But not Silver or Gold. Let there be no Pretence to say, We grow rich by the Gospel.

9] Be Punctual. Do every Thing exactly at the Time.

10] Act in all Things, not according to your own Will, but as *a Son in the Gospel*."

8

The Enlightenment

VOLTAIRE (1694–1778), the great French poet, dramatist, satirist, and philosophe, paid a prolonged visit to England in 1726, while banished by the Paris government for an early indiscretion. The Lettres philosophiques reveal the writer's enthusiasm at this time for English manners, institutions, and men of letters and learning.

In the following passages Voltaire describes Sir Isaac Newton's theories of gravitation and optics for the benefit of the French reading public and expresses his own views on the relative merits of Newtonian and Cartesian physics.

a   Voltaire's Letter on Attraction

THE DISCOVERIES, which gained Sir Isaac Newton so universal a reputation, relate to the system of the world, to light, to geometrical infinites, and lastly to chronology, with which he used to amuse himself after the fatigue of his severer studies.

I will now acquaint you (without prolixity if possible) with the few things I have been able to comprehend of all these sublime ideas. With regard to the system of our world, disputes were a long time maintained, on the cause that turns the planets, and keeps them in their orbits; and on those causes which make all bodies here below descend towards the surface of the earth.

The system of Des Cartes, explained and improved since his time, seemed to give a plausible reason for all those phaenomena; and this reason seemed more just, as it is simple, and intelligible to all capacities. But in philosophy a student ought to doubt of the things he fancies he understands too esaily, as much as of those he does not understand.

Gravity, the falling of accelerated bodies on the earth, the revolu-

From Voltaire, LETTERS CONCERNING THE ENGLISH NATION (Glasgow, 1759), Letters XV, XVI, pp. 78–95.

tion of the planets in their orbits, their rotations round their axes, all this is mere motion. Now motion cannot perhaps be conceived any otherwise than by impulsion; therefore all those bodies must be impelled. But by what are they impelled? all space is full, it therefore is filled with a very subtile matter, since this is imperceptible to us; this matter goes from west to east, since all the planets are carried from west to east. Thus from hypothesis to hypothesis, from one appearance to another, philosophers have imagined a vast whirlpool of subtile matter, in which the planets are carried round the sun: they also have created another particular vortex which floats in the great one, and which turns daily round the planets. When all this is done, it is pretended that gravity depends on this diurnal motion; for, say these, the velocity of the subtile matter that turns round our little vortex must be seventeen times more rapid than that of the earth; or, in case its velocity is seventeen times greater than that of the earth, its centrifugal force must be vastly greater, and consequently impel all bodies towards the earth. This is the cause of gravity, according to the Cartesian system. But the theorist, before he calculated the centrifugal force and velocity of the subtile matter, should first have been certain that it existed.

Sir Isaac Newton seems to have destroyed all these great and little vortices, both that which carries the planets round the sun, as well as the other which supposes every planet to turn on its own axis.

First, with regard to the pretended little vortex of the earth, it is demonstrated that it must lose its motion by insensible degrees; it is demonstrated, that if the earth swims in a fluid, its density must be equal to that of the earth; and in case its density be the same, all the bodies we endeavour to move must meet with an insuperable resistance.

With regard to the great vortices, they are still more chimerical, and it is impossible to make them agree with Kepler's law, the truth of which has been demonstrated. Sir Isaac shews, that the revolution of the fluid, in which Jupiter is supposed to be carried, is not the same with regard to the revolution of the fluid of the earth, as the revolution of Jupiter with respect to that of the earth. He proves, that as the planets make their revolutions in ellipses, and consequently being at a much greater distance one from the other in their Aphelia, and a little nearer in their Perihelia; the earth's velocity, for instance, ought to be greater, when it is nearer Venus and Mars, because the fluid that carries it along, being then more pressed, ought to have a greater motion; and yet it is even then that the earth's motion is slower.

He proves that there is no such thing as a celestial matter which goes from west to east, since the comets traverse those spaces, sometimes from east to west, and at other times from north to south.

In fine, the better to resolve, if possible, every difficulty, he proves, and even by experiments, that it is impossible there should be a plenum; and brings back the vacuum, which Aristotle and Des Cartes had banished from the world.

Having by these and several other arguments destroyed the Cartesian vortices, he despaired of ever being able to discover, whether there is a secret principle in nature, which, at the same time, is the cause of the motion of all celestial bodies, and that of gravity on the earth. But being retired in 1666, upon account of the plague, to a solitude near Cambridge; as he was walking one day in his garden, and saw some fruits fall from a tree, he fell into a profound meditation on that gravity, the cause of which had so long been sought, but in vain, by all the philosophers, whilst the vulgar think there is nothing mysterious in it. He said to himself, that from what height soever, in our hemisphere, those bodies might descend, their fall would certainly be in the progression discovered by Galileo; and the spaces they run through would be as the square of the times. Why may not this power which causes heavy bodies to descend, and is the same without any sensible diminution at the remotest distance from the center of the earth, or on the summits of the highest mountains; why, said Sir Isaac, may not this power extend as high as the moon? and in case its influence reaches so far, is it not very probable that this power retains it in its orbit, and determines its motion? but in case the moon obeys this principle, whatever it be, may we not conclude very naturally, that the rest of the planets are equally subject to it? in case this power exists, which besides is proved, it must increase in an inverse ratio of the squares of the distances. All therefore that remains is, to examine how far a heavy body, which should fall upon the earth from a moderate height, would go; and how far in the same time, a body which should fall from the orbit of the moon, would descend. To find this nothing is wanted but the measure of the earth, and the distance of the moon from it.

Thus Sir Isaac Newton reasoned. But at that time the English had but a very imperfect measure of our globe, and depended on the uncertain supposition of mariners, who computed a degree to contain but sixty English miles, whereas it consists in reality of near seventy. As this false computation did not agree with the conclusions which Sir Isaac intended to draw from them, he laid aside this pursuit. A half-learned philosopher, remarkable only for his vanity, would have made the measure of the earth agree, any how, with his system; Sir Isaac, however, chose rather to quit the researches he was then engaged in. But after Mr. Picart had measured the earth exactly, by tracing that meridian, which redounds so much to the honour of the French, Sir Isaac Newton resumed his former reflexions, and found his account in Mr. Picart's calculation.

A circumstance which has always appeared wonderful to me is, that such sublime discoveries should have been made by the sole assistance of a quadrant and a little arithmetic.

The circumference of the earth is one hundred twenty three millions, two hundred forty nine thousand six hundred feet. This, among other things, is necessary to prove the system of attraction.

The instant we know the earth's circumference, and the distance of the moon, we know that of the moon's orbit, and the diameter of this orbit. The moon performs its revolution in that orbit in twenty seven days, seven hours, forty three minutes. It is demonstrated, that the moon in its mean motion makes an hundred and four-score and seven thousand, nine hundred and sixty feet (of Paris) in a minute. It is likewise demonstrated, by a known theorem, that the central force which should make a body fall from the hight of the moon, would make its velocity no more than fifteen Paris feet in a minute of time. Now, if the law by which bodies gravitate, and attract one another in an inverse ratio of the squares of the distances be true; if the same power acts, according to that law, throughout all nature; it is evident that as the earth is sixty semi-diameters distant from the moon, a heavy body must necessarily fall (on the earth) fifteen feet in the first second, and fifty four thousand feet in the first minute.

Now a heavy body falls, in reality, fifteen feet in the first second, and goes in the first minute fifty four thousand feet, which number is the square of sixty multiplied by fifteen. Bodies therefore gravitate in an inverse ratio of the squares of the distances; consequently, what causes gravity on the earth, and keeps the moon in its orbit, is one and the same power; it being demonstrated that the moon gravitates on the earth, which is the center of its particular motion, it is demonstrated that the earth and the moon gravitate on the sun, which is the center of their annual motion.

The rest of the planets must be subject to this general law; and, if this law exists, these planets must follow the laws which Kepler discovered. All these laws, all these relations are indeed observed by the planets with the utmost exactness; therefore the power of attraction causes all the planets to gravitate towards the sun, in like manner as the moon gravitates towards our globe.

Finally, as in all bodies, re-action is equal to action, it is certain that the earth gravitates also towards the moon; and that the sun gravitates towards both: that every one of the satellites of Saturn gravitates towards the other four, and the other four towards it; all five towards Saturn, and Saturn towards all. That it is the same with regard to Jupiter; and that all these globes are attracted by the sun, which is reciprocally attracted by them.

This power of gravitation acts proportionably to the quantity of matter in bodies, a truth which Sir Isaac has demonstrated by experiments. This new discovery has been of use to shew, that the sun (the center of the planetary system) attracts them all in a direct ratio of their quantity of matter combined with their nearness. From hence Sir Isaac, rising by degrees to discoveries which seemed not to be formed for the human mind, is bold enough to compute the quantity of matter contained in the sun and in every planet; and in this manner shews, from the simple law of mechanics, that every celestial globe ought necessarily to be where it is placed.

His bare principle of the laws of gravitation accounts for all the apparent inequalities in the course of the celestial globes. The variations of the moon are a necessary consequence of those laws. Moreover the reason is evidently seen why the nodes of the moon perform their revolutions in nineteen years, and those of the earth in about twenty six thousand. The several appearances observed in the tides are also a very simple effect of this attraction. The proximity of the moon when at the full, and when it is new, and its distance in the quadratures or quarters combined with the action of the sun, exhibit a sensible reason why the ocean swells and sinks.

After having shewn, by his sublime theory, the course and inequalities of the planets, he subjects comets to the same law. The orbit of these fires (unknown for so great a series of years,) which was the terror of mankind, and the rock against which philosophy split; placed by Aristotle below the moon, and sent back by Des

Cartes above the sphere of Saturn, is at last placed in its proper seat by Sir Isaac Newton.

He proves that comets are solid bodies which move in the sphere of the sun's activity; and that they describe an ellipsis so very eccentric, and so near to parabolas, that certain comets must take up above five hundred years in their revolution.

The learned Dr. Halley is of opinion, that the comet seen in 1680, is the same which appeared in Julius Caesar's time. This shews more than any other, that comets are hard, opake bodies; for it descended so near to the sun, as to come within a sixth part of the diameter of this planet from it; and consequently might have contracted a degree of heat two thousand times stronger than that of red hot iron; and would have been soon dispersed in vapour, had it not been a firm, dense body. The guessing the course of comets began then to be very much in vogue; the celebrated Bernoulli concluded by his system, that the famous comet of 1680, would appear again the 17th of May 1719. Not a single astronomer in Europe went to bed that night; however they needed not to have broke their rest, for the famous comet never appeared. There is at least more cunning, if not more certainty, in fixing its return to so remote a distance as five hundred and seventy five years. As to Mr. Whiston, he affirmed very seriously, that in the time of the deluge a comet overflowed the terrestrial globe; and he was so unreasonable as to wonder that people laughed at him for making such an assertion. The ancients were almost in the same way of thinking with Mr. Whiston, and fancied that comets were always the forerunners of some great calamity which was to befal mankind. Sir Isaac Newton, on the contrary, suspected that they are very beneficent; and that vapours exhale from them merely to nourish and vivify the planets, which imbibe in their course the several particles the sun has detached from the comets: an opinion which at least is more probable than the former. But this is not all. If this power of gravitation or attraction acts on all the celestial globes, it acts undoubtedly on the several parts of these globes. For in case bodies attract one another in proportion to the quantity of matter contained in them, it can only be in proportion to the quantity of their parts; and if this power is found in the whole, it is undoubtedly in the half, in the quarter, in the eighth part, and so on in infinitum.

This is attraction, the great spring by which all nature is moved. Sir Isaac Newton, after having demonstrated the existence of this principle, plainly foresaw that its very name would offend; and therefore this philosopher in more places than one of his books, gives the reader some caution about it. He bids him beware of confounding this name with what the ancients called occult qualities; but to be satisfied with knowing that there is in all bodies a central force which acts to the utmost limits of the universe, according to the invariable laws of mechanics.

It is surprising, after the solemn protestations Sir Isaac made, that such eminent men as Mr. Sorin and Mr. de Fontenelle, should have imputed to this great philosopher the verbal and chimerical way of reasoning of the Aristotelians; Mr. Sorin in the memoirs of the academy of 1709, and Mr. de Fontenelle in the very elogium of Sir Isaac Newton.

Most of the French, the learned and others, have repeated this reproach. These are for ever crying out, Why did he not employ the word impulsion, which is so well understood, rather than that of attraction, which is unintelligible?

Sir Isaac might have answered these critics thus: First, you have as imperfect an idea of the word impulsion as of that of attraction; and in case you cannot conceive how one body tends towards the center of another body, neither can you conceive by what power one body can impel another.

Secondly, I could not admit of impulsion; for to do this, I must have known that a celestial matter was the agent; but so far from knowing that there is any such matter, I have proved it to be merely imaginary.

Thirdly, I use the word attraction for no other reason, but to express a defect which I discovered in nature; a certain and indisputable effect of an unknown principle; a quality inherent in matter, the cause of which persons of greater abilities than I can pretend to, may, if they can, find out.

What have you then taught us? will these people say further: and to what purpose are so many calculations to tell us what you yourself do not comprehend?

I have taught you, may Sir Isaac rejoin, that all bodies gravitate towards one another in proportion to their quantity of matter; that these central forces alone keep the planets and comets in their orbits, and cause them to move in the proportion before set down. I demonstrate to you, that it is impossible there should be any other cause which keeps the planets in their orbits, than that general phaenomenon of gravity. For heavy bodies fall on the earth according to the proportion demonstrated of central forces; and the planets finishing their course according to the same proportions, in case there were another power that acted upon all these bodies, it would either increase their velocity, or change their direction. Now not one of these bodies ever has a single degree of motion or velocity, or has any direction but what is demonstrated to be the effect of the central forces; consequently it is impossible there should be any other principle.

Give me leave once more to introduce Sir Isaac speaking: shall he not be allowed to say, My case and that of the ancients is very different? These saw, for instance, water ascend in pumps, and said, the water rises because it abhors a *vacuum*. But with regard to myself, I am in the case of a man who should have first observed that water ascends in pumps, but should leave others to explain the cause of this effect. The anatomist who first declared, that the motion of the arm is owing to the contraction of the muscles, taught mankind an indisputable truth; but are they less obliged to him because he did not know the reason why the muscles contract? The cause of the elasticity of the air is unknown, but he who first discovered this spring performed a very signal service to natural philosophy. The spring that I discovered was more hidden and more universal, and for that very reason mankind ought to thank me the more. I have discovered a new property of matter, one of the secrets of the Creator; and have calculated and discovered the effects of it. After this shall people quarrel with me about the name I gave it?

Vortices may be called an occult quality because their existence was never proved: attraction on the contrary is a real thing, because its effects are demonstrated, and the proportions of it are calculated. The cause of this cause is among the arcana of the Almighty.

> *Procedes huc, et non amplius.*
> Hither thou shalt go, and no farther.

b Voltaire's Letter on Sir Isaac Newton's Optics

THE PHILOSOPHERS of the last age found out a new universe; and a circumstance which made its discovery more difficult was, that no one had so much as suspected its existence. The most sage and judicious were of opinion, that it was a frantic rashness to dare so much as to imagine, that it was possible to guess the laws by which the celestial bodies move, and the manner how light acts. Galileo, by his astronomical discoveries, Kepler by his calculation, Des Cartes (at least in his dioptrics, and Sir Isaac Newton in all his works) severally saw the mechanism of the springs of the world. The geometricans have subjected infinity to the laws of calculation. The circulation of the blood in animals, and of the sap in vegetables, have changed the face of nature with regard to us. A new kind of existence has been given to bodies in the air-pump. By the assistance of telescopes bodies have been brought nearer to one another. Finally, the several discoveries which Sir Isaac Newton has made on light, are equal to the boldest things which the curiosity of man could expect, after so many philosophical novelties.

Till Antonio de Dominis the rainbow was considered as an inexplicable miracle. This philosopher guessed, that it was a necessary effect of the sun and rain. Des Cartes gained immortal fame by his mathematical explication of this so natural a phaenomenon. He calculated the reflections and refractions of light in drops of rain; and his sagacity on this occasion was at that time looked upon as next to divine.

But what would he have said had it been proved to him, that he was mistaken in the nature of light; that he had not the least reason to maintain that it is a globular body; that it is false to assert, that this matter, spreading itself through the whole, waits only to be projected forward by the sun, in order to be put in action, in like manner as a long staff acts at one end when pushed forward by the other; that light is certainly darted by the sun; in fine, that light is transmitted from the sun to the earth in about seven minutes, though a cannon ball, which were not to lose any of its velocity, could not go that distance in less than twenty five years? How great would have been his astonishment, had he been told, that light does not reflect directly by impinging against the solid parts of bodies; that bodies are not transparent when they have large pores; and that a man should arise, who would demonstrate all these paradoxes, and anatomize a single ray of light with more dexterity than the ablest artist dissects a human body! This man is come. Sir Isaac Newton has demonstrated to the eye, by the bare assistance of the prism, that light is a composition of coloured rays, which, being united, form white colour. A single ray is by him divided into seven, which all fall upon a piece of linen, or a sheet of white paper, in their order one above the other, and at unequal distances. The first is red, the second orange, the third yellow, the fourth green, the fifth blue, the sixth indigo, the seventh a violet purple. Each of these rays, transmitted afterwards by an hundred other prisms, will never change the colour it bears; in like manner as gold, when completely purged from its dross, will never change afterwards in the crucible. As a superabundant proof that each of these elementary rays has inherently in itself that which forms its colour to the eye, take a small piece of yellow wood for instance, and set it in the ray of a red colour, this wood will instantly be tinged red; but set it in the ray of a green colour, it assumes a green colour, and so of all the rest.

From what cause therefore do colours arise in nature? It is nothing but the disposition of bodies to reflect the rays of a certain order, and to absorb all the rest.

What then is this secret disposition? Sir Isaac Newton demonstrates, that it is nothing more than the density of the small constituent particles of which a body is composed. And how is this reflection performed? It was supposed to arise from the rebounding of the rays, in the same manner as a ball on the surface of a solid body; but this is a mistake; for Sir Isaac taught the astonished philosophers, that bodies are opake for no other reason, but because their pores are large; that light reflects on our eyes from the very bosom of those pores; that the smaller the pores of a body are, the more such a body is transparent. Thus paper, which reflects the light when dry, transmits it when oiled, because the oil, by filling its pores, makes them much smaller.

It is there that examining the vast porosity of bodies, every particle having its pores, and every particle of those particles having its own; he shews we are not certain that there is a cubic inch of solid matter in the universe, so far are we from conceiving what matter is. Having thus divided, as it were, light into its elements, and carried the sagacity of his discoveries so far, as to prove the method of distinguishing compound colours from such as are primitive; he shews, that these elementary rays separated by the prism are ranged in their order for no other reason but because they are refracted in that very order; and it is this property (unknown till he discovered it) of breaking or splitting in this proportion; it is this unequal refraction of rays, this power of refracting the red less than the orange colour, *etc.* which he calls the different refrangibility. The most reflexible rays are the most refrangible, and from hence he evinces that the same power is the cause both of the reflection and refraction of light.

But all these wonders are merely but the opening of his discoveries. He found out the secret to see the vibrations or fits of light, which come and go incessantly, and which either transmit light, or reflect it according to the density of the parts they meet with. He has presumed to calculate the density of the particles of air necessary between two glasses, the one flat, the other convex on one side, set one upon the other; in order to operate such a transmission or reflexion, or to form such and such a colour.

From all these combinations he discovers the proportion in which light acts on bodies, and bodies act on light.

He saw light so perfectly, that he has determined to what degree of perfection the art of increasing it, and of assisting our eyes by telescopes can be carried.

Des Cartes, from a noble confidence, that was very excusable, considering how strongly he was fired at the first discoveries he made in an art which he almost first found out; Des Cartes, I say, hoped to discover in the stars, by the assistance of telescopes, objects as small as those we discern upon the earth.

But Sir Isaac has shewn, that dioptric telescopes cannot be brought to a greater perfection; because of that refraction, and of that very refrangibility, which at the same time that they bring objects nearer to us, scatter too much the elementary rays; he has calculated in these glasses the proportion of the scattering of the red and of the blue rays; and proceeding so far as to demonstrate things which were not supposed even to exist, he examines the inequalities which arise from the shape or figure of the glass, and that which arises from the refrangibility. He finds, that the object glass of the telescope being convex on one side, and flat on the other, in case that flat side be turned towards the object, the error which arises from the construction and position of the glass is above five thousand times less than the error which arises from the refrangibility: and therefore, that the shape or figure of the glasses is not the cause why telescopes cannot be carried to a greater perfection, but arises wholly from the nature of light.

For this reason he invented a telescope, which discovers objects by reflexion and not by refraction. Telescopes of this new kind are very hard to make, and their use is not easy. But according to the English, a reflective telescope of but five feet has the same effect as another of an hundred feet in length.

9

"Enlightened" Despotism

CATHERINE THE GREAT of Russia (reigned 1762–1796) was in many respects the epitome of the "enlightened" despot. She combined sincere admiration for Montesquieu, Voltaire, and Diderot and authorship of an enlightened manual of education for young ladies of the nobility with savage repression of the Pugachev peasant revolt (1773) and a highly successful career as autocrat of all the Russias.

The following passage is from her Instructions, issued on the occasion of the great national assembly of 564 delegates whom she had summoned to meet in Moscow in 1767.

Catherine the Great's Instructions to the Commissioners for Composing a New Code of Laws

1] THE CHRISTIAN LAW teaches us to do mutual Good to one another, as much as possibly we can.

2] Laying this down as a fundamental Rule prescribed by that Religion, which has taken, or ought to take Root in the Hearts of the whole People; we cannot but suppose, that every honest Man in the Community is, or will be, desirous of seeing his native Country at the very Summit of Happiness, Glory, Safety, and Tranquillity.

3] And that every Individual Citizen in particular must wish to see himself protected by Laws, which should not distress him in his Circumstances, but, on the Contrary, should defend him from all Attempts of others, that are repugnant to this fundamental Rule.

4] In order therefore to proceed to a speedy Execution of what *We* expect from such a general Wish, *We,* fixing the Foundation

From W. F. Reddaway (ed.), DOCUMENTS OF CATHERINE THE GREAT (London, 1931), pp. 215–7, 219–20, 222–3, 225–7, 231–2, 248, 255, 257–8, 262, 266–7, 271, 273–5. Reprinted by permission of the Cambridge University Press.

upon the above first-mentioned Rule, ought to begin with an Inquiry into the natural Situation of this Empire.

5] For those Laws have the greatest Conformity with Nature, whose particular Regulations are best adapted to the Situation and Circumstances of the People, for whom they are instituted.

This natural Situation is described in the three following Chapters.

6] Russia is an European State.

7] This is clearly demonstrated by the following Observations: The Alterations which *Peter the Great* undertook in Russia succeeded with the greater Ease, because the Manners, which prevailed at that Time, and had been introduced amongst us by a Mixture of different Nations, and the Conquest of foreign Territories, were quite unsuitable to the Climate. *Peter the First,* by introducing the Manners and Customs of Europe among the European People in his Dominions, found at that Time such Means as even he himself was not sanguine enough to expect.

* * *

8] The Possessions of the Russian Empire extend upon the terrestrial Globe to 32 Degrees of Latitude, and to 165 of Longitude.

9] The Sovereign is absolute; for there is no other Authority but that which centers in his single Person, that can act with a Vigour proportionate to the Extent of such a vast Dominion.

10] The Extent of the Dominion requires an absolute Power to be vested in that Person who rules over it. It is expedient so to be, that the quick Dispatch of Affairs, sent from distant Parts, might make ample Amends for the Delay occasioned by the great Distance of the Places.

11] Every other Form of Government whatsover would not only have been prejudicial to Russia, but would even have proved its entire Ruin.

12] Another Reason is; That it is better to be subject to the Laws under one Master, than to be subservient to many.

13] What is the true End of Monarchy? Not to deprive People of their natural Liberty; but to correct their Actions, in order to attain the *supreme Good.*

14] The Form of Government, therefore, which best attains this End, and at the same Time sets less Bounds than others to natural Liberty, is that which coincides with the Views and Purposes of rational Creatures, and answers the End, upon which we ought to fix a stedfast Eye in the Regulations of civil Polity.

15] The Intention and the End of Monarchy, is the Glory of the Citizens, of the State, and of the Sovereign.

16] But, from this Glory, a Sense of Liberty arises in a People governed by a Monarch; which may produce in these States as much Energy in transacting the most important Affairs, and may contribute as much to the Happiness of the Subjects, as even Liberty itself.

*   *   *

17] *Of the Safety of the Institutions of Monarchy.*

18] The intermediate Powers, subordinate to, and depending upon the supreme Power, form the essential Part of monarchical Government.

19] *I* have said, that the intermediate Powers, subordinate and depending, proceed from the supreme Power; as in the very Nature of the Thing the Sovereign is the Source of all imperial and civil Power.

20] The Laws, which form the Foundation of the State, send out certain Courts of Judicature, through which, as through smaller Streams, the Power of the Government is poured out, and diffused.

21] The Laws allow these Courts of Judicature to remonstrate, that such or such an Injunction is unconstitutional, and prejudicial, obscure, and impossible to be carried into Execution; and direct, beforehand, to which Injunction one ought to pay Obedience, and in what Manner one ought to conform to it. These Laws undoubtedly constitute the firm and immoveable Basis of every State.

*   *   *

31] *Of the Situation of the People in general.*

32] It is the greatest Happiness for a Man to be so circumstanced, that, if his Passions should prompt him to be mischievous, he should still think it more for his Interest not to give Way to them.

33] The Laws ought to be so framed, as to secure the Safety of every Citizen as much as possible.

34] The Equality of the Citizens consists in this; that they should all be subject to the same Laws.

35] This Equality requires Institutions so well adapted, as to prevent the Rich from oppressing those who are not so wealthy as themselves, and converting all the Charges and Employments intrusted to them as Magistrates only, to their own private Emolument.

36] General or political Liberty does not consist in that licentious Notion, *That a Man may do whatever he pleases.*

37] In a State or Assemblage of People that live together in a Community, where there are Laws, Liberty can only consist *in doing that which every One ought to do,* and *not to be constrained to do that which One ought not to do.*

38] A Man ought to form in his own Mind an exact and clear Idea of what Liberty is. *Liberty is the Right of doing whatsoever the Laws allow:* And if any one Citizen could do what the Laws forbid, there would be no more Liberty; because others would have an equal Power of doing the same.

39] The political Liberty of a Citizen is the Peace of Mind arising from the Consciousness, that every Individual enjoys his peculiar Safety; and in order that the People might attain this Liberty, the Laws ought to be so framed, that no one Citizen should stand in Fear of another; but that all of them should stand in Fear of the same Laws.

40] *Of Laws in general.*

41] Nothing ought to be forbidden by the Laws, but what may be prejudicial, either to every Individual in particular, or to the whole Community in general.

42] All Actions, which comprehend nothing of this Nature, are in nowise cognizable by the Laws; which are made only with the View of procuring the greatest possible Advantage and Tranquillity to the People, who live under their Protection.

43] To preserve Laws from being violated, they ought to be so good, and so well furnished with all Expedients, tending to procure the greatest possible Good to the People; that every Individual might be fully convinced, that it was his Interest, as well as Duty, to preserve those Laws inviolable.

44] And this is the most exalted Pitch of Perfection which we ought to labour to attain to.

* * *

64] *Of the Laws in particular.*

65] Laws carried to the Extremity of Right, are productive of the Extremity of Evil.

66] All Laws, where the Legislation aims at the Extremity of

Rigour, may be evaded. It is Moderation which rules a People, and not Excess of Severity.

67] Civil Liberty flourishes, when the Laws deduce every Punishment from the peculiar Nature of every Crime. The Application of Punishment ought not to proceed from the arbitrary Will, or mere Caprice of the Legislator, but from the Nature of the Crime; and it is not the Man, who ought to do Violence to a Man, but the proper Action of the Man himself.

68] Crimes are divisible into four Classes.

69] The first Class of Crimes is that against Religion.

70] The second, against Manners.

71] The third, against the Peace.

72] The fourth, against the Security of the Citizens.

73] The Punishments inflicted upon these ought to flow from the specific Nature of the very Crime.

*   *   *

80] *Of Punishments.*

81] The Love of our Country, Shame, and the Dread of publick Censure, are Motives which restrain, and may deter Mankind from the Commission of a Number of Crimes.

82] The greatest Punishment for a bad Action, under a mild Administration, will be for the Party to be convinced of it. The civil Laws will there correct Vice with the more Ease, and will not be under a Necessity of employing more rigorous Means.

83] In these Governments, the Legislature will apply itself more to prevent Crime, than to punish them, and should take more Care to instil Good Manners into the Minds of the Citizens, by proper Regulations, than to dispirit them by the Terror of corporal and capital Punishments.

84] In a Word, whatever is termed Punishment in the Law, is, in Fact, nothing but Pain and Suffering.

85] Experience teaches us, that, in those Countries where Punishments are mild, they operate with the same Efficacy upon the Minds of the Citizens, as the most severe in other Places.

86] If a sensible Injury should accrue to a State from some popular Commotion, a violent Administration will be at once for a sudden Remedy, and instead of recurring to the ancient Laws, will inflict some terrible Punishment, in order to crush the growing Evil on the Spot. The Imagination of the People is affected at the Time of this greater Punishment, just as it would have been affected by the least; and when the Dread of this Punishment gradually wears off, it will be compelled to introduce a severer Punishment upon all Occasions.

87] The People ought not to be driven on by violent Methods, but we ought to make Use of the Means which Nature has given us, with the utmost Care and Caution, in order to conduct them to the End we propose.

88] Examine with Attention the Cause of all Licentiousness; and you will find, that it proceeds from the Neglect of punishing Crimes, not from the Mildness of Punishments. Let us follow Nature, which has given Shame to Man, for his Scourge, and let the greatest Part of the Punishment consist in the Infamy which accompanies the Punishment.

89] And if a Country could be found, where Infamy should not be the Consequence of Punishment; the Reason of this is to be imputed to some tyrannical Government, which inflicted the same Punishments upon the Innocent and the Guilty, without Distinction.

90] And if another Country should be known, where the People are restrained by nothing but the severest Punishments; you must again be assured, that this proceeds from the Violence of the Government, which has ordained those Punishments for the slightest Offences.

*   *   *

96] Good Laws keep strictly a just Medium: They do not always inflict pecuniary, nor always subject Malefactors to corporal Punishment.

All Punishments, by which the human Body might be maimed, ought to be abolished.

*   *   *

120] Two Witnesses are absolutely necessary, in order to form a right Judgment: For an Accuser, who affirms, and the Party accused, who denies the Fact, make the Evidence on both Sides equal; for that Reason, a Third is required in order to convict the Defendant; unless other clear collateral Proofs should fix the Credibility of the Evidence in favour of one of them.

121] The Evidence of two Witnesses is esteemed sufficient for Conviction, in every criminal Case whatsoever. The Law believes them, as if they spoke from the Mouth of Truth itself. The following Chapter will evince this more clearly.

122] In the same Manner they decide in almost every State, that every Child conceived in the Time of Wedlock is legitimate: The Law places its whole Confidence in the Mother. This is mentioned here on account of the Obscurity of the Laws in those Cases.

123] The Usage of Torture is contrary to all the Dictates of Nature and Reason; even Mankind itself cries out against it, and demands loudly the total Abolition of it. We see, at this very Time, a People greatly renowned for the Excellence of their civil Polity, who reject it without any sensible Inconveniencies. It is, therefore, by no Means necessary by its Nature. *We* will explain this more at large here below.

124] There are Laws, which do not allow the Application of Torture, except only in those Cases, where the Prisoner at the Bar refuses to plead, and will neither acknowledge himself innocent nor guilty.

125] To make an Oath too cheap by frequent Practice, is to weaken the Obligation of it, and to destroy its Efficacy. The Kissing of the Cross cannot be used upon any Occasion, but when he, that takes an Oath, has no private Interest of his own to serve; as for Instance, the Judge and the Witnesses.

126] Those who are to be tried for capital Offences, should chuse their own Judges, with the Consent of the Laws; or, at least, should have a Right of rejecting such a Number of them, that those who remain in Court may seem as chosen by the Malefactors themselves.

127] It is likewise just, that some of the Judges should be of the same Rank of Citizenship as the Defendant; that is, his Equals; that he might not think himself fallen into the Hands of such People, as would violently over-rule the Affair to his Prejudice: Of this there are already Instances in the Martial Laws.

128] When the Defendant is condemned, it is not the Judges who inflict the Punishment upon him, but the Law.

129] The Sentence ought to be as clear and distinct as possible; even so far as to preserve the very identical Words of the Law. But if they should include the private Opinion of the Judge, the People will live in Society, without knowing exactly the reciprocal Obligations they lie under to one another in that State.

*   *   *

206] Who can read, without being struck with Horror, the History of so many barbarous and useless Tortures, invented and executed without the least Remorse of Conscience, by *People* who assumed to themselves the *Name of Sages?* Who does not feel within himself a sensible Palpitation of the Heart, at the Sight of so many Thousands of unhappy Wretches, who have suffered, and still suffer: *frequently* accused of Crimes, which are *difficult, or impossible to happen,* proceeding often from *Ignorance,* and sometimes from *Superstition?* Who can look, I say, upon the Dismembering of these People, who are executed with *slow* and *studied* Barbarity, by the *very Persons* who are *their Brethren?* Countries and Times, in which the most *cruel Punishments* were made use of, are those, in which the most *inhuman Villainies* were perpetrated.

207] That a Punishment may produce the *desired* Effect, it will be sufficient; when the *Evil* it occasions exceeds the *Good* expected from the Crime, including in the Calculation the *Excess* of the Evil *over* the Good, the undoubted *Certainty* of the Punishment, and the *Privation* of all the *Advantages* hoped for from the Crime. All Severity *exceeding* these Bounds is *useless,* and consequently *tyrannical.*

208] Wherever the Laws have been extremely severe, they have either been altered, or the Impunity of the Criminals arose from the very Severity of the Laws. The *Degrees* of Punishment ought to be referred to the present *Situation* and *Circumstances* in which every People *find* itself. In *Proportion* as the *Minds* of those who live in a Community become *enlightened,* the *Sensibility* of every Individual *increases*; and if Sensibility increases amongst the Citizens, then the *Severity* of Punishments must *abate* in Proportion.

* * *

239] Q. 8. *Which are the most efficacious Means of preventing Crimes?*

240] It is better to *prevent* Crimes, than to *punish* them.

241] To *prevent* Crimes, is the *Intention,* and the *End* of every *good* Legislation; which is nothing more than the Art of conducting People to the *greatest* Good, or to leave the *least* Evil possible amongst them, if it should prove impracticable to *exterminate* the whole.

242] If we forbid many Actions, which are termed *indifferent* by the *Moralists,* we shall not prevent the Crimes, of which they *may* be productive, but shall *create* still *new* Ones.

243] Would you *prevent* Crimes? order it *so,* That the Laws might rather favor every *Individual,* than any particular Rank of Citizens, in the Community.

244] Order it so, that the People should fear the *Laws,* and *nothing* but the Laws.

245] Would you prevent Crimes? order it so, that the *Light of Knowledge* may be *diffused* among the People.

246] A Book of good Laws is nothing but a Bar to prevent the Licentiousness of injurious Men from doing Mischief to their fellow Creatures.

247] There is yet another Expedient to *prevent* Crimes, which is by *rewarding* Virtue.

248] Finally, the *most sure,* but, at the same Time, the *most difficut* Expedient to mend the Morals of the People, is a perfect System of Education.

* * *

250] A Society of Citizens, as well as every Thing else, requires a certain fixed Order: There ought to be *some to govern,* and *others to obey.*

251] And this is the Origin of every Kind of Subjection; which feels itself more or less alleviated, in Proportion to the Situation of the Subjects.

252] And, consequently, as the Law of Nature commands *Us* to take as much Care, as lies in *Our* Power, of the Prosperity of all the People; we are obliged to alleviate the Situation of the Subjects, as much as sound Reason will permit.

253] And therefore, to shun all Occasions of reducing People to a State of Slavery, except the *utmost.* Necessity should *inevitably* oblige us to do it; in that Case, it ought not to be done for our own Benefit; but for the Interest of the State: Yet even that Case is extremely uncommon.

254] Of whatever Kind Subjection may be, the civil Laws ought to guard, on the one Hand, against the *Abuse* of Slavery, and, on the other, against the *Dangers* which may arise from it.

* * *

264] *Of the Propagation of the human Species in a State.*

265] Russia is not only *greatly* deficient in the *number* of her Inhabitants; but at the same Time, extends her Dominion over *immense* Tracts of Land; which are neither peopled nor improved.

And therefore, in a Country so circumstanced, *too much* Encouragement can never be given to the *Propagation* of the human Species.

266] The Peasants generally have twelve, fifteen, and even twenty Children by one Marriage; but it rarely happens, that one *Fourth* of these ever attains to the *Age* of Maturity. There must therefore be some Fault, either in their Nourriture, in their Way of Living, or Method of Education, which occasions this *prodigious* Loss, and disappoints the *Hopes* of the Empire. How flourishing would the State of this Empire be, if we could but ward off, or *prevent* this fatal Evil by proper Regulations!

* * *

269] It seems too, that the Method of exacting their Revenues, *newly* invented by the Lords, diminishes both the *Inhabitants,* and the *Spirit of Agriculture* in Russia. Almost all the Villages are *heavily* taxed. The Lords, who seldom or never *reside* in their Villages, lay an Impost on every Head of one, two, and even five Rubles, without the least Regard to the *Means* by which their Peasants may be able to *raise* this Money.

270] It is highly necessary that the Law should prescribe a Rule to the Lords, for a more judicious Method of raising their Revenues; and oblige them to levy *such* a Tax, as *tends least* to separate the Peasant from his House and Family; this would be the Means by which Agriculture would become more extensive, and Population be more increased in the Empire.

271] Even now some Husbandmen do not see their Houses for Fifteen Years together, and yet pay the Tax annually to their respective Lords; which they procure in Towns at a vast Distance from their Families, and wander over the whole Empire for that Purpose.

272] The more happily a People live under a Government, the more easily the Number of the Inhabitants increases.

273] Countries, which abound with Meadow and Pasture Lands, are generally *very thinly* peopled; the Reason is, that *few* can find Employment in those Places: But arable Lands are much *more* populous; because they *furnish* Employment for a much greater Number of People.

274] Wherever the Inhabitants can enjoy the Conveniencies of Life, there Population will certainly increase.

275] *But a Country, which is so overwhelmed with Taxes, that the People, with all their Care and Industry, can with the utmost*

Difficulty find Means for procuring a bare Subsistance, will, in length of Time, be deserted by its Inhabitants.

* * *

293] *Of handicraft Trades, and Commerce.*

294] There can be neither skilful Handicraftsmen, nor a firmly-established Commerce, where Agriculture is neglected, or carried on with Supineness and Negligence.

295] Agriculture can never flourish there, where no Persons have any Property of their own.

296] This is founded upon a very simple Rule: *Every Man will take more Care of his own Property, than of that which belongs to another; and will not exert his utmost Endeavours upon that, which he has Reason to fear another may deprive him of.*

* * *

330] One of the best Writers upon Laws gives us his Sentiments in the following Words. *People, incited by what they see practised in some Dominions, imagine, that it would be expedient to have Laws, which should encourage the Nobility to ingage in Commerce. This would be the Means of ruining the Nobility, without the least Advantage to Commerce. The Practice indeed is extremely wise in those Countries, where Merchants, though not ennobled, are yet capable of attaining the Rank of Nobility; they have the Hopes of obtaining that Rank, without labouring under the Inconveniencies, which actually attend it. They have not a more certain Method of rising above their present Profession, than by carrying it on with the utmost Assiduity, or meeting with such Success, as is generally accompanied with an affluent Fortune. It is repugnant to the true Spirit of Trade, that the Nobility should engage in it under a monarchical Government. It would be fatal to the Cities, as the Emperors Honorius and Theodosius affirm; and would destroy the Facility of buying and selling between the Merchants and the Plebeians. It is equally contrary to the Spirit of monarchical Government, for the Nobility to engage in Trade. The Custom allowed to the Nobility, in some Countries, of engaging in Trade, is one of the Means, which contributed most to weaken the Monarchical Government.*

* * *

345] In commercial Countries, where great Numbers depend intirely upon their Art, the State is frequently obliged to provide for the Necessities of the Ancient, the Infirm, and the Orphans. A well-regulated State draws a Fund for their Subsistence from the very Arts themselves; it gives Work to some in proportion to their Abilities; and it teaches others to work, which is itself an Employment.

346] An Alms bestowed on a Beggar in the Street, can never acquit a State of the Obligation it lies under, of affording all its Citizens a certain Support during Life; such as wholesome Food, proper Cloathing, and a Way of Life not prejudicial to Health in general.

* * *

347] *Of Education.*
348] The Rules of Education are the fundamental Institutes which train us up to be Citizens.

349] Each particular Family ought to be governed upon the Plan of the great Family; which includes all the Particulars.

350] It is impossible to give a general Education to a very numerous People, and to bring up all the Children in Houses regulated for that Purpose; and, for that Reason, it will be proper to establish some *general Rules,* which may serve *by Way of Advice* to all Parents.

* * *

357] *Of the Nobility.*
358] The Husbandmen, who cultivate the Lands to produce Food for People in every Rank of Life, live in Country Towns and Villages. *This is their Lot.*

359] The Burghers, who employ their Time in mechanick Trades, Commerce, Arts, and Sciences, *inhabit the Cities.*

360] *Nobility* is an Appellation of *Honour,* which distinguishes all those who are adorned with it from every other Person of *inferior Rank.*

361] As amongst Mankind there were *some more* virtuous *than others,* and who at the same Time distinguished themselves *more* eminently by their *merit,* the People in ancient Times agreed to dignify the *most* virtuous, and the *most* deserving, by this *honourable Appellation, or Title,* and determined to *invest* them with *many Privileges* which are *founded* upon *the Principal Rules of Virtue and Honour* above mentioned.

362] They proceeded still farther, and regulated by Law *the Means* by which *this Dignity* might *be obtained* from the Sovereign, and pointed out *those bad Actions* by which it *might be forfeited.*

363] *Virtue* with *Merit raises* People to the *Rank of Nobility.*

364] Virtue and Honour ought to be the Rules, which prescribe *Love for their Country, Zeal for its Service, Obedience and Fidelity to their Sovereign*; and continually suggest, *never to be guilty of an infamous Action.*

365] There are few Ways which lead so directly to the Attainment of Honours, as the military Service. To defend their Country, and to conquer its Enemies, is the first Duty, and Proper Employment of the Nobility.

366] But though the military Art is the most ancient Way of attaining the Rank of Nobility; and though the military Virtues are essentially necessary for the Existence and Support of the State;

367] Yet still Justice is no less required in Time of Peace than in War; and the State would be destroyed without it:

368] And from hence it proceeds, that this Dignity is not attached solely to the Nobility; but may be acquired by the *civil* Virtues, as well as by the *military.*

*   *   *

376] *Of the middling Sort of People.*

377] *I* have mentioned in the xvth Chapter, *that those People who inhabit the Cities, apply themselves to handicraft Trades, Commerce, Arts, and Sciences.* In whatever *State* the *fundamental Qualification* for the Rank of Nobility is established, *conformably* with the Rules prescribed in the xvth Chapter, it is no less *useful* to establish the Qualification of Citizens upon *Principles* productive of *Good Manners and Industry,* by which the People, we here treat of, will *enjoy that Situation.*

378] This Sort of People, of whom we ought now to speak, and from whom the State expects much Benefit, are admitted into the *Middling* Rank, if their *Qualifications* are firmly *established* upon *Good Manners, and Incitements to Industry.*

379] People of *this Rank* will enjoy a State of Liberty, without intermixing either with the *Nobility* or the *Husbandmen.*

380] To this Rank of People, we ought to annex all those who are neither *Gentlemen,* nor *Husbandmen*; but employ themselves in *Arts, Sciences, Navigation, Commerce,* or *handicraft Trades.*

381] Besides these, all those, who are not of the *Nobility*, but have been educated in *Schools* or *Colleges*, of what Denomination soever, *ecclesiastical* or *civil*, founded by *Us* and *Our* Ancestors:

382] Also the Children of People belonging to the Law. But as in that *third Species*, there are different Degrees of Privilege, therefore we shall not enter into a Detail of Particulars; but only open the Way for a due Consideration of it.

383] As the whole Qualification, which intitles People to this *middling* Rank, is founded upon good Manners and Industry; the Violation of these Rules will serve, on the Contrary, for their Exclusion from it; as for Instance, *Perfidiousness* and *Breach of Promise*, especially if *caused* by *Idleness* and *Treachery*.

10

Literature and the Arts

ALEXANDER POPE (1688–1744), author of the Essay on Man, was the leading English poet of his generation and admired by Voltaire as "the English Boileau" and "the most elegant, the most correct poet and . . . the most harmonious . . . that England ever gave birth to." The views here expressed, with their emphasis on the perfection of classical models, are typical of the early Augustan Age of English literature.

The second passage is from the first of twelve lectures given in Vienna in 1808 by the German critic, orientalist, and Shakespearean translator, A. W. Schlegel (1767–1845).

a Alexander Pope's Essay on Criticism (1709)

'TIS HARD to say, if greater want of skill
Appear in writing or in judging ill;
But, of the two, less dangerous is the offence
To tire our patience, than mislead our sense.

*   *   *

First follow nature, and your judgment frame
By her just standard, which is still the same:
Unerring Nature, still divinely bright,
One clear, unchanged, and universal light,
Life, force, and beauty, must to all impart,
At once the source, and end, and test of art.
Art from that fund each just supply provides,
Works without show, and without pomp presides:
In some fair body thus the informing soul
With spirits feeds, with vigour fills the whole,
Each motion guides, and every nerve sustains;
Itself unseen, but in the effects, remains.

FROM THE POETICAL WORKS OF ALEXANDER POPE (London, n.d.), pp. 9–15, 22–3, 25–6, 28–32.

Some, to some Heaven in wit has been profuse,
Want as much more, to turn it to its use;
For wit and judgment often are at strife,
Though meant each other's aid, like man and wife.
'Tis more to guide, than spur the muse's steed;
Restrain his fury, than provoke his speed;
The winged courser, like a generous horse,
Shows most true mettle when you check his course.
　　Those rules of old discovered, not devised,
Are nature still, but nature methodized;
Nature, like liberty, is but restrained
By the same laws which first herself ordained.
　　Hear how learned Greece her useful rules indites,
When to repress, and when indulge our flights:
High on Parnassus' top her sons she showed,
And pointed out those arduous paths they trod;
Held from afar, aloft, the immortal prize,
And urged the rest by equal steps to rise.
Just precepts thus from great examples given,
She drew from them what they derived from Heaven.
The generous critic fanned the poet's fire,
And taught the world with reason to admire.
Then criticism the muse's handmaid proved,
To dress her charms, and make her more beloved.
But following wits from that intention strayed,
Who could not win the mistress, wooed the maid;
Against the poets their own arms they turned,
Sure to hate most the men from whom they learned.
So modern 'Pothecaries, taught the art
By doctor's bills to play the doctor's part,
Bold in the practice of mistaken rules,
Prescribe, apply, and call their masters fools.
Some on the leaves of ancient authors prey,
Nor time nor moths e'er spoiles so much as they,
Some dutily plain, without invention's aid,
Write dull receipts how poems may be made.
These leave the sense, their learning to display,
And those explain the meaning quite away.
　　You then whose judgment the right course would steer,
Know well each Ancient's proper character;
His fable, subject, scope in every page;

Religion, country, genius of his age:
Without all these at once before your eyes,
Cavil you may, but never criticise.
Be Homer's works your study and delight,
Read them by day, and meditate by night;
Thence form your judgment, thence your maxims bring,
And trace the muses upwards to their spring.
Still with itself compared, his text peruse;
And let your comment be the Mantuan muse.
    When first young Maro in his boundless mind
A work to outlast immortal Rome designed,
Perhaps he seemed above the critic's law,
And but from nature's fountains scorned to draw;
But when to examine every part he came,
Nature and Homer were, he found, the same.
Convinced, amazed, he checks the bold design;
And rules as strict his laboured work confine,
As if the Stagirite o'erlooked each line.
Learn hence for ancient rules a just esteem;
To copy nature is to copy them.
    Some beauties yet no precepts can declare,
For there's a happiness as well as care.
Music resembles poetry, in each
Are nameless graces which no methods teach,
And which a master-hand alone can reach.
If, where the rules not far enough extend,
(Since rules were made but to promote their end)
Some lucky licence answer to the full
The intent proposed, that licence is a rule.
Thus Pegasus, a nearer way to take,
May boldly deviate from the common track;
From vulgar bounds with brace disorder part,
And snatch a grace beyond the reach of art,
Which, without passing through the judgment, gains
The heart, and all its end at once attains.
In prospects thus, some objects please our eyes,
Which out of nature's common order rise,
The shapeless rock, or hanging precipice.
Great wits sometimes may gloriously offend,
And rise to faults true critics dare not mend.
But though the ancients thus their rules invade,

158

(As kings dispense with laws themselves have made)
Moderns, beware! or if you must offend
Against the precept, ne'er transgress its end;
Let it be seldom, and compelled by need;
And have, at least, their precedent to plead.
The critic else proceeds without remorse,
Seizes your fame, and puts his laws in force.
    I know there are, to whose presumptuous thoughts
Those freer beauties, even in them, seem faults.
Some figures monstrous and mis-shaped appear,
Considered singly, or beheld too near,
Which, but proportioned to their light or place,
Due distance reconciles to form and grace.
A prudent chief not always must display
His powers in equal ranks, and fair array.
But with the occasion and the place comply,
Conceal his force, nay seem sometimes to fly.
Those oft are stratagems which error seem,
Nor is it Homer nods, but we that dream.
    Still green with bays each ancient altar stands,
Above the reach of sacrilegious hands;
Secure from flames, from envy's fiercer rage,
Destructive war, and all-involving age.
See, from each clime the learned their incense bring!
Hear, in all tongues consenting paeans ring!
In praise so just let every voice be joined,
And fill the general chorus of mankind.
Hail, bards triumphant! born in happier days;
Immortal heirs of universal praise!
Whose honours with increase of ages grow,
As streams roll down, enlarging as they flow;
Nations unborn your mighty names shall sound,
And worlds applaud that must not yet be found!
Oh may some spark of your celestial fire,
The last, the meanest of your sons inspire,
(That on weak wings, from far, pursues your flights;
Glows while he reads, but trembles as he writes)
To teach vain wits a science little known,
To admire superior sense, and doubt their own!

*   *   *

A little learning is a dangerous thing;
Drink deep, or taste not the Pierian spring:
Their shallow draughts intoxicate the brain,
And drinking largely sobers us again.
Fired at first sight with what the muse imparts,
In fearless youth we tempt the heights of arts,
While from the bounded level of our mind
Short views we take, nor see the lengths behind;
But more advanced, behold with strange surprise
New distant scenes of endless science rise!
So pleased at first the towering Alps we try,
Mount o'er the vales, and seem to tread the sky,
The eternal snows appear already past,
And the first clouds and mountains seem the last;
But, those attained, we tremble to survey
The growing labours of the lengthened way,
The increasing prospect tires our wandering eyes,
Hills peep o'er hills, and Alps on Alps arise!
A perfect judge will read each work of wit
With the same spirit that its author writ:
Survey the whole, nor seek slight faults to find
Where nature moves, and rapture warms the mind;
Nor lose, for that malignant dull delight,
The generous pleasure to be charmed with wit.
But in such lays as neither ebb, nor flow,
Correctly cold, and regularly low,
That shunning faults, one quiet tenor keep;
We cannot blame indeed — but we may sleep.
In wit, as nature, what affects our hearts
Is not the exactness of peculiar parts;
'Tis not a lip, or eye, we beauty call,
But the joint force and full result of all.
Thus when we view some well-proportioned dome,
(The world's just wonder, and even thine, O Rome!)
No single parts unequally surprise,
All comes united to the admiring eyes;
No monstrous height or breadth, or length appear;
The whole at once is bold, and regular.
Whoever thinks a faultless piece to see,
Thinks what ne'er was, nor is, nor e'er shall be.

In every work regard the writer's end,
Since none can compass more than they intend;
And if the means be just, the conduct true,
Applause, in spite of trivial faults, is due;
As men of breeding, sometimes men of wit,
To avoid great errors, must the less commit:
Neglect the rules each verbal critic lays,
For not to know some trifles, is a praise.
Most critics, fond of some subservient art,
Still make the whole depend upon a part:
They talk of principles, but notions prize,
And all to one loved folly sacrifice.

*   *   *

Be thou the first true merit to befriend;
His praise is lost, who stays, till all commend.
Short is the date, alas, of modern rhymes,
And 'tis but just to let them live betimes.
No longer now that golden age appears,
When patriarch-wits survived a thousand years:
Now length of fame (our second life) is lost,
And bar threescore is all even that can boast;
Our sons their fathers' failing language see,
And such as is, shall Dryden be.
So when the faithful pencil has designed
Some bright idea of the master's mind,
Where a new world leaps out at his command,
And ready nature waits upon his hand;
When the ripe colours soften and unite,
And sweetly melt into just shade and light;
When mellowing years their full perfection give,
And each bold figure just begins to live,
The treacherous colours the fair art betray,
And all the bright creation fades away!

*   *   *

Learn then what morals critics ought to show,
For 'tis but half a judge's task, to know.
'Tis not enough, taste, judgment, learning, join;
In all you speak, let truth and candour shine:

That not alone what to your sense is due
All may allow; but seek your friendship too.
    Be silent always when you doubt your sense;
And speak, though sure, with seeming diffidence.
Some positive, persisting fops we know,
Who, if once wrong, will needs be always so;
But you, with pleasure own your errors past,
And make each day a critic on the last.
    'Tis not enough, your counsel still be true;
Blunt truths more mischief than nice falsehoods do;
Men must be taught as if you taught them not,
And things unknown proposed as things forgot.
Without good breeding, truth is disapproved;
That only makes superior sense beloved.
    Be niggards of advice on no pretence;
For the worst avarice is that of sense.
With mean complacence ne'er betray your trust,
Nor be so civil as to prove unjust.
Fear not the anger of the wise to raise;
Those best can bear reproof, who merit praise.

*   *   *

    Thus long succeeding critics justly reigned,
Licence repressed, and useful laws ordained.
Learning and Rome alike in empire grew;
And arts still followed where her eagles flew;
From the same foes, at last, both felt their doom,
And the same age saw learning fall, and Rome.
With tyranny, then superstition joined,
As that the body, this enslaved the mind;
Much was believed, but little understood,
And to be dull was construed to be good;
A second deluge learning thus o'er-run,
And the Monks finished what the Goths begun.
    At length Erasmus, that great injured name,
(The glory of the priesthood, and the shame!)
Stemmed the wild torrent of a barbarous age,
And drove those holy Vandals off the stage.
    But see! each muse, in Leo's golden days,
Starts from her trance, and trims her withered bays,

Rome's ancient genius, o'er its ruins spread,
Shakes off the dust, and rears his reverend head.
The sculpture and her sister-arts revive;
Stones leaped to form, and rocks began to live;
With sweeter notes each rising temple rung;
A Raphael painted, and a Vida sung.
Immortal Vida; on whose honoured brow
The poet's bays and critic's ivy grow:
Cremona now shall ever boast thy name,
As next in place to Mantua, next in fame!
   But soon by impious arms from Latium chased,
Their ancient bounds the banished muses passed;
Thence arts o'er all the northern world advance,
But we, brave Britons, foreign laws despised,
And kept unconquered, and uncivilized;
Fierce for the liberties of wit, and bold,
We still defy the Romans, as of old.
Yet some there were, among the sounder few
Of those who less presumed, and better knew,
Who durst assert the juster ancient cause,
And here restored wit's fundamental laws.
Such was the muse, whose rules and practice tell,
"Nature's chief master-piece is writing well."
Such was Roscommon, not more learned than good,
With manners generous as his noble blood;
To him the wit of Greece and Rome was known,
And every author's merit, but his own.
Such late was Walsh — the muse's judge and friend,
Who justly knew to blame or to commend;
To failings mild, but zealous for desert;
The clearest head, and the sincerest heart.
This humble praise, lamented shade! receive,
This praise at least a grateful muse may give:
The muse, whose early voice you taught to sing,
Prescribed her heights, and pruned her tender wing,
(Her guide now lost) no more attempts to rise,
But in low numbers short excursions tries:
Content, if hence the unlearned their wants may view,
The learned reflect on what before they knew:
Careless of censure, nor too fond of fame;

Still pleased to praise, yet not afraid to blame,
Averse alike to flatter, or offend;
Not free from faults, nor yet too vain to mend.

b   A. W. Schlegel on the Relative Merits of Classical and Romantic Art and Literature (*1808*)

WE SEE numbers of men, and even whole nations, so fettered by the conventions of education and habits of life, that, even in the appreciation of the fine arts, they cannot shake them off. Nothing to them appears natural, appropriate, or beautiful, which is alien to their own language, manners, and social relations. With this exclusive mode of seeing and feeling, it is no doubt possible to attain, by means of cultivation, to great nicety of discrimination within the narrow circle to which it limits and circumscribes them. But no man can be a true critic or connoisseur without universality of mind, without that flexibility which enables him, by renouncing all personal predilections and blind habits, to adapt himself to the peculiarities of other ages and nations — to feel them, as it were, from their proper central point, and, what ennobles human nature, to recognise and duly appreciate whatever is beautiful and grand under the external accessories which were necessary to its embodying, even though occasionally they may seem to disguise and distort it. There is no monopoly of poetry for particular ages and nations; and consequently that despotism in taste, which would seek to invest with universal authority the rules which at first, perhaps, were but arbitrarily advanced, is but a vain and empty pretension. . . .

Let us now apply the idea which we have been developing, of the universality of true criticism, to the history of poetry and the fine arts. This, like the so-called universal history, we generally limit (even though beyond this range there may be much that is both remarkable and worth knowing) to whatever has had a nearer or more remote influence on the present civilisation of Europe: consequently, to the works of the Greeks and Romans, and of those of the modern European nations, who first and chiefly distinguished themselves in art and literature. It is well known that, three centuries

From John Black (trans.), LECTURES ON DRAMATIC ART AND LITERATURE (London, 1892), pp. 18–27.

and a-half ago, the study of ancient literature received a new life, by the diffusion of the Grecian language (for the Latin never became extinct); the classical authors were brought to light, and rendered universally accessible by means of the press; and the monuments of ancient art were diligently disinterred and preserved. All this powerfully excited the human mind, and formed a decided epoch in the history of human civilisation; its manifold effects have extended to our times, and will yet extend to an incalculable series of ages. But the study of the ancients was forthwith most fatally perverted. The learned, who were chiefly in the possession of this knowledge, and who were incapable of distinguishing themselves by works of their own, claimed for the ancients an unlimited authority, and with great appearance of reason, since they are models in their kind. Maintaining that nothing could be hoped for the human mind but from an imitation of antiquity, in the works of the moderns they only valued what resembled, or seemed to bear a resemblance to, those of the ancients. Everything else they rejected as barbarous and unnatural. With the great poets and artists it was quite otherwise. However strong their enthusiasm for the ancients, and however determined their purpose of entering into competition with them, they were compelled by their independence and originality of mind, to strike out a path of their own, and to impress upon their productions the stamp of their own genius. Such was the case with Dante among the Italians, the father of modern poetry; acknowledging Virgil for his master, he has produced a work which, of all others, most differs from the Æneid, and in our opinion far excels its pretended model in power, truth, compass, and profundity. It was the same afterwards with Ariosto, who has most unaccountably been compared to Homer, for nothing can be more unlike. So in art with Michael Angelo and Raphael, who had no doubt deeply studied the antique. When we ground our judgment of modern painters merely on their greater or less resemblance to the ancients, we must necessarily be unjust towards them, as Winkelmann undoubtedly was in the case of Raphael. As the poets for the most part had their share of scholarship, it gave rise to a curious struggle between their natural inclination and their imaginary duty. When they sacrificed to the latter, they were praised by the learned; but by yielding to the former, they became the favourites of the people. What preserves the heroic poems of a Tasso and a Camoëns to this day alive in the hearts and on the lips of their countrymen, is by no means their imperfect resemblance to Virgil, or even to Homer, but in Tasso the tender feeling of chivalrous love and honour, and in Camoëns the glowing inspiration of heroic patriotism.

Those very ages, nations, and ranks, who felt least the want of a poetry of their own, were the most assiduous in their imitation of the ancients; accordingly, its results are but dull school exercises, which at best excite a frigid admiration. But in the fine arts, mere imitation is always fruitless; even what we borrow from others, to assume a true poetical shape, must, as it were, be born again within us. Of what avail is all foreign imitation? Art cannot exist without nature, and man can give nothing to his fellow-man but himself.

Genuine successors and true rivals of the ancients, who, by virtue of congenial talents and cultivation have walked in their path and worked in their spirit, have ever been as rare as their mechanical spiritless copyists are common. Seduced by the form, the great body of critics have been but too indulgent to these servile imitators. These were held up as correct modern classics, while the great truly living and popular poets, whose reputation was a part of their nations' glory, and to whose sublimity it was impossible to be altogether blind, were at best but tolerated as rude and wild natural geniuses. But the unqualified separation of genius and taste on which such a judgment proceeds, is altogether untenable. Genius is the almost unconscious choice of the highest degree of excellence, and, consequently, it is taste in its highest activity.

In this state, nearly, matters continued till a period not far back, when several inquiring minds, chiefly Germans, endeavoured to clear up the misconception, and to give the ancients their due, without being insensible to the merits of the moderns, although of a totally different kind. The apparent contradiction did not intimidate them. The groundwork of human nature is no doubt everywhere the same; but in all our investigations, we may observe that, throughout the whole range of nature, there is no elementary power so simple, but that it is capable of dividing and diverging into opposite directions. The whole play of vital motion hinges on harmony and contrast. Why, then, should not this phenomenon recur on a grander scale in the history of man? In this idea we have perhaps discovered the true key to the ancient and modern history of poetry and the fine arts. Those who adopted it, gave to the peculiar spirit of *modern* art, as contrasted with the *antique* or *classical,* the name of *romantic.* The term is certainly not inappropriate; the word is derived from *romance* — the name originally given to the languages which were formed from the mixture of the Latin and the old Teutonic dialects, in the same manner as modern civilisation is the fruit of the heterogeneous union of the peculiarities of the northern nations and the fragments of antiquity; whereas the civilisation of the ancients was much more of a piece.

The distinction which we have just stated can hardly fail to appear well founded, if it can be shown, so far as our knowledge of antiquity extends, that the same contrast in the labours of the ancients and moderns runs symmetrically, I might almost say systematically, throughout every branch of art — that it is as evident in music and the plastic arts as in poetry. This is a problem which, in its full extent, still remains to be demonstrated, though, on particular portions of it, many excellent observations have been advanced already.

Among the foreign authors who wrote before this school can be said to have been formed in Germany, we may mention Rousseau, who acknowledged the contrast in music, and showed that rhythm and melody were the prevailing principles of ancient, as harmony is that of modern music. In his prejudices against harmony, however, we cannot at all concur. On the subject of the arts of design an ingenious observation was made by Hemsterhuys, that the ancient painters were perhaps too much of sculptors, and the modern sculptors too much of painters. This is the exact point of difference; for, as I shall distinctly show in the sequel, the spirit of ancient art and poetry is *plastic,* but that of the moderns *picturesque.*

By an example taken from another art, that of architecture, I shall endeavour to illustrate what I mean by this contrast. Throughout the Middle Ages there prevailed, and in the latter centuries of that aera was carried to perfection, a style of architecture, which has been called Gothic, but ought really to have been termed old German. When, on the general revival of classical antiquity, the imitation of Grecian architecture became prevalent, and but too frequently without a due regard to the difference of climate and manners or to the purpose of the building, the zealots of this new taste, passing a sweeping sentence of condemnation on the Gothic, reprobated it as tasteless, gloomy, and barbarous. This was in some degree pardonable in the Italians, among whom a love for ancient architecture, cherished by hereditary remains of classical edifices, and the similarity of their climate to that of the Greeks and Romans, might, in some sort, be said to be innate. But we Northerns are not so easily to be talked out of the powerful, solemn impressions which seize upon the mind at entering a Gothic cathedral. We feel, on the contrary, a strong desire to investigate and to justify the source of this impression. A very slight attention will convince us, that the Gothic architecture displays not only an extraordinary degree of mechanical skill, but also a marvellous power of invention; and, on a closer examination, we recognise its profound significance, and perceive that as well as the Grecian it constitutes in itself a complete and finished system.

To the application! — The Pantheon is not more different from Westminster Abbey or the church of St. Stephen at Vienna, than the structure of a tragedy of Sophocles from a drama of Shakspeare. The comparison between these wonderful productions of poetry and architecture might be carried still farther. But does our admiration of the one compel us to depreciate the other? May we not admit that each is great and admirable in its kind, although the one is, and is meant to be, different from the other? The experiment is worth attempting. We will quarrel with no man for his predilection either for the Grecian or the Gothic. The world is wide, and affords room for a great diversity of objects. Narrow and blindly adopted pre-possessions will never constitute a genuine critic or connoisseur, who ought, on the contrary, to possess the power of dwelling with liberal impartiality on the most discrepant views, renouncing the while all personal inclinations.

For our present object, the justification, namely, of the grand division which we lay down in the history of art, and according to which we conceive ourselves equally warranted in establishing the same division in dramatic literature, it might be sufficient merely to have stated this contrast between the ancient, or classical, and the romantic. But as there are exclusive admirers of the ancients, who never cease asserting that all deviation from them is merely the whim of a new school of critics, who, expressing themselves in language full of mystery, cautiously avoid conveying their sentiments in a tangible shape, I shall endeavour to explain the origin and spirit of the *romantic,* and then leave the world to judge if the use of the word, and of the idea which it is intended to convey, be thereby justified.

The mental culture of the Greeks was a finished education in the school of Nature. Of a beautiful and noble race, endowed with susceptible senses and a cheerful spirit under a mild sky, they lived and bloomed in the full health of existence; and, favoured by a rare combination of circumstances, accomplished all that the finite nature of man is capable of. The whole of their art and poetry is the expression of a consciousness of this harmony of all their faculties. They invented the poetry of joy.

Their religion was the deification of the powers of nature and of the earthly life; but this worship, which, among other nations, clouded the imagination with hideous shapes, and hardened the heart to cruelty, assumed, among the Greeks, a mild, a grand, and a dignified form. Superstition, too often the tyrant of the human faculties, seemed to have here contributed to their freest development. It cherished the arts by which it was adorned, and its idols became the models of ideal beauty.

But however highly the Greeks may have succeeded in the Beautiful, and even in the Moral, we cannot concede any higher character to their civilisation than that of a defined and ennobled sensuality. Of course this must be understood generally. The conjectures of a few philosophers, and the irradiations of poetical inspiration, constitute an occasional exception. Man can never altogether turn aside his thoughts from infinity, and some obscure recollections will always remind him of the home he has lost; but we are now speaking of the predominant tendency of his endeavours.

Religion is the root of human existence. Were it possible for man to renounce all religion, including that which is unconscious, independent of the will, he would become a mere surface without any internal substance. When this centre is disturbed, the whole system of the mental faculties and feelings takes a new shape.

And this is what has actually taken place in modern Europe through the introduction of Christianity. This sublime and beneficent religion has regenerated the ancient world from its state of exhaustion and debasement; it is the guiding principle in the history of modern nations, and even at this day, when many suppose they have shaken off its authority, they still find themselves much more influenced by it in their views of human affairs than they themselves are aware.

After Christianity, the character of Europe has, since the commencement of the Middle Ages, been chiefly influenced by the Germanic race of northern conquerors, who infused new life and vigour into a degenerated people. The stern nature of the North drives man back within himself; and what is lost in the free sportive development of the senses, must, in noble dispositions, be compensated by earnestness of mind. Hence the honest cordiality with which Christianity was welcomed by all the Teutonic tribes, so that among no other race of men has it penetrated more deeply into the inner man, displayed more powerful effects, or become more interwoven with all human feelings and sensibilities.

* * *

Chivalry, love, and honour, together with religion itself, are the subjects of that poetry of nature which poured itself out in the Middle Ages with incredible fulness, and preceded the more artistic cultivation of the romantic spirit. This age had also its mythology, consisting of chivalrous tales and legends; but its wonders and its heroism were the very reverse of those of the ancient mythology.

Several inquirers who, in other respects, entertain the same conception of the peculiarities of the moderns, and trace them to the same source that we do, have placed the essence of the northern poetry in melancholy; and to this, when properly understood, we have nothing to object.

Among the Greeks human nature was in itself all-sufficient; it was conscious of no defects, and aspired to no higher perfection than that which it could actually attain by the exercise of its own energies. We, however, are taught by superior wisdom that man, through a grievous transgression, forfeited the place for which he was originally destined; and that the sole destination of his earthly existence is to struggle to regain his lost position, which, if left to his own strength, he can never accomplish. The old religion of the senses sought no higher possession than outward and perishable blessings; and immortality, so far as it was believed, stood shadow-like in the obscure distance, a faint dream of this sunny waking life. The very reverse of all this is the case with the Christian view: every thing finite and mortal is lost in the contemplation of infinity; life has become shadow and darkness, and the first day of our real existence dawns in the world beyond the grave. Such a religion must waken the vague foreboding, which slumbers in every feeling heart, into a distinct consciousness that the happiness after which we are here striving is unattainable; that no external object can ever entirely fill our souls; and that all earthly enjoyment is but a fleeting and momentary illusion. When the soul, resting as it were under the willows of exile, breathes out its longing for its distant home, what else but melancholy can be the key-note of its songs? Hence the poetry of the ancients was the poetry of enjoyment, and ours is that of desire: the former has its foundation in the scene which is present, while the latter hovers betwixt recollection and hope. . . . The feeling of the moderns is, upon the whole, more inward, their fancy more incorporeal, and their thoughts more contemplative. In nature, it is true, the boundaries of objects run more into one another, and things are not so distinctly separated as we must exhibit them in order to convey distinct notions of them.

11

The Parliamentary Reform
Movement in England

SIR ROBERT WALPOLE (1676–1745) held the post of Chief Minister to
George I and George II, virtually without a break from 1722 to 1742.
He has been called England's "first Prime Minister"; certainly he was the
first English statesman to hold so prolonged an ascendancy over king,
cabinet, and Commons.

The eyewitness account of a Wilkite riot in London on March 22,
1769 was sent from St. James's Street, London, on March 24, by Mrs.
James Harris, wife of the M.P. for Christchurch (Hampshire), to her
son, James, the future first Earl of Malmesbury, at Madrid. At this time,
John Wilkes (1725?–97) was serving his sentence at the King's Bench
prison. His supporters were demonstrating against a cavalcade of City
merchants, who were bearing a "loyal" (that is, anti-Wilkite) address to
the King at St. James's Palace.

John Wilkes's speech in favor of parliamentary reform was made in the
House of Commons on March 21, 1776.

a Sir Robert Walpole Defends the Septennial
Act (March 13, 1734)

"I HOPE the house will indulge me the liberty of giving some
of those reasons which induce me to be against the motion.
In general I must take notice, that the nature of our constitution
seems to be very much mistaken by the gentlemen who have spoken
in favour of this motion. It is certain, that our's is a mixed government, and the perfection of our constitution consists in this, that the
monarchical, aristocratical, and democratical forms of government
are mixed and interwoven in our's, so as to give us all the advan-

From William Coxe, MEMOIRS OF THE LIFE AND ADMINISTRATION OF SIR
ROBERT WALPOLE, 3 vols. (London, 1798), vol. i, pp. 422–6.

tages of each, without subjecting us to the dangers and inconveniences of either. The democratical form of government, which is the only one I have now occasion to take notice of, is liable to these inconveniences, that they are generally too tedious in their coming to any resolution, and seldom brisk and expeditious enough in carrying their resolutions into execution; that they are always wavering in their resolutions, and never steady in any of the measures they resolve to pursue; and that they are often involved in factions, seditions and insurrections, which exposes them to be made the tools, if not the prey of their neighbours. Therefore in all the regulations we make, with respect to our constitution, we are to guard against running too much into that form of government which is properly called democratical: this was, in my opinion, the effect of the triennial law, and will again be the effect, if ever it should be restored.

"That triennial elections would make our government too tedious in all their resolves is evident; because in such case, no prudent administration would ever resolve upon any measure of consequence, till they had felt not only the pulse of the parliament, but the pulse of the people; and the ministers of state would always labour under this disadvantage, that as secrets of state must not be immediately divulged, their enemies (and enemies they will always have) would have a handle for exposing their measures, and rendering them disagreeable to the people, and thereby carrying perhaps a new election against them, before they could have an opportunity of justifying their measures, by divulging those facts and circumstances from whence the justice and the wisdom of their measures would clearly appear.

"Then, it is by experience well known, that what is called the populace of every country, are apt to be too much elated with success, and too much dejected with every misfortune. This makes them wavering in their opinions about affairs of state, and never long of the same mind; and as this house is chosen by the free and unbiassed voice of the people in general, if this choice were so often renewed, we might expect, that this house would be as wavering and as unsteady as the people usually are; and it being impossible to carry on the public affairs of the nation without the concurrence of this house, the ministers would always be obliged to comply, and consequently would be obliged to change their measures as often as the people changed their minds.

"With septennial parliaments we are not exposed to either of these misfortunes, because, if the ministers, after having felt the pulse of the parliament, which they can always soon do, resolve upon any measures, they have generally time enough before the new election comes on, to give the people a proper information, in order to shew them, the justice and the wisdom of the measures they have pursued; and if the people should at any time be too much elated, or too much dejected, or should without a cause change their minds, those at the helm of affairs have time to set them right, before a new election comes on.

"As to faction and sedition, I will grant, that in monarchical and aristocratical governments, it generally arises from violence and oppression; but in democratical governments, it always arises from the people's having too great a share in the government. For in all countries, and in all governments, there always will be many factious and unquiet spirits, who can never be at rest, either in power or out of power. When in power they are never easy, unless every man submits entirely to their direction; and when out of power, they are always working and intriguing against those that are in, without any regard to justice, or to the interest of their country. In popular governments such men have too much game, they have too many opportunities for working upon and corrupting the minds of the people, in order to give them a bad impression of, and to raise discontents against those that have the management of the public affairs for the time; and these discontents often break out into seditions and insurrections. This would, in my opinion, be our misfortune, if our parliaments were either annual or triennial: by such frequent elections, there would be so much power thrown into the hands of the people, as would destroy that equal mixture, which is the beauty of our constitution. In short, our government would really become a democratical government, and might from thence very probably diverge into a tyrannical. Therefore, in order to preserve our constitution, in order to prevent our falling under tyranny and arbitrary power, we ought to preserve that law, which I really think has brought our constitution to a more equal mixture, and consequently to a greater perfection than it was ever in before that law took place.

"As to bribery and corruption, if it were possible to influence, by such base means, the majority of the electors of Great Britain, to chuse such men as would probably give up their liberties; if it were possible to influence, by such means, a majority of the members of this house to consent to the establishment of arbitrary power, I should readily allow, that the calculations made by the gentlemen of the other side were just, and their inference true; but I am persuaded that neither of these is possible. As the members of this house generally are, and must always be, gentlemen of fortune and figure in their country, is it possible to suppose, that any of them could by a pension or a post be influenced to consent to the overthrow of our constitution, by which the enjoyment, not only of what he got, but of what he before had, would be rendered altogether precarious. I will allow, that with respect to bribery, the price must be higher or lower, generally in proportion to the virtue of the man who is to be bribed; but it must likewise be granted, that the humour he happens to be in at the time, and the spirit he happens to be endowed with, adds a great deal to his virtue. When no encroachments are made upon the rights of the people, when the people do not think themselves in any danger, there may be many of the electors, who, by a bribe of ten guineas, might be induced to vote for one candidate rather than another; but if the court were making any encroachments upon the rights of the people, a proper spirit would, without doubt, arise in the nation, and in such a case I am persuaded that none, or very few, even of such electors, could be induced to vote for a court candidate, no not for ten times the sum.

"There may be some bribery and corruption in the nation, I am afraid there will always be some. But it is no proof of it that strangers are sometimes chosen; for a gentleman may have so much natural influence over a borough in his neighbourhood, as to be able to prevail with them to chuse any person he pleases to recommend; and if upon such recommendation they chuse one or two of his friends, who are perhaps strangers to them, it is not from thence to be inferred, that the two strangers were chosen their representatives by the means of bribery and corruption.

"To insinuate that money may be issued from the public treasury for bribing elections, is really something very extraordinary, especially in those gentlemen who know how many checks are upon every shilling that can be issued from thence; and how regularly the money granted in one year for the service of the nation, must always be accounted for the very next sessions in this house, and likewise in the other, if they have a mind to call for any such account. And as to gentlemen in offices, if they have any advantage over country gentlemen, in having something else to depend on besides their own private fortunes, they have likewise many disadvantages: they are obliged to live here at London with their families, by which they are put to a much greater expence, than gentlemen of equal fortune who live in the country. This lays them under a very great disadvantage in supporting their interest in the country. The country gentleman, by living among the electors, and purchasing the necessaries for his family from them, keeps up an acquaintance and correspondence with them, without putting himself to any extraordinary charge; whereas a gentleman who lives in London, has no other way of keeping up an acquaintance and correspondence among his friends in the country, but by going down once or twice a year, at a very extraordinary expence, and often without any other business; so that we may conclude, a gentleman in office cannot, even in seven years, save much for distributing in ready money at the time of an election; and I really believe, if the fact were narrowly inquired into, it would appear, that the gentlemen in office are as little guilty of bribing their electors with ready money, as any other set of gentlemen in the kingdom.

"That there are ferments often raised among the people without any just cause, is what I am surprised to hear controverted, since very late experience may convince us of the contrary: do not we know what a ferment was raised in the nation towards the latter end of the late queen's reign? And it is well known what a fatal change in the affairs of this nation was introduced, or at least confirmed, by an election coming on while the nation was in that ferment. Do not we know what a ferment was raised in the nation soon after his late majesty's accession? And if an election had then been allowed to come on while the nation was in that ferment, it might perhaps have had as fatal effects as the former; but, thank God, this was wisely provided against by the very law which is now wanted to be repealed.

"It has, indeed, been said, that the chief motive for enacting that law now no longer exists: I cannot admit that the motive they mean was the chief motive; but even that motive is very far from having entirely ceased. Can gentlemen imagine, that in the spirit raised in the nation not above a twelve-month since, Jacobitism and disaffection to the present government had no share? Perhaps some who might wish well to the present establishment did co-operate, nay, I do not know but they were the first movers of that spirit; but it cannot be supposed that the spirit then raised should have grown up to such a ferment, merely from a proposition which was honestly and fairly laid before the parliament, and left entirely to their determination! No, the spirit was, perhaps, begun by those who are truly friends to the illustrious family we have now upon the throne; but it was raised to a much greater height than, I believe, even they designed, by Jacobites, and such as are enemies to our present establishment, who thought they never had a fairer opportunity of bringing about what they have so long and so unsuccessfully wished for, than that which had been furnished them by those who first raised that spirit. I hope the people have now in a great measure come to themselves, and therefore I doubt not but the next elections will shew, that when they are left to judge coolly, they can distinguish between the real and the pretended friends to the government. But I must say, if the ferment then raised in the nation had not already greatly subsided, I should have thought a new election a very dangerous experiment; and as such ferments may hereafter often happen, I must think that frequent elections will always be dangerous; for which reason, in so far as I can see at present, I shall, I believe, at all times think it a very dangerous experiment to repeal the septennial bill."

b A Wilkite Riot in London (March 22, 1769)

WEDNESDAY, the 22nd, the merchants were to carry a loyal address to his Majesty. About noon, a hearse attended by an immense Mob came down Pall Mall; the hearse was decorated with prints and two pictures, one of which represented the killing of Allen in St. George's Fields, the other the killing of Clarke in the riot at Brentford;[1] it was drawn by one black, and one white horse, the coachman dressed in black, with a fur cap and a quantity of blue ribbon. This hearse, amid the acclamation of the mob, went close to Palace Gate, and then up St. James's Street. It had taken its place just before the procession of merchants, who came up with their address, and who, when they arrived, appear to have been pelted with dirt and stones, all their glasses and many wooden blinds broken in, the coachman and footmen covered with dirt as

From J. H. Harris (ed.), LETTERS OF THE FIRST EARL OF MALMESBURY FROM 1745 TO 1820, 2 vols. (London, 1870), vol. i, pp. 176–9.

well as the masters. The same insults continued when the merchants alighted; on which a party of Grenadiers were placed at the gate of St. James's. Lord Talbot as Lord Steward with his staff, Lord Despencer and some others of the Court came down and assisted the merchants and kept off the rabble, advancing some paces before the gate for that purpose. One rioter was seized by Justice Walsh, but was soon rescued by his friends and carried off in triumph. One coach with the address was stopped, not being allowed to put down company. The Duke of Northumberland was severely pelted, as he went back to the Palace; the ammunition of these rioters consisted chiefly of dirt, but many stones were seen to be thrown, and one glass bottle. The Riot Act was read without any effect, Lord Talbot harangued at the gate, one Mr. Whitworth (not Sir Charles) was haranguing from St. James's coffee-house, and a drunken woman in a third place: they each had their audience, but the Wilkism and obscenity of the woman proved the greatest attraction. The tumult still continued at its height, when from the Palace Yard issued the Horse Guards and Horse Grenadiers, with their swords drawn, and commanded by three officers. The rabble, whose spirit of mischief is only equalled by their timidity, immediately retired and left a large vacancy before the Palace. The Horse formed into two fronts, one up St. James's Street, the other up Pall Mall; soon after the Horse came, several rioters were seized and carried into custody.

During this period all the shops in the neighbourhood were shut. The merchants, when they got to St. James's, could not find their address. The gates of Temple Bar having been shut against them, a most infamous riot took place there. Mr. Boheme, the chairman, was insulted and forced to quit his coach, and got into a coffee-house; in the hustle he left the address in the coach, which was carried back to his coach-house; this was made known to his Majesty, who said he *would wait for it, if it was till the next day.* At last, I believe, it was brought privately by water from Whitehall; it was four o'clock before it could be presented. The Guards patrolled the streets that afternoon and evening. It was said that, amongst the mob, there were men of better appearance, supposed to be their leaders, but this is not certain.

Your father was in St. James's coffee-house all the morning, so saw the whole. Your sisters and I were at Clapham in the morning, and came down to Pall Mall in the midst of the mob. We let down our glasses, they cried *Wilkes and Liberty* enough to us, but did not

178

insist on our joining them, so we got safe home, though I was a great deal flurried at the time. Many of the mob cried *Wilkes, and no King,* which is shocking to think on.

'Tis reported some of these rioters are sent to Newgate, and that seventeen are taken.

ORIGINAL NOTE

1. William Allen, a publican's son of Southwark, was mistakenly shot by the Foot Guards in the course of a demonstration outside the King's Bench prison in St. George's Fields (where John Wilkes was held prisoner) on 10 May 1768; George Clarke, a young Wilkite lawyer, was killed by Irish chairmen, hired to 'protect' Sir William Proctor, the anti-Wilkite candidate, at the Middlesex election of December of the same year.

c *Speech of John Wilkes in Favor of Parliamentary Reform (1776)*

MR. WILKES rose and said:
   ... This House is at this hour composed of the same representation it was at his [Charles II] demise, notwithstanding the many and important changes which have since happened. It becomes us therefore to enquire, whether the sense of parliament can be now, on solid grounds, from the present representation, said to be the sense of the nation, as in the time of our forefathers. I am satisfied Sir, the sentiments of the people cannot be justly known at this time from the resolutions of a parliament, composed as the present is, even though no undue influence was practised after the return of the members to the House, even supposing for a moment the influence of all the baneful arts of corruption to be suspended, which, for a moment, I believe, they have not been, under the present profligate administration. Let us examine, Sir, with exactness and candour, if the representation is fair and perfect; let us consider of what the efficient parts of this House are composed, and what proportion they bear, on the large scale, to the body of the people of England, who are supposed to be represented.

The Southern part of this island, to which I now confine my ideas,

From E. N. Williams, THE EIGHTEENTH CENTURY CONSTITUTION 1688–1815 (London, 1960), pp. 215–7. Reprinted by permission of the Cambridge University Press.

consists of about five millions of people, according to the most received calculation. I will state by what numbers the majority of this House is elected, and I propose the largest number present of any recorded in our Journals, which was in the famous year 1741. In that year the three largest divisions appear on our Journals. The first is that of the 21st of January, when the numbers were 253 to 250; the second on the 28th of the same month, 236 to 235; the third on the 9th of March, 244 to 243. In these divisions the members for Scotland are included; but I will state my calculations only for England, because it gives the argument more force. The division therefore, I adopt, is that of January 21. The number of members present on that day were 503. Let me, however, suppose the number of 254 to be the majority of members, who will ever be able to attend in their places. I state it high, from the accidents of sickness, service in foreign parts, travelling and necessary avocations. From the majority of electors only in the boroughs, which return members to this House, it has been demonstrated, that this number of 254 is elected by no more than 5,723 persons, generally the inhabitants of Cornish, and other very insignificant boroughs, perhaps by not the most respectable part of the community. Is our sovereign, then, to learn the sense of his whole people from these few persons? Are these men to give laws to this vast empire, and to tax this wealthy nation? I do not mention all the tedious calculations, because gentlemen may find them at length in the works of the incomparable Dr Price, in Postlethwaite, and in Burgh's Political Disquisitions. Figures afford the clearest demonstration, incapable of cavil and sophistry. . . .

. . . I am aware, Sir, that the power, *de jure,* of the legislature to disfranchise a number of boroughs, upon the general grounds of improving the constitution, has been doubted; and gentlemen will ask, whether a power is lodged in the representative to destroy his immediate constituent? Such a question is best answered by another, How originated the right, and upon what ground was it first granted? Old Sarum and Gatton, for instance, were populous towns, and therefore the right of representation was first given them. They are now desolate, and of consequence ought not to retain a privilege, which they acquired only by their extent and populousness. We ought in every thing, as far as we can to make the theory and practice of the constitution coincide. The supreme legislative body of a state must surely have this power inherent in itself. It was *de facto* lately exercised to its full extent by parliament in the case of Shoreham with universal approbation, for near a hundred corrupt voters were disfranchised, and about twice that number of freeholders admitted from the county of Sussex. . . .

. . . The disfranchising of the mean, venal, and dependent boroughs would be laying the axe to the root of corruption and treasury influence, as well as aristocratical tyranny. We ought equally to guard against those, who sell themselves, or whose lords sell them. Burgage tenures, and private property in a share of the legislature, are monstrous absurdities in a free state, as well as an insult on common sense. I wish, Sir, an English parliament to speak the free, unbiassed sense of the body of the English people, and of every man among us, of each individual, who may justly be supposed to be comprehended in a fair majority. The meanest mechanic, the poorest peasant and day labourer, has important rights respecting his personal liberty, that of his wife and children, his property, however inconsiderable, his wages, his earnings, the very price and value of each day's hard labour, which are in many trades and manufactures regulated by the power of parliament. Every law relative to marriage, to the protection of a wife, sister, or daughter, against violence and brutal lust, to every contract or agreement with a rapacious or unjust master, is of importance to the manufacturer, the cottager, the servant, as well as to the rich subjects of the state. Some share therefore in the power of making those laws, which deeply interest them, and to which they are expected to pay obedience, should be reserved even to this inferior, but most useful, set of men in the community. We ought always to remember this important truth, acknowledged by every free state, that all government is instituted for the good of the mass of the people to be governed; that they are the original fountain of power, and even of the revenue, and in all events the last resource. . . .

. . . Without a true representation of the Commons our constitution is essentially defective, our parliament is a delusive name, a mere phantom, and all other remedies to recover the pristine purity of the form of government established by our ancestors would be ineffectual, even the shortening the periods of parliaments, and a place and pension Bill, both which I highly approve, and think absolutely necessary. I therefore flatter myself, Sir, that I shall have the concurrence of the House with the motion, which I have now the honour of making, "That leave be given to bring in a Bill for a just and equal Representation of the People of England in Parliament."

12

The American Revolution

THE STAMP ACT CONGRESS marked the culmination of the protest movement in America against the stamp duties imposed in 1765 by George Grenville.

Jefferson rewrote his notes, first jotted down in rough during the summer of 1776, and sent a copy of this transcript to James Madison in June, 1783. Subsequently he incorporated it in his "Autobiography" of 1821. The notes are important as the only significant account of the debate of June 8 and 10.

John Dickinson, though he declined to sign the Declaration of July 4, later played a prominent part in winning the independence that he had opposed in 1776.

a The Declarations of the Stamp Act Congress (October 19, 1765)

THE MEMBERS of this congress, sincerely devoted, with the warmest sentiments of affection and duty to his Majesty's person and government; inviolably attached to the present happy establishment of the Protestant succession, and with minds deeply impressed by a sense of the present and impending misfortunes of the British colonies on this continent; having considered as maturely as time would permit, the circumstances of the said colonies, esteem it our indispensable duty to make the following declarations, of our humble opinion, respecting the most essential rights and liberties of the colonists, and of the grievances under which they labour, by reason of several late acts of Parliament.

I] That his Majesty's subjects in these colonies, owe the same allegiance to the Crown of Great Britain, that is owing from his

From Merril Jensen (ed.), ENGLISH HISTORICAL DOCUMENTS (London, 1955), vol. ix, AMERICAN COLONIAL DOCUMENTS TO 1776, pp. 672-3, 868-73, 868, 877-80. Reprinted by permission of Eyre and Spottiswoode.

subjects born within the realm, and all due subordination to that august body, the Parliament of Great Britain.

II] That his Majesty's liege subjects in these colonies are entitled to all the inherent rights and liberties of his natural born subjects within the kingdom of Great Britain.

III] That it is inseparably essential to the freedom of a people, and the undoubted right of Englishmen, that no taxes should be imposed on them, but with their own consent, given personally, or by their representatives.

IV] That the people of these colonies are not, and from their local circumstances, cannot be represented in the House of Commons in Great Britain.

V] That the only representatives of the people of these colonies, are persons chosen therein, by themselves; and that no taxes ever have been, or can be constitutionally imposed on them, but by their respective legislature.

VI] That all supplies to the Crown, being free gifts of the people, it is unreasonable and inconsistent with the principles and spirit of the British constitution, for the people of Great Britain to grant to his Majesty the property of the colonists.

VII] That trial by jury is the inherent and invaluable right of every British subject in these colonies.

VIII] That the late Act of Parliament, entitled, An Act for granting and applying certain Stamp Duties, and other Duties in the British Colonies and Plantations in America, etc., by imposing taxes on the inhabitants of these colonies, and the said Act, and several other Acts, by extending the jurisdiction of the courts of admiralty beyond its ancient limits, have a manifest tendency to subvert the rights and liberties of the colonists.

IX] That the duties imposed by several late Acts of Parliament, from the peculiar circumstances of these colonies, will be extremely burdensome and grievous, and from the scarcity of specie, the payment of them absolutely impracticable.

X] That as the profits of the trade of these colonies ultimately centre in Great Britain, to pay for the manufactures which they are obliged to take from thence, they eventually contribute very largely to all supplies granted there to the Crown.

XI] That the restrictions imposed by several late Acts of Parliament, on the trade of these colonies, will render them unable to purchase the manufactures of Great Britain.

XII] That the increase, prosperity and happiness of these colonies, depend on the full and free enjoyment of their rights and liberties, and an intercourse with Great Britain, mutually affectionate and advantageous.

XIII] That it is the right of the British subjects in these colonies, to petition the king or either house of Parliament.

Lastly, that it is the indispensable duty of these colonies to the best of sovereigns, to the mother country, and to themselves, to endeavour by a loyal and dutiful address to his Majesty, and humble applications to both houses of Parliament, to procure the repeal of the Act for granting and applying certain stamp duties, of all clauses of any other Acts of Parliament, whereby the jurisdiction of the admiralty is extended as aforesaid, and of the other late Acts for the restriction of American commerce.

b Thomas Jefferson's Notes on the Debates and Proceedings on the Virginia Resolution of Independence (June 8, 10; July 1776)

In Congress, Friday, June 7, 1776

THE DELEGATES from Virginia moved in obedience to instructions from their constituents that the Congress should declare that these United Colonies are and of right ought to be free and independent states; that they are absolved from all obedience to the British Crown, and that all political connection between them and the state of Great Britain is and ought to be totally dissolved; that measures should be immediately taken for procuring the assistance of foreign powers, and a confederation be formed to bind the colonies more closely together.

The house being obliged to attend at that time to some other business, the proposition was referred to the next day when the members were ordered to attend punctually at ten o'clock.

Saturday June 8th they proceeded to take it into consideration, and referred it to a committee of the whole, into which they immediately resolved themselves, and passed that day and Monday the 10th in debating on the subject.

It was argued by [James] Wilson, Robert R. Livingston, E[dward] Rutledge, [John] Dickinson, and others:

That though they were friends to the measures themselves and saw the impossibility that we should ever again be united with Great Britain, yet they were against adopting them at this time;

That the conduct we had formerly observed was wise and proper now, of deferring to take any capital step till the voice of the people drove us into it;

That they were our power and without them our declarations could not be carried into effect;

That the people of the middle colonies (Maryland, Delaware, Pennsylvania, the Jersies, and N[ew] York) were not yet ripe for bidding adieu to British connection; but that they were fast ripening and in a short time would join in the general voice of America;

That the resolution entered into by this house on the 15th of May for suppressing the exercise of all powers derived from the Crown had shown, by the ferment into which it had thrown these middle colonies, that they had not yet accommodated their minds to a separation from the mother country;

That some of them had expressly forbidden their delegates to consent to such a declaration, and others had given no instructions, and consequently no powers to give such consent;

That if the delegates of any particular colony had no power to declare such colony independent, certain they were the others could not declare it for them, the colonies being as yet perfectly independent of each other;

That the Assembly of Pennsylvania was now sitting above stairs, their convention would sit within a few days; the convention of New York was now sitting, and those of the Jersies and Delaware counties would meet on the Monday following, and it was probable these bodies would take up the question of independence, and would declare to their delegates the voice of their state;

That if such a declaration should now be agreed to, these delegates must retire and possibly their colonies might secede from the union;

That such a secession would weaken us more than could be compensated by any foreign alliance;

That in the event of such a division foreign powers would either refuse to join themselves to our fortunes, or having us so much in their power as that desperate declaration would place us, they would insist on terms proportionably more hard and prejudicial;

That we had little reason to expect an alliance with those to whom alone as yet we had cast our eyes;

That France and Spain had reason to be jealous of that rising power which would one day certainly strip them of all their American possessions;

That it was more likely they should form a connection with the British court who, if they should find themselves unable otherwise to extricate themselves from their difficulties, would agree to a partition of our territories, restoring Canada to France and the Floridas to Spain to accomplish for themselves a recovery of these colonies;

That it would not be long before we should receive certain information of the disposition of the French court from the agent whom we had sent to Paris for that purpose;

That if this disposition should be favourable, by waiting the event of the present campaign, which we all hoped would be successful, we should have reason to expect an alliance on better terms;

That this would in fact work no delay of any effectual aid from such ally, as, from the advance of the season and distance of our situation, it was impossible we could receive any assistance during this campaign;

That it was prudent to fix among ourselves the terms on which we would form alliance before we declared we would form one at all events;

And that if these were agreed on and our declaration of independence ready by the time our ambassador should be ready to sail, it would be as well as to go into that declaration at this day.

On the other side it was urged by J[ohn] Adams, [Richard Henry] Lee, [George] Wythe, and others:

That no gentleman had argued against the policy or the right of separation from Britain, nor had supposed it possible we should ever renew our connection; that they had only opposed its being now declared;

That the question was not whether, by a declaration of independence we should make ourselves what we are not, but whether we should declare a fact which already exists;

That as to the people or Parliament of England, we had always been independent of them, their restraints on our trade deriving efficacy from our acquiescence only and not from any rights they possessed of imposing them, and that so far our connection had been federal only and was now dissolved by the commencement of hostilities;

That as to the king, we had been bound to him by allegiance, but that this bond was now dissolved by his assent to the late Act of Parliament by which he declares us out of his protection and by his levying war on us, a fact which had long ago proved us out of his protection, it being a certain position in law that allegiance and protection are reciprocal, the one ceasing when the other is withdrawn;

That James II never declared the people of England out of his protection; yet his actions proved it, and the Parliament declared it;

No delegates then can be denied, or ever want a power of declaring an existent truth;

That the delegates from the Delaware counties having declared their constituents ready to join, there are only two colonies, Pennsylvania and Maryland, whose delegates are absolutely tied up, and that these had by their instructions only reserved a right of confirming or rejecting the measure;

That the instructions from Pennsylvania might be accounted for from the times in which they were drawn, near a twelvemonth ago, since which the face of affairs has totally changed;

That within that time it had become apparent that Britain was determined to accept nothing less than a carte blanche, and that the king's answer to the lord mayor, aldermen, and common council of London, which had come to hand four days ago, must have satisfied everyone of this point;

That the people wait for us to lead the way;

That *they* are in favour of the measure, though the instructions given by some of their *representatives* are not;

That the voice of the representatives is not always consonant with the voice of the people, and that this is remarkably the case in these middle colonies;

That the effect of the resolution of the 15th of May has proved this, which, raising the murmurs of some in the colonies of Pennsylvania and Maryland, called forth the opposing voice of the freer part of the people and proved them to be the majority, even in these colonies;

That the backwardness of these two colonies might be ascribed partly to the influence of proprietary power and connections, and partly to their having not yet been attacked by the enemy;

That these causes were not likely to be soon removed, as there seemed no probability that the enemy would make either of these the seat of this summer's war;

That it would be vain to wait either weeks or months for perfect unanimity, since it was impossible that all men should ever become of one sentiment on any question;

That the conduct of some colonies from the beginning of this contest had given reason to suspect it was their settled policy to keep in the rear of the confederacy, that their particular prospect might be better, even in the worst event;

That therefore it was necessary for those colonies who had thrown themselves forward and hazarded all from the beginning to come forward now also and put all again to their own hazard;

That the history of the Dutch revolution, of whom three states only confederated at first, proved that a secession of some colonies would not be so dangerous as some apprehended;

That a declaration of independence alone could render it consistent with European delicacy for European powers to treat with us, or even to receive an ambassador from us;

That till this they would not receive our vessels into their ports nor acknowledge the adjudications of our courts of admiralty to be legitimate in cases of capture of British vessels;

That though France and Spain may be jealous of our rising power, they must think it will be much more formidable with the addition of Great Britain and will therefore see it their interest to prevent a coalition; but should they refuse, we shall be but where we are; whereas without trying we shall never know whether they will aid us or not;

That the present campaign may be unsuccessful, and therefore we had better propose an alliance while our affairs wear a hopeful aspect;

That to wait the event of this campaign will certainly work delay because during this summer France may assist us effectually by cutting off those supplies of provisions from England and Ireland on which the enemy's armies here are to depend, or by setting in motion the great power they have collected in the West Indies and calling our enemy to the defence of the possessions they have there;

That it would be idle to lose time in settling the terms of alliance, till we had first determined we would enter into alliance;

That it is necessary to lose no time in opening a trade for our people, who will want clothes and will want money too for the payment of taxes;

And that the only misfortune is that we did not enter into alliance with France six months sooner, as, besides opening their ports for the vent of our last year's produce, they might have marched an army into Germany and prevented the petty princes there from selling their unhappy subjects to subdue us.

It appearing in the course of these debates that the colonies of N[ew] York, N[ew] Jersey, Pennsylvania, Delaware, and Maryland were not yet matured for falling from the parent stem, but that they were fast advancing to that state, it was thought most prudent to wait a while for them, and to postpone the final decision to July 1. But that this might occasion as little delay as possible, a committee was appointed to prepare a declaration of independence. The committee were J[ohn] Adams, Dr. Franklin, Roger Sherman, Robert R. Livingston, and myself. Committees were also appointed at the same time to prepare a plan of confederation for the colonies, and to state the terms proper to be proposed for foreign alliance. The committee for drawing the declaration of independence desired me to do it. It was accordingly done, and being approved by them, I reported it to the house on Friday the 28th of June, when it was read and ordered to lie on the table. On Monday the 1st of July the house resolved itself into a committee of the whole and resumed the consideration of the original motion made by the delegates of Virginia, which being again debated through the day, was carried in the affirmative by the votes of N[ew] Hampshire, Connecticut, Massachusetts, Rhode Island, N[ew] Jersey, Maryland, Virginia, N[orth] Carolina, and Georgia. S[outh] Carolina and Pennsylvania voted against it. Delaware having but two members present, they were divided. The delegates for N[ew] York declared they were for it themselves and were assured their constituents were for it but that their instructions, having been drawn near a twelvemonth before, when reconciliation was still the general object, they were enjoined by them to do nothing which should impede that object. They therefore thought themselves not justifiable in voting on either side and asked leave to withdraw from the question which was given them. The committee rose and reported their resolution to the house. Mr. Rutledge of S[outh] Carolina then requested the determination might be put off to the next day as he believed his colleagues, though they disapproved of the resolution, would then join in it for the sake of unanimity. The ultimate question whether the house would agree to the resolution of the committee, was accordingly postponed to the next day, when it was again moved and S[outh] Carolina concurred in voting for it. In the meantime a third member had come post from the Delaware counties and turned the vote of that colony in favour of the resolution. Members of a different sentiment attending that morning from Pennsylvania also, their vote was changed so that the whole twelve colonies who were authorized to vote at all gave their voices for it; and within a few days the convention of N[ew] York approved of it, and thus supplied the void occasioned by the withdrawing of their delegates from the vote.

c *John Dickinson's Speech Against Independence (July 1, 1776)*

THE CONSEQUENCES involved in the motion now lying before you are of such magnitude that I tremble under the oppressive honour of sharing in its determination. I feel myself unequal to the burden assigned me. I believe; I had almost said, I rejoice, that the time is approaching when I shall be relieved from its weight. While the trust remains with me I must discharge the duties of it as well as I can — and I hope I shall be the more favourably heard, as I am convinced that I shall hold such language as will sacrifice my private emolument to general interests. My conduct this day I expect will give the finishing blow to my once too great, and my integrity considered now, too diminished popularity. It will be my lot to know that I had rather vote away the enjoyment of that dazzling display, that pleasing possession, than the blood and happiness of my countrymen — too fortunate amidst their calamities, if I prove (a truth known in Heaven) that I had rather they should hate me than that I should hurt them. I might indeed practise an artful, an advantageous reserve upon this occasion. But thinking as I do on the subject of debate, silence would be guilt. I despise its arts, I detest its advantages. I must speak, though I should lose my life, though I should lose the affections of my country. Happy at present, however, I shall esteem myself if I can so far rise to the height of this great argument as to offer to this honourable assembly, in a full and clear manner, those reasons that have so invariably fixed my own opinion.

It was a custom in a wise and virtuous state to preface propositions in council with a prayer, that they might redound to the public
benefit. I beg leave to imitate the laudable example. And I do most
humbly implore Almighty God, with whom dwells wisdom itself, so
to enlighten the members of this house that their decision may be
such as will best promote the liberty, safety, and prosperity of these
colonies, and for myself, that his divine goodness may be graciously
pleased to enable me to speak the precepts of sound policy on the
important question that now engages our attention.

Sir, gentlemen of very distinguished abilities and knowledge differ
widely in their sentiments upon the point now agitated. They all
agree that the utmost prudence is required in forming our decision,
but immediately disagree in their notion of that prudence. Some cautiously insist that we ought to obtain that previous information which
we are likely quickly to obtain, and to make those previous establishments that are acknowledged to be necessary. Others strenuously assert
that though regularly such information and establishment ought to
precede the measure proposed, yet, confiding in our fortune more
boldly than Caesar himself, we ought to brave the storm in a skiff
made of paper.

In all such cases where every argument is adorned with an elo-
quence that may please and yet mislead, it seems to me the proper
method of discovering the right path, to inquire which of the parties
is probably the most warmed by passion. Other circumstances being
equal or nearly equal, that consideration would have influence with
me. I fear the virtue of Americans. Resentment of the injuries offered
to their country may irritate them to counsels and to actions that may
be detrimental to the cause they would die to advance.

What advantages could it be claimed would follow from the
adoption of this resolution? (1) It might animate the people. (2) It
would convince foreign powers of our strength and unanimity and
we would receive their aid in consequence thereof. As to the first
point, it is unnecessary. The preservation of life, liberty, and property is a sufficient motive to animate the people. The general spirit
of America is animated. As to the second, foreign powers will not
rely on words.

The event of the campaign will be the best evidence of our
strength and unanimity. This properly the first campaign. Who has
received intelligence that such a proof of our strength and daring
spirit will be agreeable to France? What must she expect from a

JOHN DICKINSON: *The American Revolution*

people that begin their empire in so high a style when on the point of being invaded by the whole power of Great Britain aided by formidable afor [foreign?] aid, unconnected with foreign powers? She and Spain must perceive the immediate danger of their colonies lying at our doors, their seat of empire is in another world. Masserano — Intelligence from Cadiz.

It would be more respectful to act in conformity to the views of France. Let us take advantage of their pride; let us give them reason to believe that we confide in them; that we deseire to act in conjunction with their policies and interests. Let us know how they would regard this stranger in the states of the world. People are fond of what they have attained in producing; they regard it as a child. A cement of affection exists between them. Let us allow them the glory of appearing the vindicators of liberty. It will please them.

It is treating them with contempt to act otherwise, especially after the application made to France which by this time has reached them. Bermuda, 5 May. Consider the abilities of the persons sent. What will they think if now so quickly afterwards, without waiting for their determination, totally slighting their sentiments on such a prodigious issue, we haughtily pursue our own measures?

May they not say to us: Gentlemen, you falsely pretended to consult us and disrespectfully proceeded without waiting our resolution. You must abide the consequences. We are not ready for a rupture. You should have negotiated till we were. We will not be hurried by your impetuosity. We know it is our interest to support you but we shall be in no haste about it. Try your own strength and resources in which you have such confidence. We know now you dare not look back. Reconciliation is impossible without declaring independence, now that you have reached the stage you have. Yours is the most rash and at the same time, the most contemptible senate that ever existed on earth! Suppose on this event Great Britain should offer Canada to France and Florida to Spain with an extension of the old limits. Would not France and Spain accept them? Gentlemen say the trade of all America is more valuable to France than Canada. I grant it; but suppose she may get both? If she is politic, and none doubt that, I aver she has the easiest game to play for attaining both that ever presented itself to a nation.

When we have bound ourselves to a stern quarrel with Great Britain by a declaration of independence, France has nothing to do but to hold back and intimidate Great Britain till Canada is put into her hands; then to intimidate us into a most disadvantageous grant of our trade. It is my firm opinion these events will take place, and arise naturally from our declaring independence.

As to aid from foreign powers: our declaration can procure us none during this present campaign though made today. It is impossible.

Now let us consider if all the advantages expected from foreign powers cannot be attained in a more unexceptional manner. Is there no way of giving notice of a nation's resolution than by proclaiming it to all the world? Let us in the most solemn manner inform the House of Bourbon, at least France, that we wait only for her determination to declare our independence. We must not talk generally of foreign powers but only of those we expect to favour us. Let us assure Spain that we never will give any assistance to her colonies. Let France become guarantee for us in arrangements of this kind.

Besides, first we ought to establish our governments and take the regular form of a state. These preventive measures will show deliberation, wisdom, caution, and unanimity.

It is our interest to keep Great Britain in the opinion that we mean reconciliation as long as possible. The wealth of London, etc., is poured into the treasury. The whole nation is ardent against us. We oblige her by our attitude to persevere in her spirit. See the last petition of London.

Suppose we shall ruin her. France must rise on her ruins. Her ambition. Her religion. Our dangers from thence. We shall weep at our [?]. We shall be overwhelmed with debt. Compute that debt at 6 millions of Pennsylvania money a year.

The war will be carried on with more severity. The burning of towns, the setting loose of Indians on our frontiers has not yet been done. Boston might have been burned, though it was not.

What advantage is to be expected from a declaration?

1] The animating of our troops? I answer, it is unnecessary.

2] Union of the colonies? I answer, this is also unnecessary. It may weaken that union when the people find themselves engaged in a cause rendered more cruel by such a declaration without prospect of an end to their calamities, by a continuation of the war.

People are changeable. In bitterness of soul they may complain against our rashness and ask why we did not apply first to foreign powers; why we did not settle differences among ourselves; why we did not take care to secure unsettled lands for easing their burdens instead of leaving them to colonies; why we did not wait till we were better prepared, or till we had made an experiment of our strength.

3] A third advantage to be expected from a declaration is said to be the proof it would furnish of our strength of spirit. But this is possibly only the first campaign of the war. France and Spain may be alarmed and provoked with each other; Masserano was an insult to France. There is not the least evidence of her granting us favourable terms. Her probable condition. The glory of recovering Canada will be enough for her. She will get that and then dictate terms to us.

A partition of these colonies will take place if Great Britain can't conquer us. To escape from the protection we have in British rule by declaring independence would be like destroying a house before we have got another in winter with a small family; then asking a neighbour to take us in and finding he is unprepared.

4] It is claimed that the spirit of the colonies calls for such a declaration. I answer that the spirit of the colonies is not to be relied on. Not only treaties with foreign powers but among ourselves should precede this declaration. We should know on what grounds we are to stand with regard to one another. We ought to settle the issues raised by the declaration of Virginia about colonists in their limits. And too, the committee on confederation dispute almost every article. Some of us totally despair of any reasonable terms of confederation.

We cannot look back. Men generally sell their goods to most advantage when they have several chapmen. We have but two to rely on. We exclude one by this declaration without knowing what the other will give.

Great Britain after one or more unsuccessful campaigns may be induced to offer us such a share of commerce as would satisfy us, to appoint councillors during good behaviour, to withdraw her armies, to protect our commerce, establish our militias — in short to redress all the grievances complained of in our first petition. Let us know if we can get terms from France that will be more beneficial than these. If we can, let us declare independence. If we cannot, let us at least withhold that declaration till we obtain terms that are tolerable.

We have many points of the utmost moment to settle with France — Canada, Acadia, and Cape Breton. What will content her? Trade or territory? What conditions of trade? Barbary pirates, Spain, Portugal? Will she demand an exclusive trade as a compensation, or grant us protection against piratical states only for a share of our commerce?

When our enemies are pressing us so vigorously; when we are in so wretched a state of preparation; when the sentiments and designs of our expected friends are so unknown to us, I am alarmed at this declaration being so vehemently presented. A worthy gentleman told us that people in this house have had different views for more than a twelvemonth. This is amazing after what they have so repeatedly declared in this house and private conversations, that they meant only reconciliation. But since they can conceal their views so dextrously, I should be glad to read a little more in the Doomsday Book of America — not all — that, like the Book of Fate, might be too dreadful —title page — binding. I should be glad to know whether in 20 or 30 years this commonwealth of colonies may not be thought too unwieldy, and Hudson's River be a proper boundary for a separate commonwealth to the northward. I have a strong impression on my mind that this will take place.

d The Declaration of Independence (July 4, 1776)

The Unanimous Declaration of the Thirteen United States of America

WHEN IN THE Course of human events, it becomes necessary for one people to dissolve the political bands which have connected them with another, and to assume among the powers of the earth, the separate and equal station to which the Laws of Nature and of Nature's God entitle them, a decent respect to the opinions of mankind requires that they should declare the causes which impel them to the separation. We hold these truths to be self-evident, that all men are created equal, that they are endowed by their Creator with certain unalienable Rights, that among these are Life, Liberty and the pursuit of Happiness. That to secure these rights, Governments are instituted among Men, deriving their just powers from the consent of the governed, That whenever any Form of Government becomes destructive of these ends, it is the Right of the People to alter or to abolish it, and to institute new Government, laying its foundation on such principles and organizing its powers in such form, as to them shall seem most likely to effect their Safety and Happiness. Prudence, indeed, will dictate that Governments long established should not be changed for light and transient causes; and accordingly all experience hath shewn, that mankind are more disposed to suffer, while evils are sufferable, than to right themselves by abolishing the forms to which they are accustomed. But when a long train of abuses and usurpations, pursuing invariably the same Object evinces a design to reduce them under absolute Depotism, it is their right, it is their duty, to throw off such Government, and to provide new Guards for their future security. Such has been the patient sufferance of these Colonies; and such is now the necessity which constrains them to alter their former Systems of Government. The history of the present King of Great Britain is a history of repeated injuries and usurpations, all having in direct object the establishment of an absolute Tyranny over these States. To prove this, let Facts be submitted to a candid world. He has refused his Assent to Laws, the most wholesome and necessary for the public good. He has forbidden his Governors to pass Laws of immediate and pressing importance, unless suspended in their operation till his Assent should be obtained; and when so suspended, he has utterly neglected to attend to them. He has refused to pass other Laws for the accommodation of large districts of people, unless those people would relinquish the right of Representation in the Legislature, a right inestimable to them and formidable to tyrants only. He has called together legislative bodies at places unusual, uncomfortable, and distant from the depository of their public Records, for the sole purpose of fatiguing them into compliance with his measures. He has dissolved Representative Houses repeatedly, for opposing with manly firmness his invasions on the rights of the people. He has refused for a long time, after such dissolutions, to cause others to be elected; whereby the Legislative powers, incapable of Annihilation, have returned to the People at large for their exercise; the State remaining in the mean time exposed to all the dangers of invasion from without, and convulsions within. He has endeavoured to prevent the population of these States; for that purpose obstructing the Laws for Naturalization of Foreigners; refusing to pass others to encourage their migrations hither, and raising the conditions of new Appropriations of Lands. He has obstructed the Administration of Justice, by refusing his Assent to Laws for establishing Judiciary powers. He has made Judges dependent on his Will alone, for the tenure of their offices, and the amount and payment of their salaries. He has erected a multitude of New Offices, and sent hither swarms of Officers to harass our people, and eat out their substance. He has kept among us, in times of peace, standing Armies without the Consent of our legislatures. He has affected to render the Military independent of and superior to the Civil power. He has combined with others to subject us to a jurisdiction foreign to our constitution, and unacknowledged by our laws; giving his Assent to their Acts of pretended Legislation: For Quartering large bodies of armed troops among us: For protecting them, by a mock Trial, from punishment for any Murders which they should commit on the Inhabitants of these States: For cutting off our Trade with all parts of the world: For imposing Taxes on us without our Consent: For depriving us in many cases of the benefits of Trial by Jury: For transporting us beyond Seas to be tried for pretended offences: For abolishing the free System of English Laws in a neighbouring Province, establishing therein an Arbitrary government, and enlarging its Boundaries so as to render it at once an example and fit instrument for introducing the same absolute rule into these Colonies: For taking away our Charters, abolishing our most valuable Laws, and altering fundamentally the Forms of our Governments: For suspending our own Legislatures, and declaring themselves invested with power to legislate for us in all cases whatsoever. He has abdicated Government here, by declaring us out of his Protection and waging War against us. He has plundered our seas, ravaged our Coasts, burnt our towns, and destroyed the Lives of our people. He is at this time transporting large Armies of foreign Mercenaries to compleat the works of death, desolation and tyranny, already begun with circumstances of Cruelty & perfidy scarcely paralleled in the most barbarous ages, and totally unworthy the Head of a civilized nation. He has constrained our fellow Citizens taken Captive on the high Seas to bear Arms against their Country, to become the executioners of their friends and Brethren, or to fall themselves by their Hands. He has excited domestic insurrections amongst us, and has endeavoured to bring on the inhabitants of our frontiers, the merciless Indian Savages, whose known rule of warfare, is an undistinguished destruction of all ages, sexes and conditions. In every stage of these Oppressions We have Petitioned for Redress in the most humble terms: Our repeated Petitions have been answered only by repeated injury. A Prince, whose character is thus marked by every act which may define a Tyrant, is unfit to be the ruler of a free people. Nor have We been wanting in attentions to our Brittish brethren. We have warned them from time to time of attempts by their legislature to extend an unwarrantable jurisdiction over us. We have reminded them of the circumstances of our emigration and settlement here. We have appealed to their native justice and magnanimity, and we have conjured them by the ties of our common kindred to disavow these usurpations, which would inevitably interrupt our connections and correspondence. They too have been deaf to the voice of justice and of consanguinity. We must, therefore, acquiesce in the necessity, which denounces our Separation, and hold them, as we hold the rest of mankind, Enemies in War, in Peace Friends.

We, therefore, the Representatives of the united States of America, in General Congress, Assembled, appealing to the Supreme Judge of the world for the rectitude of our intentions, do, in the Name, and by Authority of the good People of these Colonies, solemnly publish and declare, That these United Colonies are, and of Right ought to be Free and Independent States; that they are Absolved from all Allegiance to the British Crown, and that all political connection between them and the State of Great Britain, is and ought to be totally dissolved; and that as Free and Independent States, they have full Power to levy War, conclude Peace, contract Alliances, establish Commerce, and to do all other Acts and Things which Independent States may of right do. And for the support of this Declaration, with a firm reliance on the protection of divine Providence, we mutually pledge to each other our Lives, our Fortunes and our sacred Honour.

Button Gwinnett	John Hancock	Lewis Morris
Lyman Hall	Thos. Nelson jr.	Richd. Stockton
Geo Walton	Francis Lightfoot Lee	Jno Witherspoon
Wm. Hooper	Carter Braxton	Fras. Hopkinson
Joseph Hewes	Robt. Morris	John Hart
John Penn	Benjamin Rush	Abra Clark
Edward Rutledge	Benja. Franklin	Josiah Bartlett
Thos. Heyward Junr.	John Morton	Wm: Whipple
Thomas Lynch Junr.	Geo Clymer	Saml. Adams
Arthur Middleton	Jas. Smith	John Adams
Samuel Chase	Geo. Taylor	Robt. Treat Paine
Wm. Paca	James Wilson	Elbridge Gerry
Thos. Stone	Geo. Ross	Step. Hopkins
Charles Carroll of	Caesar Rodney	William Ellery
Carrollton	Geo Read	Roger Sherman
George Wythe	Tho M: Kean	Saml. Huntington
Richard Henry Lee	Wm. Floyd	Wm. Williams
Th: Jefferson	Phil. Livingston	Oliver Wolcott
Benja. Harrison	Frans. Lewis	Matthew Thornton

13

The French Revolution

MAILLARD, a sheriff's officer who had played a leading part in the capture of the Bastille, testified before the Commission set up by the Châtelet in Paris in 1790 to prosecute those responsible for the Versailles disturbances of October 6, 1789.

The first version of the Declaration of the Rights of Man and Citizen proclaimed the "principles of 1789" as conceived by the first revolutionary Assembly, in which constitutional monarchists predominated. The second was drafted after the Jacobins had, in June, 1793, excluded the "Girondin" deputies, with the aid of the Paris sans-culottes and National Guard, and taken control of the National Convention.

The "Instruction" was addressed by the Temporary Commission, set up at Lyons in November, 1793, to the local revolutionary authorities of the departments of Rhone and Loire. The Commission had been entrusted by the Representatives of the People with the Army of the Alps with the task of restoring revolutionary authority in the disaffected areas after the defeat of the "federalist" rebellion at Lyons of May 1793. The document clearly reflects the (short-lived) Jacobin-sans-culotte alliance of the summer and autumn of 1793.

a Stanislas Maillard on the Women's March to Versailles (October 5, 1789)

STANISLAS-MARIE MAILLARD, twenty-six years of age, captain in the Bastille Volunteers, residing in the Rue Béthizi at Paris, in the parish of St. Germain l'Auxerrois, testified

That at seven o'clock in the morning of 5th October last he went to the City Hall to lodge a complaint on behalf of the Volunteers. The city council was not in session, but the rooms were filled with women who were trying to break in all the doors of the rooms in the City Hall. This determined him to go down to the headquarters

From PROCÉDURE CRIMINELLE INSTRUITE AU CHÂTELET DE PARIS, 2 vols. (Paris, 1790), vol. 1, pp. 117–32. Translation by the editor.

of the National Guard in order to receive the instructions of M. de Gouvion as how best to remedy and prevent the destruction that might be wrought by these women. M. de Gouvion requested him immediately to stay with him and to help him to calm the people. At that moment news was brought to M. de Gouvion of a riot that had broken out in the Faubourg St. Antoine; and, fearing that the company of Volunteers stationed at the Bastille, at the entrance to the Faubourg, had not been supplied with ammunition, M. de Gouvion gave him an order for the delivery of three hundred cartridges for the Volunteers. He (the present witness) then made off to the district of St. Louis-la-Culture, where he had the order countersigned; went on to the place where the Volunteers were stationed; found, on inspection and after enquiry, that they had enough ammunition for their defence; and consequently made no use of the order. The workers at the Bastille now advanced on the Volunteers standing under arms in the courtyard; but Mr. Hulin, their commanding officer, and he himself addressed the workers with courtesy and assured them that their arms would only be used against the enemies of freedom, and not against themselves as they appeared to fear, and to convince them of this they ordered the Volunteers to lower their arms. When calm had been restored and the workers had left the Place de la Bastille, he left Mr. Hulin and, in accordance with M. de Gouvion's request to give him assistance (M. de Gouvion being alone), returned alone to the City Hall. On arrival, he found it at first impossible to enter the building, which was occupied by a large crowd of women who refused to let any men come in among them and kept repeating that the city council was composed of aristocrats. He himself was taken for a member of the council, as he was dressed in black, and entry being refused him he was obliged to go and change his clothes. But as he went down the steps of the building he was stopped by five or six women, who made him go up again, shouting to their comrades that he was a Bastille Volunteer and that there was nothing to fear from him. After this, having mingled with the women, he found some forcing the downstairs doors, others snatching papers in the offices, saying that that was all the city council had done since the revolution began and that they would burn them. Supported by a certain Richard Dupin, he urged them to keep calm, but these women kept saying that the men were not strong enough to be revenged on their enemies and that they (the women) would do better. While he was in the courtyard, he looked round and saw a large number of men go up, armed with pikes, lances, pitchforks and other weapons, having compelled the women to let them in. They then flung themselves on the doors that the women had begun to beat, broke them down with great hammers that they had with them and with crowbars that they found in the City Hall, and took all the arms they could find and gave some to the women. He then received word that a number of women had arrived with torches to burn the papers in the building; so he dashed out, flung himself upon them (there were but two), as they approached the City Hall, each bearing a lighted torch; he snatched the torches from their hands, which nearly cost him his life as they were intent on carrying out their design. He prayed them to send a deputation to the council to demand justice and to describe their plight, as they were all in need of bread; but they replied that the whole council was composed of bad citizens who deserved to be hanged from lamp-posts, M. Bailly and M. de Lafayette first of all. . . .

. . . Mr. Maillard . . . , continuing his evidence, said that to avert the danger and misfortune that threatened both Mm. de Lafayette and Bailly and the City Hall he thought it best to go once more to staff headquarters, where he only found present M. Derminy, M. de Gouvion's aide. Whereupon he (the witness) told M. Derminy that these women would not listen to reason and that, having destroyed the City Hall, they intended to proceed to the National Assembly in order to learn all that had been done and decreed up to the present date. He told these ladies that the National Assembly owed them no reckoning, and that if they went there they would cause a disturbance and would prevent the deputies from paying serious attention to the important business arising from the present situation. As the women persisted in their plans, he thought it wise to repair once more to M. Derminy and acquaint him with their resolution, adding that if the latter thought fit he would accompany them to Versailles in order to prevent and to apprize them of the danger to which they were exposing themselves by embarking on so rash a venture. To this M. Derminy replied that he could not give him an order of this nature, which would be against the citizens' interests, but that he (the witness) might do as he pleased, provided that what he did did not endanger the public peace. In reply, he assured M. Derminy that the proposed action would have no such results and that it was, in fact, the only means of relieving the City Hall and the capital; moreover, by these means the districts could be alerted and, while the women marched four leagues, the army would have time to avert the evils that these ladies were proposing to commit.

The witness now seized a drum at the entrance to the City Hall, where the women were already assembled in very large numbers; detachments went off into different districts to recruit other women, who were instructed to meet them at the Place Louis XV. . . . But as the people were assembled in great numbers and this square was no longer suited as a place of meeting, they decided to proceed to the Place d'Armes, in the middle of the Champs Elysées, whence he saw detachments of women coming up from every direction, armed with broomsticks, lances, pitchforks, swords, pistols and muskets. As they had no ammunition, they wanted to compel him to go with a detachment of them to the arsenal to fetch powder; but he made use of the order given him by M. de Gouvion and displayed it to them, claiming that the order had been made out for them but there was no powder in the arsenal (though he knew that the contrary was true). . . . And now by means of prayers and protestations he succeeded in persuading the women to lay down their arms, with the exception of a few who refused, but whom wiser heads among them compelled to yield. . . .

Meanwhile, he had acquired the confidence of these women to the extent that they all said unanimously that they would have only him to lead them. A score of them left the ranks to compel all the other men to march behind them; and so they took the road to Versailles with eight or ten drums at their head. They now numbered about six or seven thousand and passed through Chaillot along the river. Here all houses were closed up, for fear no doubt of pillage; but, in spite of this, women went knocking at all the doors; and when people refused to open, they wanted to beat them in, and removed all sign-boards. Observing this and wishing to prevent the ruin of the inhabitants, he gave the order to halt and told them that they would discredit themselves by behaving in such a manner, and that if they continued to do so he would no longer march at their head, that their actions would be looked on unfavourably, whereas if they proceeded peaceably and honestly all the citizens of the capital would be grateful to them. They yielded at length to his remonstrances and opinions and discreetly continued on their way to Sèvres. On the way, however, they stopped several couriers and carriages of the court coming from the direction of Versailles, for fear (as they said) that the Pont de Sèvres be closed to stop them passing — but without harming these persons in any way. Arriving at the Pont de Sèvres, he gave the order to halt and, to prevent mischief, he asked if there were any armed men there; but instead of the inhabitants of Sèvres to whom he addressed this question giving any satisfactory reply, they merely stated that Sèvres was in a state of the greatest consternation, that all houses were closed, and that it would be impossible to find any refreshment for these ladies. . . .

[Several of the men having been left behind at Sèvres,] he and the women continued on their journey to Versailles. Past Viroflay, they met a number of individuals on horseback, who appeared to be *bourgeois* and wore black cockades in their hats. The women stopped them and made as if to commit violence against them, saying that they must die as punishment for having insulted, and for insulting, the national cockade; one they struck and pulled him off his horse, tearing off his black cockade which one of the women handed to him (the witness). He ordered the other women to halt . . . and came to the aid of the man whom they were ill-using; he obtained his release on condition that he should surrender his horse, that he should march behind them, and that at the first place they came to he should be made to carry on his back a placard, proclaiming that he had insulted the national cockade. . . . [The same treatment having been meted out to two other passers-by and two of the women having mounted their horses,] he drew the women up (as far as it was in his power to do so) in three ranks and made them form a circle, and told them that the two cannons that they had with them must be removed from the head of their procession; that although they had no ammunition, they might be suspected of evil intentions; that they would do better to give an air of gaiety than to occasion a riot in Versailles; that as the city had not been warned of their proceedings, its inhabitants might mistake their purpose and they might become the victims of their own zeal. They consented to do as he wished; consequently, the cannons were placed behind them and he invited the women to chant "Long live Henri IV!" as they entered Versailles and to cry "Long live the King!" — a cry which they did not cease to repeat in the midst of the citizens awaiting them, who greeted them with cries of *"Long live our Parisiennes!"* So they arrived at the door of the National Assembly, where he told them that it would be imprudent for more than five or six of them to appear. They refused, all wanting to go in; whereupon a Guards' officer, on duty at the National Assembly, joined him and urged that not more than twelve of the women should enter. . . .

After much discussion among the women, fifteen were chosen to appear with him at the bar of the National Assembly; of these fifteen he only knew the *femme* Lavarenne, who has just been awarded a medal by the Paris city council. Entering the Assembly, he urged the women to be silent and to leave to him the task of communicating to the Assembly their demands, as they had explained them to him on the way; to this they consented. He then asked the president's leave to speak. M. Mounier, who was then president, granted him leave and he told them that two or three persons, whom they had met on the way driving in a carriage from the court, had informed him that they had learned that an abbé, a member of the Assembly, had given a miller two hundred *livres* to stop him grinding corn with the promise to give him the same every week. The National Assembly insisted that he should name this individual; but he could not satisfy their wishes, as he could remember neither the names of those whom these persons denounced nor the names of the accusers themselves: all that he could remember was that the latter lived in the Rue du Plâtre Ste. Avoye. As the Assembly persisted in demanding the name of the accused, M. de Robespierre, deputy of Arras, rose to speak and said that the stranger admitted to their august assembly was absolutely right, that he believed there had been talk of it that very morning, and that the Abbé Gregoire could throw further light on the matter; hence he (the witness) was relieved of the obligation of doing so. He (the witness) now once more addressed the Assembly and said that to restore calm, allay public disquiet and avert disaster, he begged the gentlemen of the Assembly to appoint a deputation to go to the Life-Guards in order to enjoin them to adopt the national cockade and make amends for the injury they were said to have done to it. Several members raised their voices and said it was false that the Life-Guards had ever insulted the national cockade, that all who wished to be citizens could be so freely, and that no one could be forced to be so. Speaking again and displaying three black cockades (the same that were spoken of earlier), he said that, on the contrary, there should be no person who did not take pride in being so and that if there were, within this august Assembly, any members that felt dishonoured by this title they should be excluded immediately. Many applauded these words and the hall rang with cries of "Yes, all should be so and we are all citizens". In the midst of this applause, he was handed a national cockade, sent in by the Life-Guards, which he showed to all the women as a proof of their submission; and all the women cried "Long live the King and the Life-Guards!" He once more asked leave to speak and said that it was essential also, in order to avert misfortune and to allay the suspicions that had been spread in the capital concerning the arrival of the Flanders Regiment at Versailles, to withdraw this regiment because the citizens feared they might start a revolution. [The Assembly now agreed to appoint a deputation to wait upon the King and put forward the women's demands. Meanwhile, angry words were exchanged with the clerical members of the Assembly and it was rumoured that the Life-Guards had fired on the women outside.]

As he spoke, a dozen women entered the National Assembly and said that the Life-Guards had just fired on them, that one had been arrested, and that they were waiting for him (the witness) to come down before deciding on the manner of the death he had merited. At that moment, the sound of musket-fire could be heard; this caused alarm in the Assembly and he was urged by several deputies to hasten down in order to put a stop to these mischiefs. He went down surrounded by the women and observed a Life-Guard, who was being held by the bridle of his horse; the man wished to dismount, but the women prevented him, though without doing him any injury other than to hurl abuse at him. When the Life-Guard saw him advance to speak to him, he drew a sword and cut through his reins; the point of the sword struck a woman on the shoulder, and he fled. He (the witness) made to run after him, but he could not catch him, and the Life-Guard, as he fled, discharged his pistol at him but failed to hit him. He (the witness) then returned to the National Assembly, having enjoined the women not to approach closer to the royal palace. At eight o'clock in the evening, the president returned with his deputation from their audience with the King. He repeated the King's words before the Assembly; the women listened respectfully as their intent was to restore calm among his people. Then the president read aloud five papers relative to the demands addressed by the Parisian National Guard to the National Assembly and to the King concerning the food-supply. His Majesty had commanded that two officers should accompany him (the witness) back to Paris, but the women objected to this and all said that they alone should escort him. The five papers were entered in the registers of the Assembly and copies were handed to him by Viscount Mirabeau; and, immediately afterwards, he returned to Paris with a part of the women in a carriage of the court. In the Avenue de Versailles, as they rode, they encountered the Parisian National Guard.

Arriving in Paris, he gave orders to be taken directly to the City

Hall, which he entered escorted by some hundred and fifty women who went ahead of him into the hall where sat the representatives of the Commune, the mayor presiding. He (the witness) gave an account of all that had taken place and, having first read them aloud, handed to the mayor the five papers entrusted to his care (as has been related above). . . . At six o'clock in the morning of Tuesday, 6th October, the mayor besought the women to withdraw to their homes, which they did; but eight or ten of them escorted him (the witness) to his dwelling, which was then the Hôtel de Grenelle St. Honoré in the street of the same name. At eight o'clock in the morning of this same day, ten to twelve women came to fetch him, and compelled him to march with them to meet the National Guard and present the Marquis de Lafayette with a laurel branch on his return from Versailles. But a messenger whom they encountered told them that he was ordered to have the Tuileries palace prepared to receive His Majesty, who was coming to Paris that evening. The women urged him (the witness) to go with them to meet His Majesty. So he went with them and they met the King at Viroflay. They mingled with the women who escorted the King's carriage and returned to Paris to the City Hall, and here he left all these women. And that is all he knew of the matter.

b Two Versions of the Declaration of the Rights of Man and Citizen

August 27, 1789

THE REPRESENTATIVES of the French people, organized in National Assembly, considering that ignorance, forgetfulness, or contempt of the rights of man are the sole causes of public misfortunes and of the corruption of governments, have resolved to set forth in a solemn declaration the natural, inalienable, and sacred rights of man, in order that such declaration, continually before all members of the social body, may be a perpetual reminder of their rights and duties; in order that the acts of the legislative power and those of the executive power may constantly be compared with the aim of every political institution and may accordingly be more re-

From John Hall Stewart, A DOCUMENTARY SURVEY OF THE FRENCH REVOLUTION (New York, 1951), pp. 113–5, 455–8. Reprinted by permission of The Macmillan Company.

spected; in order that the demands of the citizens, founded hence-forth upon simple and incontestable principles, may always be directed towards the maintenance of the Constitution and the wel-fare of all.

Accordingly, the National Assembly recognizes and proclaims, in the presence and under the auspices of the Supreme Being, the fol-lowing rights of man and citizen.

1] Men are born and remain free and equal in rights; social distinctions may be based only upon general usefulness.

2] The aim of every political association is the preservation of the natural and inalienable rights of man; these rights are liberty, prop-erty, security, and resistance to oppression.

3] The source of all sovereignty resides essentially in the nation; no group, no individual may exercise authority not emanating ex-pressly therefrom.

4] Liberty consists of the power to do whatever is not injurious to others; thus the enjoyment of the natural rights of every man has for its limits only those that assure other members of society the en-joyment of those same rights; such limits may be determined only by law.

5] The law has the right to forbid only actions which are injurious to society. Whatever is not forbidden by law may not be prevented, and no one may be constrained to do what it does not prescribe.

6] Law is the expression of the general will; all citizens have the right to concur personally, or through their representatives, in its formation; it must be the same for all, whether it protects or punishes. All citizens, being equal before it, are equally admissible to all public offices, positions, and employments, according to their capacity, and without other distinction than that of virtues and talents.

7] No man may be accused, arrested, or detained except in the cases determined by law, and according to the forms prescribed thereby. Whoever solicit, expedite, or execute arbitrary orders, or have them executed, must be punished; but every citizen summoned or apprehended in pursuance of the law must obey immediately; he renders himself culpable by resistance.

8] The law is to establish only penalties that are absolutely and obviously necessary; and no one may be punished except by virtue of a law established and promulgated prior to the offence and legally applied.

9] Since every man is presumed innocent until declared guilty, if arrest be deemed indispensable, all unnecessary severity for securing the person of the accused must be severely repressed by law.

10] No one is to be disquieted because of his opinions, even religious, provided their manifestation does not disturb the public order established by law.

11] Free communication of ideas and opinions is one of the most precious of the rights of man. Consequently, every citizen may speak, write, and print freely, subject to responsibility for the abuse of such liberty in the cases determined by law.

12] The guarantee of the rights of man and citizen necessitates a public force; such a force, therefore, is instituted for the advantage of all and not for the particular benefit of those to whom it is entrusted.

13] For the maintenance of the public force and for the expenses of administration a common tax is indispensable; it must be assessed equally on all citizens in proportion to their means.

14] Citizens have the right to ascertain, by themselves or through their representatives, the necessity of the public tax, to consent to it freely, to supervise its use, and to determine its quota, assessment, payment, and duration.

15] Society has the right to require of every public agent an accounting of his administration.

16] Every society in which the guarantee of rights is not assured or the separation of powers not determined has no constitution at all.

17] Since property is a sacred and inviolable right, no one may be deprived thereof unless a legally established public necessity obviously requires it, and upon condition of a just and previous indemnity.

June 24, 1793

The French people, convinced that forgetfulness of and contempt for the natural rights of man are the sole causes of the misfortunes of the world, have resolved to set forth these sacred and inalienable rights in a solemn declaration, in order that all citizens, being able constantly to compare the acts of the government with the aim of every social institution, may never permit themselves to be oppressed and degraded by tyranny, in order that the people may always have before their eyes the bases of their liberty and their happiness, the magistrate the guide to his duties, the legislator the object of his mission.

Accordingly, in the presence of the Supreme Being, they proclaim the following declaration of the rights of man and citizen.

1] The aim of society is the general welfare. Government is instituted to guarantee man the enjoyment of his natural and inalienable rights.

2] These rights are equality, liberty, security, and property.

3] All men are equal by nature and before the law.

4] Law is the free and solemn expression of the general will; it is the same for all, whether it protects or punishes; it may order only what is just and useful to society; it may prohibit only what is injurious thereto.

5] All citizens are equally admissible to public office. Free peoples recognize no grounds for preference in their elections other than virtues and talents.

6] Liberty is the power appertaining to man to do whatever is not injurious to the rights of others. It has nature for its principle, justice for its rule, law for its safeguard. Its moral limit lies in this maxim: *Do not to others that which you do not wish to be done to you.*

7] The right of manifesting ideas and opinions, either through the press or in any other manner, the right of peaceful assembly, and the free exercise of worship may not be forbidden. The necessity of enunciating these rights implies either the presence or the recent memory of despotism.

8] Security consists of the protection accorded by society to each one of its members for the preservation of his person, his rights, and his property.

9] The law must protect public and individual liberty against the oppression of those who govern.

10] No one is to be accused, arrested, or detained, except in the cases determined by law and according to the forms prescribed thereby. Any citizen, summoned or seized by authority of the law, must obey immediately; he renders himself culpable by resistance.

11] Any act directed against a person, apart from the cases and without the forms determined by law, is arbitrary and tyrannical; if attempt is made to execute such act by force, the person who is the object thereof has the right to resist it by force.

12] Those who incite, dispatch, sign, or execute arbitrary acts, or cause them to be executed, are guilty and must be punished.

13] Since every man is presumed innocent until declared guilty, if his arrest is deemed indispensable, all severity unnecessary for securing his person must be severely curbed by law.

14] No one is to be tried and punished until after having been heard or legally summoned, and except by virtue of a law promulgated prior to the offence. A law that would punish offences committed before it existed would be tyranny; the retroactive effect of such a law would be a crime.

15] The law is to enact only penalties which are strictly and obviously necessary. Penalties must be proportionate to offences and useful to society.

16] The right of property is the right appertaining to every citizen to enjoy and dispose at will of his goods, his income, and the product of his labor and skill.

17] No kind of labor, tillage, or commerce may be forbidden the industry of citizens.

18] Every man may contract his services or his time; but he may not sell himself or be sold; his person is not an alienable property. The law does not recognize the status of servant; only a bond of solicitude and acknowledgment may exist between the employee and his employer.

19] No one may be deprived of the least portion of his property without his consent, unless a legally established public necessity requires it, and upon condition of a just and previous indemnity.

20] No tax may be established except for general utility. All citizens have the right to concur in the establishment of taxes, to supervise their use, and to have an account rendered thereof.

21] Public relief is a sacred obligation. Society owes subsistence to unfortunate citizens, either by procuring work for them or by providing the means of existence for those unable to work.

22] Education is necessary for everyone. Society must promote with all its power the advancement of public reason, and must place education within reach of all citizens.

23] The social guarantee consists of the effort of all to assure to each the enjoyment and preservation of his rights; this guarantee is based upon national sovereignty.

24] It cannot exist if the limits of public functions are not clearly determined by law, and if the responsibility of all functionaries is not assured.

25] Sovereignty resides in the people; it is one and indivisible, imprescriptible, and inalienable.

26] No portion of the people may exercise the power of the entire people; but every section of the sovereign assembled is to enjoy the right to express its will with complete liberty.

27] Let any individual who would usurp sovereignty be put to death instantly by free men.

28] A people always has the right to review, reform, and amend its constitution. One generation may not subject future generations to its laws.

29] Every citizen has an equal right to concur in the formation of the law and in the selection of its mandataries or agents.

30] Public functions are essentially temporary; they may be considered as neither distinctions nor rewards, but only as duties.

31] Offences of mandataries and agents of the people must never go unpunished. No one has the right to consider himself more inviolable than others.

32] The right of presenting petitions to the depositaries of public authority may not be forbidden, suspended, or limited under any circumstances.

33] Resistance to oppression is the consequence of the other rights of man.

34] There is oppression against the social body when a single one of its members is oppressed. There is oppression against every member when the social body is oppressed.

35] When the government violates the rights of the people, insurrection is for the people, and for every portion thereof, the most sacred of rights and the most indispensable of duties.

c *Instruction Addressed by the "Temporary Commission" to the Authorities of the Departments of Rhone and Loire (November 16, 1793)*

✿ THE REPRESENTATIVES of the People with the Army of the Alps and in the various departments of the Republic are striving with indefatigable zeal to restore order, disturbed by the infamous rebellion at Lyons; to punish the traitors and prosecute the conspirators; to revive the energies of the *sans-culottes;* to assure the

From W. Markov and A. Soboul (eds.), DIE SANSCULOTTEN VON PARIS (Berlin, 1957), pp. 218–36. Translation from the French text by George Rudé. Reprinted by permission of Akademie Verlag.

food-supplies of the army and civilian population; and, above all, to compensate the poor and needy for the losses that they have suffered from the crimes of rich counter-revolutionaries.

To aid them in these manifold and important tasks, they have built around them a core of pure and tested patriots; they have organised a Commission of *sans-culottes,* whose task it is to cooperate with them, to relieve them of a multitude of detail that would take up time which should be devoted to over-all planning and direction; and, under their guidance, to draw the reconstituted local authorities into the revolutionary movement and, in association with themselves, to adopt such measures of public safety as circumstances will demand and provident patriotism will suggest.

The Commission is fully conscious of the magnitude of the task it is called upon to discharge and will respond to the trust and realize the designs of the Representatives of the People; but, from the start, it is also conscious of the vital need to supplement its own watchfulness with that of the local authorities, the revolutionary committees, popular societies and of every citizen; it deems it necessary to make known to them the spirit that must animate them today, the principal operations that they must undertake, and all that the Republic has the right to expect not only of their civic virtue, but of that profound feeling of indignation and of that generous desire for vengeance that the crimes and rebellion lately ravishing their country have imprinted in their hearts.

SECTION ONE. *The Revolutionary Spirit*

The Revolution is made for the people; the people's happiness is its aim; love of the people is the touchstone of the revolutionary spirit.

It is easy enough to realize that by the people is not intended that class that, privileged by wealth, had usurped all the pleasures of life and all the benefits of society. The people is the sum total of all French citizens; above all, it is the immense class of the poor, they who give their sons to the fatherland and send them to defend its frontiers, who feed society with the fruits of their labour, and who embellish and honour it by their virtues. The Revolution would be a moral and political monster if its aim were to safeguard the happiness of a few score individuals, while maintaining twenty-four million citizens in hunger and want; it would have been a hollow sham, contemptuous of humanity, to have invoked incessantly the name of equality while maintaining in being the vast gulf in human happiness that has separated man from man and, by preserving the old distinctions of wealth and poverty and of happiness and wretchedness, stifling the declaration of rights, which recognizes no distinction other than that of talent and virtue.

Those who, from the earliest days of the Revolution, have divined its true spirit and have promoted its progress must have seen that it would tend to drive such inhuman monstrosities from the face of France; they have seen that, even if it were impossible to establish a perfect equality among men, it would at least be possible to narrow the gulf; they have seen that there was a terrible disproportion between the labour of the peasant and craftsman and the modest earnings that it yielded; they have seen with indignation that the man whose strong hands provided his fellow-citizens with bread often lacked it for himself, and bathed it with his tears even more than with his sweat; they have cast a glance of compassion and humanity on the fields, the workshops, and on the garrets and the subterranean hovels of the poor and, as the accompaniment of labour which should be rewarded with affluence, they have seen the rags of poverty, the pallor of hunger, and they have heard the doleful plaints of the needy and the sharp cries of the sick.

On the other hand, they have seen in the houses of the rich, the idle and the vicious every refinement of barbarous luxury; and they have seen what should have been the reward of industry and virtue squandered among the bloodsuckers of the people, among rogues flaunting their shame and finery, who have grown fatter on the substance of the poor and wretched than on the insolent luxury of their meals and banquets . . .

Had the *bourgeois* aristocracy been allowed to live, it would soon have begotten a financial aristocracy which, in turn, would have engendered an aristocracy of nobles; for the man of wealth soon comes to regard himself as of a different kind from other men. And so by progressive usurpation the need would eventually have been felt to consecrate these new distinctions by newly-created institutions; so the clergy and its dogmas would be reborn; and that is not all. A solitary altar erected in a Republic may, by suffering a swift blow, be overthrown; but give it a throne to bear it up, by their mutual support, the monarchy is re-created: that is the inevitable sequence. And so from one catastrophe to another France would have been led back under the hateful yoke that she had just shaken off; and do not doubt, citizens, that the monsters would have made it heavier than before and added to the weight of your chains to prevent you from breaking free. They would have punished you for your earlier strivings for liberty. The wheel, prison, forced labour, serfdom, tithe, taxes — that is the prospect, the consummation of a half-completed Revolution. . . .

SECTION TWO. *The Arrest of Suspected Persons*

It follows from the simple and illuminating principles that we have just recalled to you that the Republican can no longer live with slaves; such have, by their crimes and baseness, exhausted our patience. For five years we have held out our hands to help them; they have rejected our advances, and it is time that they atone for their indifference and learn, at least, the price of liberty by the forced sacrifice of their own. Here the desire for legitimate vengeance becomes an imperative need for him who considers the public interest; for the public interest requires that our enemies be visited by terror, that the threats of their conspiracies be broken, that they be punished for their crimes, and that they be made to forfeit the happiness that they want nothing of. It is in response to this great measure decreed by the National Convention that the municipalities and revolutionary authorities must display their true zeal and engage in patriotic activity; in this cause all personal considerations and private loyalties must be submerged; the voice of blood itself must be stilled before the voice of the fatherland; for you live in a land stained by an infamous rebellion. Well then, citizens and magistrates of the people, all those who have played a direct or indirect part in the rebellion must perish on the scaffold. It is your duty to hand them over to national vengeance.

We are not speaking here merely of the priests, nobles, relatives of *émigrés*, administrators and other perjured officials on whom the law has already expressly passed sentence; we assume that, in their case, you have already done your duty; your own heads will answer for it. But we speak here, more particularly, of all those who, though not mentioned by name in the decrees, are recommended by them to the watchful eye of the nation; we speak of those hypocrites who have always mouthed, but only mouthed, their respect for the law and the person and yet who, every day, oppressed you and, in the case of the poor, violated the most sacred of laws, those of humanity and nature; we speak to you of men, made hard and insensitive by habit and condition, who cannot love the Revolution because it thwarts their prejudices, destroys their hopes and stifles their greed; they are men that called themselves men of law but should have called themselves *men of blood,* that only lived by the dissension among their fellows and the perpetual fuel that they gave to discord and hatred. . . .

REPUBLICANS, these are your duties. Let no consideration of age or sex or kinship hold you back. Act without fear, spare only the *sans-culottes;* and so that the avenging thunderbolt shall never falter in your hands, remember the device inscribed on the banners of the *sans-culottes:* PEACE TO THE COTTAGES, WAR ON THE PALACES.

SECTION THREE. *The Revolutionary Taxation of the Rich*

Money must be found to pay the cost of the war and meet the expenses of the Revolution; and who shall come to the aid of the fatherland and provide for its needs if it be not the rich? If they are aristocrats, it is only just that they should pay for a war that only they and their supporters have provoked; if they are patriots, you will anticipate their wishes by calling on them to put their wealth to the only use that befits Republicans: that is, to use it in the service of the Republic. So nothing can excuse you for not raising this tax forthwith. And there must be no exemptions: every man who is not in need must contribute to this extraordinary relief. The tax must be proportionate to the overriding needs of the country; and so you must begin by determining, in broad outline and in a truly revolutionary manner, the sum that every individual must place at the disposal of the common weal. There is no call here for mathematical exactitude or for such timorous scruples as one must display in assessing citizens for general taxation: this is an extraordinary measure which must bear the stamp of the circumstances that gave rise to it. Act, therefore, boldly and take all that a citizen does not need for his personal use; for superfluity is an evident and gratuitous violation of the rights of the people. All that a man has beyond his needs he cannot use, he can only abuse; so, in leaving him what is strictly necessary the rest belongs to the Republic and its poorer citizens. . . .

SECTION FOUR. *Supplying the Markets and Measures to be Taken with Regard to Food*

The counter-revolutionaries' great hope was to starve the people; they counted on the rich proprietors, the large farmers and the hoarders, and they dared believe that famine would reduce France to slavery. The National Convention has foiled their plans. It has decreed, or rather proclaimed, the great principle that the produce of French soil, while allowing for the compensation due to the producer, belongs to France. The people have, therefore, a guaranteed right to the fruits of their labours and are no longer liable to see the produce of their own toil and sweat go to swell the bellies of a few privileged tyrants, or a handful of oppressive landowners; no longer, therefore, can an iniquitous proprietor dictate to the people and maintain himself in idle luxury by exploiting the labour of industrious men. Such are the fundamental principles that local authorities and citizens must make their own; for a man will never be free as long as he believes that his whole existence, and that of his family, depends on the whim of another man.

It is with these principles in mind that revolutionary committees or food-supply committees must especially concern themselves with supplying the markets. . . .

SECTION FIVE. *Rooting Out Fanaticism*

The priests are the sole cause of the misfortunes of France; it is they who, for the past thirteen hundred years, have progressively erected the edifice of our slavery, adorned it with all the sacred bauble that could hide its faults from the eye of reason and the sharp cutting edge of philosophy; they have enslaved the mind of man to their own foolish prejudices and, to crown their infamies, have hallowed by their sanctified deceptions the errors with which they have beguiled the centuries. It is clear that the Revolution, the very triumph of enlightenment, is outraged by the prolonged agony of this handful of deceivers; their reign is drawing to a close and giving way to the dominion of good sense and reason; it is the duty of patriots to accelerate this process and to instil in the minds of their less enlightened fellow-citizens the reforming principles of the French Revolution. . . .

Republicans, in presenting you with this rapid sketch of your duties, the Temporary Commission of Republican Vigilance repeats that it neither claims, nor has it been able, to tell you all. There are matters of which mention has only to be made for the penetrating eye of the patriot to grasp them and to turn them to good use. Be vigilant, you all have great wrongs to atone for, the crimes of the Lyons rebels are your crimes. Had you been imbued with that proud, Republican spirit that is the hallmark of the free man, never would these rascals have dared to attempt to strike a blow against our country, or at least they would have had not a single minute to rejoice in its success. Return then promptly to the path of liberty and make up for the ground that you have lost; regain, by the exertion of your patriotic virtues and efforts, the esteem and confidence of France. The National Convention and the Representatives of the People have their eyes on you and on your magistrates; the reckoning that they demand of you will be the more severe the greater the number of the faults for which you seek their pardon. . . . The time for half-measures and evasion of responsibility is past. Help us to strike great blows, or you will be the first to suffer them. *Liberty or Death;* consider and make your choice. [Signed *Duhamel,* president, *Perrotin,* vice-president, *Duviquet,* general secretary, and 11 others; and approved by *Collot d'Herbois* and *Fouché,* Representatives of the People.]

14

The Debate on the French Revolution

THESE TWO SELECTIONS from the writings of the two main protagonists in the debate — Edmund Burke, M.P. (1730–1797), and Thomas Paine (1737–1809) — illustrate the sharp cleavage of opinion that developed in England over the French Revolution some months after its outbreak. Paine later became a member of the French National Convention.

a Edmund Burke Castigates the French Revolution (1790)

FRANCE, by the perfidy of her leaders, has utterly disgraced the tone of lenient council in the cabinets of princes, and disarmed it of its most potent topics. She has sanctified the dark, suspicious maximums of tyrannous distrust; and taught kings to tremble at (what will hereafter be called) the delusive plausibilities of moral politicians. Sovereigns will consider those, who advise them to place an unlimited confidence in their people, as subverters of their thrones; as traitors who aim at their destruction, by leading their easy good-nature, under specious pretences, to admit combinations of bold and faithless men into a participation of their power. This alone (if there were nothing else) is an irreparable calamity to you and to mankind. Remember that your parliament of Paris told your king, that, in calling the states together, he had nothing to fear but the prodigal excess of their zeal in providing for the support of the throne. It is right that these men should hide their heads. It is right that they should bear their part in the ruin which their counsel has brought on

From Edmund Burke, REFLECTIONS ON THE REVOLUTION IN FRANCE (London and New York, Everyman's Library Edition), pp. 36–7, 52–3, 55–9. Reprinted by permission of J. M. Dent & Sons and E. P. Dutton & Co., Inc.

their sovereign and their country. Such sanguine declarations tend to lull authority asleep; to encourage it rashly to engage in perilous adventures of untried policy; to neglect those provisions, preparations, and precautions, which distinguish benevolence from imbecility; and without which no man can answer for the salutary effect of any abstract plan of government or of freedom. For want of these, they have seen the medicine of the state corrupted into its poison. They have seen the French rebel against a mild and lawful monarch, with more fury, outrage, and insult, than ever any people has been known to rise against the most illegal usurper, or the most sanguinary tyrant. Their resistance was made to concession; their revolt was from protection; their blow was aimed at a hand holding out graces, favours, and immunities.

This was unnatural. The rest is in order. They have found their punishment in their success. Laws overturned; tribunals subverted; industry without vigour; commerce expiring; the revenue unpaid, yet the people impoverished; a church pillaged, and a state not relieved; civil and military anarchy made the constitution of the kingdom; everything human and divine sacrificed to the idol of public credit, and national bankruptcy the consequence; and, to crown all, the paper securities of new, precarious, tottering power, the discredited paper securities of impoverished fraud and beggared rapine, held out as a currency for the support of an empire, in lieu of the two great recognized species that represent the lasting, conventional credit of mankind, which disappeared and hid themselves in the earth from whence they came, when the principle of property, whose creatures and representatives they are, was systematically subverted.

Were all these dreadful things necessary? Were they the inevitable results of the desperate struggle of determined patriots, compelled to wade through blood and tumult, to the quiet shore of a tranquil and prosperous liberty? No! nothing like it. The fresh ruins of France, which shock our feelings wherever we can turn our eyes, are not the devastation of civil war; they are the sad but instructive monuments of rash and ignorant counsel in time of profound peace. They are the display of inconsiderate and presumptuous, because unresisted and irresistible, authority. . . .

* * *

I see that your example is held out to shame us. I know that we are supposed a dull, sluggish race, rendered passive by finding our situation tolerable, and prevented by a mediocrity of freedom from ever attaining to its full perfection. Your leaders in France began by affecting to admire, almost to adore, the British constitution; but as they advanced, they came to look upon it with a sovereign contempt. The friends of your National Assembly amongst us have full as mean an opinion of what was formerly thought the glory of their country. The Revolution Society has discovered that the English nation is not free. . . .

* * *

It is no wonder therefore, that with these ideas of everything in their constitution and government at home, either in church or state, as illegitimate and usurped, or at best as a vain mockery, they look abroad with an eager and passionate enthusiasm. Whilst they are possessed by these notions, it is vain to talk to them of the practice of their ancestors, the fundamental laws of their country, the fixed form of a constitution, whose merits are confirmed by the solid test of long experience, and an increasing public strength and national prosperity. They despise experience as the wisdom of unlettered men; and as for the rest, they have wrought under ground a mine that will blow up, at one grand explosion, all examples of antiquity, all precedents, charters, and acts of parliament. They have "the rights of men." Against these there can be no prescription; against these no agreement is binding; these admit no temperament and no compromise; anything withheld from their full demand is so much of fraud and injustice. Against these their rights of men let no government look for security in the length of its continuance, or in the justice and lenity of its administration. The objections of these speculatists, if its forms do not quadrate with their theories, are as valid against such an old and beneficent government, as against the most violent tyranny, or the greenest usurpation. They are always at issue with governments, not on a question of abuse, but a question of competency, and a question of title. I have nothing to say to the clumsy subtilty of their political metaphysics. Let them be their amusement in the schools. — "Illa *se jactat in aula — Æolus, et clauso ventorum carcere regnet.*" — But let them not break prison to burst like a *Levanter,* to sweep the earth with their hurricane, and to break up the fountains of the great deep to overwhelm us.

Far am I from denying in theory, full as far is my heart from withholding in practice (if I were of power to give or to withhold), the *real* rights of men. In denying their false claims of right, I do not mean to injure those which are real, and are such as their pretended rights would totally destroy. If civil society be made for the advantage of man, all the advantages for which it is made become his right. It is an institution of beneficence; and law itself is only beneficence acting by a rule. Men have a right to live by that rule; they have a right to do justice, as between their fellows, whether their fellows are in public function or in ordinary occupation. They have a right to the fruits of their industry; and to the means of making their industry fruitful. They have a right to the acquisitions of their parents; to the nourishment and improvement of their offspring; to instruction in life, and to consolation in death. Whatever each man can separately do, without trespassing upon others, he has a right to do for himself; and he has a right to a fair portion of all which society, with all its combinations of skill and force, can do in his favour. In this patrnership all men have equal rights; but not to equal things. He that has but five shillings in the partnership, has as good a right to it, as he that has five hundred pounds has to his larger proportion. But he has not a right to an equal dividend in the product of the joint stock; and as to the share of power, authority, and direction which each individual ought to have in the management of the state, that I must deny to be amongst the direct original rights of man in civil society; for I have in my contemplation the civil social man, and no other. It is a thing to be settled by convention.

If civil society be the offspring of convention, that convention must be its law. That convention must limit and modify all the descriptions of constitution which are formed under it. Every sort of legislative, judicial, or executory power are its creatures. They can have no being in any other state of things; and how can any man claim under the conventions of civil society, rights which do not so much as suppose its existence? rights which are absolutely repugnant to it? One of the first motives to civil society, and which becomes one of its fundamental rules, is, *that no man should be judge in his own cause.* By this each person has at once divested himself of the first fundamental right of uncovenanted man, that is, to judge for himself, and to assert his own cause. He abdicates all right to be his own governor. He inclusively, in a great measure, abandons the right of self-defence, the first law of nature. Men cannot enjoy the rights of an uncivil and of a civil state together. That he may obtain justice, he gives up his right of determining what it is in points the most essential to him. That he may secure some liberty, he makes a surrender in trust of the whole of it.

Government is not made in virtue of natural rights, which may and do exist in total independence of it; and exist in much greater clearness, and in a much greater degree of abstract perfection; but their abstract perfection is their practical defect. By having a right to everything they want everything. Government is a contrivance of human wisdom to provide for human *wants*. Men have a right that these wants should be provided for by this wisdom. Among these wants is to be reckoned the want, out of civil society, of a sufficient restraint upon their passions. Society requires not only that the passions of individuals should be subjected, but that even in the mass and body, as well as in the individuals, the inclinations of men should frequently be thwarted, their will controlled, and their passions brought into subjection. This can only be done *by a power out of themselves;* and not, in the exercise of its function, subject to that will and to those passions which it is its office to bridle and subdue. In this sense the restraints on men, as well as their liberties, are to be reckoned among their rights. But as the liberties and the restrictions vary with times and circumstances, and admit of infinite modifications, they cannot be settled upon any abstract rule; and nothing is so foolish as to discuss them upon that principle.

The moment you abate anything from the full rights of men, each to govern himself, and suffer any artificial, positive limitation upon those rights, from that moment the whole organization of government becomes a consideration of convenience. This it is which makes the constitution of a state, and the due distribution of its powers, a matter of the most delicate and complicated skill. It requires a deep knowledge of human nature and human necessities, and of the things which facilitate or obstruct the various ends, which are to be pursued by the mechanism of civil institutions. The state is to have recruits to its strength, and remedies to its distempers. What is the use of discussing a man's abstract right to food or medicine? The question is upon the method of procuring and administering them. In that deliberation I shall always advise to call in the aid of the farmer and the physician, rather than the professor of metaphysics.

The science of constructing a commonwealth, or renovating it, or reforming it, is, like every other experimental science, not to be taught *à priori*. Nor is it a short experience that can instruct us in that practical science; because the real effects of moral causes are not always immediate; but that which in the first instance is prejudicial may be excellent in its remoter operation; and its excellence may arise even from the ill effects it produces in the beginning. The reverse also happens; and very plausible schemes, with very pleasing commencements, have often shameful and lamentable conclusions. In states there are often some obscure and almost latent causes, things which appear at first view of little moment, on which a very great part of its prosperity or adversity may most essentially depend. The science of government being therefore so practical in itself, and intended for such practical purposes, a matter which requires experience, and even more experience than any prson can gain in his whole life, however sagacious and observing he may be, it is with infinite caution that any man ought to venture upon pulling down an edifice, which has answered in any tolerable degree for ages the common purposes of society, or on building it up again, without having models and patterns of approved utility before his eyes.

b *Tom Paine Defends the Rights of Man (1791)*

🎗 THERE NEVER did, there never will, and there never can exist a parliament, or any description of men, or any generation of men, in any country, possessed of the right or the power of binding and controlling posterity to the *"end of time,"* or of commanding forever how the world shall be governed, or who shall govern it; and therefore, all such clauses, acts or declarations, by which the makers of them attempt to do what they have neither the right nor the power to do, nor the power to execute, are in themselves null and void.

Every age and generation must be as free to act for itself, *in all cases,* as the ages and generation which preceded it. The vanity and presumption of governing beyond the grave, is the most ridiculous and insolent of all tyrannies.

Man has no property in man; neither has any generation a property in the generations which are to follow. The Parliament or the

From D. E. Wheeler (ed.), LIFE AND WRITINGS OF THOMAS PAINE, 10 vols. (New York, 1908), vol. iv, pp. 7–9, 25–6, 51–60.

people of 1688, or of any other period, had no more right to dispose of the people of the present day, or to bind or to control them *in any shape whatever,* than the Parliament or the people of the present day have to dispose of, bind, or control those who are to live a hundred or a thousand years hence.

Every generation is, and must be, competent to all the purposes which its occasions require. It is the living, and not the dead, that are to be accommodated. When man ceases to be, his power and his wants cease with him; and having no longer any participation in the concerns of this world, he has no longer any authority in directing who shall be its governors, or how its government shall be organized, or how administered.

I am not contending for nor against any form of government, nor for nor against any party here or elsewhere. That which a whole nation chooses to do, it has a right to do. Mr. Burke says, No. Where then *does* the right exist? I am contending for the rights of the *living,* and against their being willed away, and controlled and contracted for, by the manuscript assumed authority of the dead; and Mr. Burke is contending for the authority of the dead over the rights and freedom of the living.

There was a time when kings disposed of their crowns by will upon their death-beds, and consigned the people, like beasts of the field, to whatever successor they appointed. This is now so exploded as scarcely to be remembered, and so monstrous as hardly to be believed. But the parliamentary clauses upon which Mr. Burke builds his political church, are of the same nature.

The laws of every country must be analogous to some common principle. In England, no parent or master, nor all the authority of Parliament, omnipotent as it has called itself, can bind or control the personal freedom even of an individual beyond the age of twenty-one years. On what ground of right, then, could the Parliament of 1688, or any other parliament, bind all posterity for ever?

Those who have quitted the world, and those who are not yet arrived at it, are as remote from each other, as the utmost stretch of moral imagination can conceive. What possible obligation, then, can exist between them; what rule or principle can be laid down, that two nonentities, the one out of existence, and the other not in, and who never can meet in this world, that the one should control the other to the end of time?

*   *   *

The circumstances of the world are continually changing, and the opinions of men change also; and as government is for the living, and not for the dead, it is the living only that has any right in it. That which may be thought right and found convenient in one age, may be thought wrong and found inconvenient in another. In such cases, who is to decide, the living or the dead?

* * *

From his violence and his grief, his silence on some points, and his excess on others, it is difficult not to believe that Mr. Burke is sorry, extremely sorry, that arbitrary power, the power of the Pope, and the Bastille, are pulled down.

Not one glance of compassion, not one commiserating reflection, that I can find throughout his book, has he bestowed on those who lingered out the most wretched of lives, a life without hope, in the most miserable of prisons.

It is painful to behold a man employing his talents to corrupt himself. Nature has been kinder to Mr. Burke than he is to her. He is not affected by the reality of distress touching his heart, but by the showy resemblance of it striking his imagination. He pities the plumage, but forgets the dying bird.

Accustomed to kiss the aristocratical hand that hath purloined him from himself, he degenerates into a composition of art, and the genuine soul of nature forsakes him. His hero or his heroine must be a tragedy-victim expiring in show, and not the real prisoner of mystery, sinking into death in the silence of a dungeon.

* * *

I have now to follow Mr. Burke through a pathless wilderness of rhapsodies, and a sort of descant upon governments, in which he asserts whatever he pleases, on the presumption of its being believed, without offering either evidence or reasons for so doing.

Before anything can be reasoned upon to a conclusion, certain facts, principles, or data, to reason from, must be established, admitted, or denied. Mr. Burke, with his usual outrage, abuses the *Declaration of the Rights of Man,* published by the National Assembly of France, as the basis on which the Constitution of France is built. This he calls "paltry and blurred sheets of paper about the rights of man."

Does Mr. Burke mean to deny that *man* has any rights? If he does, then he must mean that there are no such things as rights any where, and that he has none himself; for who is there in the world but man? But if Mr. Burke means to admit that man has rights, the question then will be, what are those rights, and how came man by them originally?

The error of those who reason by precedents drawn from antiquity, respecting the rights of man, is that they do not go far enough into antiquity. They do not go the whole way. They stop in some of the intermediate stages of an hundred or a thousand years, and produce what was then done as a rule for the present day. This is no authority at all.

If we travel still further into antiquity, we shall find a directly contrary opinion and practise prevailing; and, if antiquity is to be authority, a thousand such authorities may be produced, successively contradicting each other; but if we proceed on, we shall at last come out right; we shall come to the time when man came from the hand of his Maker. What was he then? Man. Man was his high and only title, and a higher cannot be given him. But of titles I shall speak hereafter.

We have now arrived at the origin of man, and at the origin of his rights. As to the manner in which the world has been governed from that day to this, it is no further any concern of ours than to make a proper use of the errors or the improvements which the history of it presents. Those who lived a hundred or a thousand years ago, were then moderns as we are now. They had *their* ancients, and those ancients had others, and we also shall be ancients in our turn.

If the mere name of antiquity is to govern in the affairs of life, the people who are to live an hundred or a thousand years hence, may as well take us for a precedent, as we made a precedent of those who lived an hundred or a thousand years ago.

The fact is, that portions of antiquity, by proving every thing, establish nothing. It is authority against authority all the way, till we come to the divine origin of the rights of man, at the Creation. Here our inquiries find a resting-place, and our reason finds a home.

If a dispute about the rights of man had arisen at a distance of an hundred years from the Creation, it is to this source of authority they must have referred, and it is to the same source of authority that we must now refer.

Though I mean not to touch upon any sectarian principle of

religion, yet it may be worth observing, that the genealogy of Christ is traced to Adam. Why then not trace the rights of man to the creation of man? I will answer the question. Because there have been upstart governments, thrusting themselves between, and presumptuously working to *un-make* man.

If any generation of men ever possessed the right of dictating the mode by which the world should be governed for ever, it was the first generation that existed; and if that generation did it not, no succeeding generation can show any authority for doing it, nor can set any up.

* * *

It is also to be observed, that all the religions known in the world are founded, so far as they relate to man, on the *unity of man,* as being all of one degree. Whether in heaven or in hell, or in whatever state man may be supposed to exist hereafter, the good and the bad are the only distinctions. Nay, even the laws of governments are obliged to slide into this principle, by making degrees to consist in crimes and not in persons.

It is one of the greatest of all truths, and of the highest advantage to cultivate. By considering man in this light, and by instructing him to consider himself in this light, it places him in a close connection with all his duties, whether to his Creator or to the creation, of which he is a part; and it is only when he forgets his origin, or, to use a more fashionable phrase, his *birth and family,* that he becomes dissolute.

It is not among the least of the evils of the present existing governments in all parts of Europe, that man, considered as man, is thrown back to a vast distance from his Maker, and the artificial chasm filled up by a succession of barriers, or a sort of turnpike gates, through which he has to pass.

The duty of man is not a wilderness of turnpike gates, through which he is to pass by tickets from one to the other. It is plain and simple, and consists but of two points. His duty to God, which every man must feel; and with respect to his neighbor, to do as he would be done by. If those to whom power is delegated do well, they will be respected; if not, they will be despised; and with regard to those to whom no power is delegated, but who assume it, the rational world can know nothing of them.

Hitherto we have spoken only (and that but in part) of the

natural rights of man. We have now to consider the civil rights of man, and to show how the one originates from the other. Man did not enter into society to become *worse* than he was before, nor to have fewer rights than he had before, but to have those rights better secured. His natural rights are the foundation of all his civil rights. But in order to pursue this distinction with more precision, it is necessary to make the different qualities of natural and civil rights.

A few words will explain this. Natural rights are those which appertain to man in right of his existence. Of this kind are all the intellectual rights, or rights of the mind, and also all those rights of acting as an individual for his own comfort and happiness, which are not injurious to the natural rights of others. Civil rights are those which appertain to man in right of his being a member of society.

Every civil right has for its foundation some natural right pre-existing in the individual, but to the enjoyment of which his individual power is not, in all cases, sufficiently competent. Of this kind are all those which relate to security and protection.

From this short review, it will be easy to distinguish between that class of natural rights which man retains after entering into society, and those which he throws into the common stock as a member of society.

The natural rights which he retains, are all those in which the *power* to execute is as perfect in the individual as the right itself. Among this class, as is before mentioned, are all the intellectual rights, or rights of the mind: consequently, religion is one of those rights.

The natural rights which are not retained, are all those in which, though the right is perfect in the individual, the power to execute them is defective. They answer not his purpose. A man, by natural right, has a right to judge in his own cause; and so far as the right of the mind is concerned, he never surrenders it but what availeth it him to judge, if he has not power to redress? He therefore deposits his right in the common stock of society, and takes the arm of society, of which he is a part, in preference and in addition to his own. Society *grants* him nothing. Every man is proprietor in society, and draws on the capital as a matter of right.

From these premises, two or three certain conclusions will follow.

First, That every civil right grows out of a natural right; or, in other words, is a natural right exchanged.

Secondly, That civil power, properly considered as such, is made up of the aggregate of that class of the natural rights of man, which becomes defective in the individual in point of power, and answers not his purpose, but when collected to a focus, becomes competent to the purpose of every one.

Thirdly, That the power produced from the aggregate of natural rights, imperfect in power in the individual, cannot be applied to invade the natural rights which are retained in the individual, and in which the power to execute is as perfect as the right itself.

15

Napoleon

THE ACCOUNT of the battle of Arcola is by the young revolutionary general whom the Directory had appointed eight months before to command the Army of Italy.

Napoleon's observations on the study of history and geography form part of his "remarks on a scheme for establishing a Faculty of Literature and History at the Collège de France," which he sent to his Minister of the Interior from his headquarters at Finkenstein in Germany on April 19, 1807.

Napoleon's conversations with his companion-in-exile and confidant, the Count de Las Cases, at St. Helena in August and September, 1816, were later recorded by the Count in Le Mémorial de Sainte-Hélène (1823), which became one of the main sources of the "Napoleonic legend."

a Bonaparte in Italy (1796)

To the Executive Directory

H.Q., Verona, 29 Brumaire, Year V (19 Nov, 1796)

I AM SO worn out with fatigue, Citizen Directors, that I cannot inform you of all the military events preceding the battle of Arcola, which has just decided the fate of Italy.

Learning that Field-Marshal Alvinzi was approaching Verona so as to join up with his divisions in the Tyrol, I marched down the Adige with the Augereau and Masséna divisions. During the night of the 4th to 25th I had a boat bridge built at Ronco, where we crossed. I hoped to reach Villanova in the morning and from there capture the enemy's artillery parks and baggage and attack his army on the flank and rear. General Alvinzi's headquarters were at Caldiero. But the enemy had heard of our movement and had sent a

From J. E. Howard (ed. and trans.), LETTERS AND DOCUMENTS OF NAPOLEON, 2 vols. (London, 1961), vol. i, pp. 161–3. Reprinted by permission of the Cresset Press and Oxford University Press, Inc.

Croat and some Hungarian regiments into the village of Arcola, a very strong position in the midst of marshes and canals. This village held up the advanceguard the whole day. In vain did the generals, knowing the importance of time, rush to the front to force our columns to cross the little bridge: too much courage did only harm; almost all were wounded and General Verdier, Bon, Verne and Lannes were put out of action. Seizing a flag, Augereau carried it to the very end of the bridge: "Cowards," he cried to his troops, "are you so afraid of death?" and he stayed there several minutes without producing any effect. Yet we had to cross this bridge or make a detour of several leagues which would have nullified our whole operation; I went up myself and asked the soldiers if they were still the victors of Lodi; my presence had an effect that decided me to attempt the crossing once more.

Already twice wounded, General Lannes returned and received a third and more dangerous wound; General Vignolle was also wounded. We had to give up the idea of taking the village by frontal assault and await the arrival of a column commanded by General Guieu that I had sent by Albaredo. It did not come up until the night, but it occupied the village and took four guns and several hundred prisoners. Meanwhile General Masséna was attacking a division which the enemy had sent from his headquarters onto our left; he drove it back and routed it completely.

During the night we decided to evacuate the village of Arcola, and we prepared to be attacked at dawn by the whole enemy army, which had had time to bring up its artillery and supplies and to fall back to meet us.

At first light the action began everywhere with the greatest violence. Masséna, who was on the left, put the enemy to flight and pursued him to the gates of Caldiero. General Robert, who was on the central causeway with the 75th, overthrew the enemy with the bayonet and covered the battlefield with dead.

I ordered Adjutant-general Vial to move down the Adige with a demi-brigade so as to turn the enemy's left. But the terrain presents insuperable obstacles. The brave adjutant-general plunged into the water up to his neck, but in vain, for only eighty grenadiers were able to follow him and that could not make a sufficient diversion. During the night of the 26th to 27th I had bridges thrown over the canals and marshes, and General Augereau crossed with his division. At 10.0 a.m. we were in action, General Masséna being on the left, General Robert in the centre, General Augereau on the right.

The enemy attacked the centre vigorously and forced it to give ground. I then withdrew the 32nd from the left and placed it in ambush in some woods, and at the moment when the enemy by driving back our centre was on the point of turning our right General Gardanne left his ambush at the head of the 32nd taking the enemy in the flank and doing a horrible slaughter. The enemy's left was supported by marshes and was overpowering our right by superior numbers. I ordered Citizen Hercule, an officer of my Guides, to choose twenty-five men of his company and ride half a league down the Adige and round the marshes covering the enemy's left flank and then to fall upon him from behind at the gallop sounding several trumpets. This manoeuvre succeeded perfectly: the enemy infantry wavered, and General Augereau seized the moment. But although retreating, it still resisted until a little force of 800 or 900 men with four guns which I had sent through Porto-Legnano to take up position behind the enemy fell upon his rear and completed the rout. General Masséna, who had moved to the centre, marched straight on the village of Arcola, occupied it and pursued the enemy up to the village of San Bonifacio; but nightfall prevented us from going further.

The fruits of the battle of Arcola are 4,000 to 5,000 prisoners, 4 flags, 18 guns. The enemy has lost at least 4,000 dead and as many wounded; we have had 900 men wounded and about 200 killed. . . .

Meanwhile General Vaubois was attacked and defeated at Rivoli, an important position covering Mantua. We left Arcola at dawn; I sent the cavalry through Vicenza to pursue the enemy and went myself to Verona where I had left General Kilmaine with 3,000 men.

I have now rallied and reinforced the Vaubois division, which is at Castelnovo, 8,000 strong. Augereau is at Verona, Masséna at Villanova. Tomorrow I shall attack the division which beat Vaubois, chase it into the Tyrol and await the surrender of Mantua, which cannot hold more than a fortnight. If, as things now are, you send me the help you have long promised, I will promise to force the Emperor to make peace within six weeks and also go to Rome.

I cannot hide from you that I have not found among the soldiers my phalanxes of Lodi, Millesimo, Castiglione; fatigue and the loss of the brave have removed that dash with which I could have hoped to catch Alvinzi and the greater part of his army. General Vaubois lacks character and experience in handling big divisions. . . .

The generals and officers of the staff showed unexampled energy

and courage; twelve or fifteen have been killed: it was indeed a fight
to the death. . . .

Bonaparte

b Napoleon on Higher Education (1807)

HISTORY, for similar reasons, can be classed with the sciences
which would benefit by a school of advanced study. The reading of history is a science in itself. Everything has been said over
and over again. There is such a glut of apocryphal histories, and so
much difference exists between one book written at an earlier date,
and another written at a later date, and making use of the labours
and the ideas of previous historians, that a man who wants to look
up the best account of some event, and plunges into a big historical
library, loses himself in a regular maze. To know what remains of
the ancient historians, and what has been lost, and to distinguish
original authorities from the additions made to them by good or bad
commentators — this alone, if not a science, is at least an important
subject of study. Thus the knowledge and selection of good historians,
good memoirs, and genuine chronicles, is a real and useful acquisition. If, in a great capital like Paris, there were a school of advanced
study in history, and if its first course were one in bibliography, a
young man need no longer waste months in the misleading study of
inadequate or untrustworthy authorities; he would be directed to the
best books, and would, with less time and trouble, acquire a better
knowledge of the subject.

There is, besides, a part of history, namely the most recent periods,
which cannot be learnt from books. No historian comes down to our
own day. For every man of 25 there is a period of 50 years before
his birth of which no history has been written. This gap presents
many difficulties. It needs hard work — work that is always imperfect,
and often unremunerative — to link up past events with the present
day. To do so would be an important duty of the professors at the
advanced school. They ought to know not only what has happened
from the beginnings of national life up to the point at which historians stop writing, but also up to the time at which they are
teaching.

From J. M. Thompson (ed.), LETTERS OF NAPOLEON (Oxford, 1934), pp.
183–7. Reprinted by permission of Basil Blackwell.

There should be a number of such professors — in Roman history, Greek history, the history of the Empire, Church history, American history, and several more for the history of France, England, Germany, Italy, and Spain.

History would also be divided into the various branches suitable for teaching. First would come the history of legislation. The professor of this subject would have to go back to the Romans, and follow on from that period, dealing with the reigns of the French kings in chronological order, down to the Consulate. Then would come the history of the art of war in France. The professor would expound the different plans of campaign adopted at various periods of our history, whether for invading other countries or for defending our own; the causes of victory and of defeat; with the authors and memoirs in which his facts can be found, and his conclusions verified. This branch of history, which interests everyone, and is essential for soldiers, would also be extremely useful to statesmen. The art of attacking and defending fortified positions can be explained at the specialised School of Engineering: the art of war as a whole can't be expounded, because it has never yet been put on paper — if, indeed, it ever will be. But a chair of history devoted to explaining how the great commanders defended our frontiers in various wars could not fail to be of the greatest benefit.

One might, then, consider the organisation of a sort of Literary University, including in this term not merely *belles-lettres,* but also history and geography — for one cannot think of the former without the latter. . . .

* * *

I want this University: it has been in my mind a long time, because I have done so much work myself, and have felt the need of it. I have read a lot of history, and I have often wasted a deal of time in useless reading, just for lack of direction. And I have paid enough attention to geography to know that there is no single man in Paris who is perfectly up to date in the discoveries which are made every day, and in the ceaseless changes of that subject. I am certain that the proposed institution would be a great help to education in general, even for the best educated people; whereas courses in literature would have none of these advantages — my experience being that they teach nothing more than one knows at the age of 14. . . .

* * *

One objection is constantly raised in this connexion: it is said that contemporaries are bad historians. I don't agree. I should, if what is meant is a satirical treatment of current events; I should, if it were the history of a living man, or of one whom the historian had known personally; for history must not be turned into panegyric. But it is as easy one year as it is a hundred years after the event to say when or under what circumstances a state was forced to take up arms; at what moment it compelled the enemy to make peace; or in what month such and such a fleet sailed on such and such an expedition, and what engagements it lost or won. It makes little difference whether the historian is near the facts, or far away from them. If he is really close to the facts he is likely to be all the more truthful, because he knows that his readers can judge of what happened in their own life-time. There is no inconvenience in this, whilst there is a real advantage, especially for young people, who can find nobody to instruct them in the events of 20 or 30 years ago. For instance, without this type of teaching, soldiers will have to wait a long time before they can learn to profit by the faults which have led to defeat, or to appreciate the dispositions which would have prevented it. The whole Revolutionary war should be full of lessons; yet one often devotes long hours to persistent research, and fails to gather them. The reason is, not that there is no detailed description of the facts — for they have been described in all kinds of ways and in all kinds of places, but that it is nobody's business to make research easy, and to give the guidance which is needed if it is to be done intelligently.

c Napoleon as Peace-Maker and the Prophet of European Union

August 24, 1816]

"PEACE, concluded at Moscow, would have fulfilled and wound up my hostile expeditions. It would have been, with respect to the grand cause, the term of casualties and the commencement of security. A new horizon, new undertakings, would have unfolded themselves, adapted, in every respect, to the well-being and prosper-

From JOURNAL OF THE PRIVATE LIFE AND CONVERSATIONS OF THE EMPEROR NAPOLEON AT SAINT HELENA, 8 vols. (London, 1823), vol. v, pp. 265–7; vol. vii, pp. 133–9.

ity of all. The foundation of the European system would have been laid, and my only remaining task would have been its organisation.

"Satisfied on these grand points, and every where at peace, I should have also had my congress and my holy alliance. These are plans which were stolen from me. In that assembly of all the sovereigns, we should have discussed our interest in a family way, and settled our accounts with the people, as a clerk does with his master.

"The cause of the age was victorious, the revolution accomplished; the only point in question was to reconcile it with what it had not destroyed. But that task belonged to me; I had for a long time been making preparations for it, *at the expence, perhaps, of my popularity.* No matter. I became the arch of the old and new alliance, the natural mediator between the ancient and modern order of things. I maintained the principles and possessed the confidence of the one; I had identified myself with the other. I belonged to them both; I should have acted conscientiously in favour of each:

'My glory would have consisted in my equity'."

And, after having enumerated what he would have proposed between sovereign and sovereign, and between sovereigns and their people, he continued: "Powerful as we were, all that we might have conceded would have appeared grand. It would have gained us the gratitude of the people. At present, what they may extort will never seem enough to them, and they will be uniformly distrustful and discontented."

He next took a review of what he would have proposed for the prosperity, the interests, the enjoyments and the well-being of the European confederacy. He wished to establish the same principles, the same system everywhere. An European code; a court of European appeal, with full powers to redress all wrong decisions, as ours redresses at home those of our tribunals. Money of the same value but with different coins; the same weights, the same measures, the same laws, etc. etc.

"Europe would soon in that manner," he said, "have really been but the same people, and every one, who travelled, would have every where found himself in one common country."

He would have required that all the rivers should be navigable in common; that the seas should be thrown open; that the great armies should, in future, be reduced to the single establishment of a guard for the sovereign, etc. etc.

In fine, a crowd of ideas fell from him, the greater part of which were new; some of the simplest nature, others altogether sublime, relative to the different political, civil, and legislative branches, to religion, to the arts, and commerce: they embraced every subject.

He concluded: "On my return to France, in the bosom of my country, at once great, powerful, magnificent, at peace and glorious, I would have proclaimed the immutability of boundaries, all future wars purely *defensive;* all new aggrandizement *anti-national.* I would have associated my son with the empire; my dictatorship would have terminated, and his constitutional reign commenced. . . .

"Paris would have been the capital of the world, and the French the envy of nations! . . .

"My leisure and my old age would have been consecrated, in company with the Empress, and, during the royal apprenticeship of my son, in visiting, with my own horses, like a plain country couple, every corner of the empire; in receiving compliments, in redressing wrongs, in founding monuments, and in doing good every where and by every means! . . . These also, my dear Las Cases, were among my dreams!"

November 11, 1816]

"They speak incessantly of my love of war; but have I not been constantly occupied in defending myself? Did I ever win a single great victory without immediately offering peace?

"The truth is that I have never been master of my own movements; I have never really been entirely myself.

"I may have had many plans, but I was never at liberty to carry out any. However much I might hold the helm, however strong my hand, the sudden and numberless waves that beset my craft were stronger still, and I had the wisdom to yield to them rather than to founder by wishing obstinately to resist them. I have, therefore, never been truly my own master, but I have always been governed by circumstances. . . ."

And having treated many other subjects besides, the Emperor said: "One of my great plans was the rejoining, the concentration of those same geographical nations which have been disunited and parcelled out by revolution and policy. There are dispersed in Europe upwards of 30,000,000 of French, 15,000,000 of Spaniards, 15,000,000 of Italians, and 30,000,000 of Germans; and it was my intention to incorporate these people each into one nation. It would have been a noble thing to have advanced into posterity with such a train, and attended by the blessings of future ages. I felt myself worthy of this glory!

"After this summary simplification, it would have been possible to indulge the chimera of the *beau ideal* of civilization. In this state of things, there would have been some chance of establishing, in every country, a unity of codes, principles, opinions, sentiments, views, and interests. Then, perhaps, by the help of the universal diffusion of knowledge, one might have thought of attempting, in the great European family, the application of the American Congress, or the amphictyons of Greece. What a perspective of power, grandeur, happiness, and prosperity would thus have appeared! . . .

"The concentration of 30,000,000 or 40,000,000 of Frenchmen was completed and perfected; and that of 15,000,000 of Spaniards was nearly accomplished; for nothing is more common than to convert accident into principle. As I did not subdue the Spaniards, people will argue henceforth as though they were incapable of being subdued; but the fact is that they were subdued, and that at the very moment that they escaped the Cortès of Cadiz were secretly treating with us. And so it was neither their own resistance, nor the efforts of the English, that delivered them, but my mistakes and my distant reverses: the mistake, above all, of having transported myself and all my forces a thousand leagues away and suffering ruin in the attempt. For none will deny that if, when I entered that country, Austria, by not declaring war, had left me a further four months' stay in Spain, all would have been ended: the Spanish government would have been strengthened, popular agitation would have been calmed, the different parties would have rallied to me; and, after three or four years, there would have ensued a lasting peace, brilliant prosperity, a united nation; and I should have deserved well of them, and spared them the terrible tyranny that crushes them and the terrible convulsions that await them.

"With regard to the 15,000,000 of Italians, their concentration was already far advanced: it only wanted maturity. The people were daily becoming more firmly established in the unity of principles and legislation; and also in the unity of thought and feeling, that certain and infallible cement of human concentration. The union of Piedmont to France, and the junction of Parma, Tuscany and Rome were, in my mind, only temporary measures, intended merely to guarantee and promote the national education of the Italians. And see how right I was, and how great is the influence of common laws! The parties that we joined together, although this might appear as the forcible unification of an invader, and in spite of all their Italian patriotism, have been precisely those that have, by far, remained the most deeply attached to us. Now that they have been separated once more, they believe themselves to have been invaded and disinherited; and so they have been! . . .

"The whole of the south of Europe would, then, soon have become united in a common bond of geography, aims, opinions, sentiment and interests. In this state of affairs, what counter-balance would have been formed by all the nations of the north? What human effort would not have come to grief in attempting to pierce such a barrier! . . .

"The concentration of the Germans must have been effected more gradually; and therefore I had done no more than simplify their monstrous complication. Not that they were unprepared for concentration; on the contrary, they were too well prepared for it, and they might have blindly risen in reaction against us, before they had comprehended our designs. How happens it that no German Prince has yet formed a just notion of the spirit of his nation, and turned it to good account? Certainly, if heaven had made me a Prince of Germany, amidst the many critical events of our times, I should, infallibly, have governed the 30,000,000 of Germans combined; and from what I know of them, I think I may venture to affirm that, if they had once elected and proclaimed me, they would not have forsaken me, and I should never have been at St. Helena. . . .

"At all events, this concentration will be brought about, sooner or later, by the very force of events. The impulse is given; and I think that, since my fall and the destruction of my system, no grand equilibrium can possibly be established in Europe, except by the concentration and confederation of the principal nations. The sovereign who, in the first great conflict, shall sincerely embrace the cause of the people, will find himself at the head of all Europe, and may attempt whatever he pleases.

"And if people ask me now why I did not then give expression to such ideas; why I did not offer them for public discussion? They would have been so popular, I shall be told, and the public support that they would have elicited would have been an enormous addition of strength to me! My answer is that ill-will is always far more active than good-will; that we have wit in such plenty that it readily drives out good sense, and it tends to shed darkness on the most brightly-lit corners; and that to offer such lofty designs for public discussion would be to expose them to the spirit of faction, to passion, intrigue and gossip, and, inevitably, to meet with discredit and opposition. I believed, therefore, that it would be a far wiser course to keep them secret; and so I created around myself, like an aura, that atmosphere of uncertainty that beguiles and delights the multitude; those mysterious speculations that fill and occupy every mind; and, in fine, those sudden and brilliant solutions that were so enthusiastically acclaimed and strengthened my hold over men's minds."

16

The Settlement of Europe

BEFORE THE FINAL DEFEAT of Napoleon and his banishment to St. Helena, *the victorious powers and their allies concluded their negotiations at Vienna and agreed on the main terms of the territorial re-settlement of Europe. The following is an abridged version of the general treaty signed in Congress at Vienna on June 9, 1815.*

The Treaty of Vienna (1815)

In the Name of the Most Holy and Undivided Trinity

THE POWERS who signed the Treaty concluded at Paris on the 30th of May 1814, having assembled at Vienna, in pursuance of the 32d Article of that Act, with the Princes and States their Allies, to complete the provisions of the said Treaty, and to add to them the arrangements rendered necessary by the state in which Europe was left at the termination of the last war, being now desirous to embrace, in common transaction, the various results of their negotiations, for the purpose of confirming them by their reciprocal ratifications, have authorised their Plenipotentiaries to unite, in a general instrument, the regulations of superior and permanent interest, and to join to that act, as integral parts of the arrangements of Congress, the Treaties, Conventions, Declarations, Regulations, and other particular acts, as cited in the present Treaty. And the above-mentioned Powers having appointed Plenipotentiaries to the Congress, that is to say: H.M. the Emperor of Austria, King of Hungary and Bohemia, the . . . Prince de Metternich . . . and the . . . Baron de Wessenberg . . . H.M. the King of Spain and the Indies, Don Peter Gomez Labrador . . . H.M. the King of France and Navarre,

From A. Aspinall and E. Antony Smith, ENGLISH HISTORICAL DOCUMENTS (London, 1959), vol. xi (1783–1832), pp. 938–49. Reprinted by permission of Eyre and Spottiswoode and Oxford University Press, Inc.

the Sieur Charles Maurice de Talleyrand-Périgord, Prince of Talley-
rand . . . the Sieur Duke d'Alberg . . . the Sieur Count Gouvernet de
Latour du Pin . . . and the Sieur Alexis Count de Noailles . . . H.M.
the King of the United Kingdom of Great Britain and Ireland, . . .
Viscount Castlereagh . . . the Duke . . . of Wellington, . . . the . . .
Earl of Clancarty . . . , Earl Cathcart . . . and . . . Lord Stewart . . .
H.R.H. the Prince Regent of the Kingdoms of Portugal and the
Brazils, the . . . Count of Palmella, . . . the Sieur Antonio de Saldanha
da Gama . . . and the Sieur Don Joachim Lobo da Silveira . . . H.M.
the King of Prussia, the Prince Hardenberg . . . and the . . . Baron
de Humboldt . . . H.M. the Emperor of all the Russias, the . . .
Prince de Rasoumoffsky . . . , the . . . Count de Stackelberg . . . and
the . . . Count de Nesselrode . . . H.M. the King of Sweden and
Norway, the . . . Count de Lowenhielm . . .

Article I] The Duchy of Warsaw, with the exception of the provinces and districts which are otherwise disposed of by the following
Articles, is united to the Russian Empire, to which it shall be irrev-
ocably attached by its Constitution, and be possessed by H.M. the
Emperor of all the Russias, his heirs and successors in perpetuity.
His Imperial Majesty reserves to himself to give to this State, enjoying a distinct Administration, the interior improvement which he
shall judge proper. He shall assume with his other titles that of
Czar, King of Poland, agreeably to the form established for the titles
attached to his other possessions. The Poles, who are respective subjects of Russia, Austria and Prussia, shall obtain a representation,
and national institutions, regulated according to the degree of political consideration, that each of the Governments to which they
belong shall judge expedient and proper to grant them.

* * *

Article VI] The town of Cracow, with territory, is declared to
be for ever a free, independent, and strictly neutral city, under the
protection of Austria, Russia and Prussia.

* * *

Article XIV] The principles established for the free navigation of
rivers and canals, in the whole extent of ancient Poland, as well as
for the trade to the ports, for the circulation of articles, the growth
and produce of the different Polish provinces, and for the commerce,
relative to goods in transitu, such as they are specified in the 24th,

25th, 26th, 28th and 29th Articles of the Treaty between Austria and Russia . . . shall be invariably maintained.

Article XV] H.M. the King of Saxony renounces in perpetuity for himself and all his descendants and successors, in favour of H.M. the King of Prussia, all his right and title to the provinces, districts and territories . . . of the kingdom of Saxony.

* * *

Article XVII] Austria, Russia, Great Britain and France guarantee to H.M. the King of Prussia, his descendants and successors, the possession of the countries marked out in the 15th Article, in full property and sovereignty.

* * *

Article XIX] H.M. the King of Prussia and H.M. the King of Saxony . . . renounce . . . all feudal rights or pretensions which they might exercise . . . beyond the frontiers fixed by the present treaty.

* * *

Article XXVI] H.M. the King of the United Kingdom of Great Britain and Ireland, having substituted to his ancient title of Elector of the Holy Roman Empire, that of King of Hanover, and this title having been acknowledged by all the Powers of Europe, and by the Princes and free towns of Germany, the countries which have till now composed the Electorate of Brunswick-Lüneburg, according as their limits have been recognised and fixed for the future, by the following Articles, shall henceforth form the Kingdom of Hanover.

[*Articles XXVII–XXXIII* further concern Hanover.]

[*Articles XXXIV–LII* further concern the German principalities.]

Article LIII] The Sovereign Princes and Free Towns of Germany, under which denomination, for the present purpose, are comprehended their Majesties the Emperor of Austria, the Kings of Prussia, of Denmark and of the Netherlands; that is to say, the Emperor of Austria and the King of Prussia for all their possessions which anciently belonged to the German Empire, the King of Denmark for the Duchy of Holstein, and the King of the Netherlands for the Grand Duchy of Luxemburg, establish among themselves a perpetual Confederation, which shall be called 'the Germanic Confederation'.

Article LIV] The object of this Confederation is the maintenance of the external and internal safety of Germany, and of the independence and inviolability of the confederated States.

* * *

Article LVI] The affairs of the Confederation shall be confided to a Federative Diet, in which all the Members shall vote by their Plenipotentiaries, either individually or collectively, in the following manner, without prejudice to their rank [each to have one vote]: 1] Austria. 2] Prussia. 3] Bavaria. 4] Saxony. 5] Hanover. 6] Würtemberg. 7] Baden. 8] Electoral Hesse. 9] Grand Duchy of Hesse. 10] Denmark, for Holstein. 11] The Netherlands, for Luxemburg. 12] Grand-Ducal and Ducal Houses of Saxony. 13] Brunswick and Nassau. 14] Mecklenburg-Schwerin and Strelitz. 15] Holstein-Oldenburg, Anhalt and Schwartzburg. 16] Hohenzollern, Lichtenstein, Reuss, Schaumburg, Lippe, Lippe and Waldeck. 17] The Free Towns of Lübeck, Frankfort, Bremen and Hamburg.
Article LVII] Austria shall preside at the Federative Diet. Each State of the Confederation has the right of making propositions, and the presiding State shall bring them under deliberation within a definitive time.
Article LVIII] Whenever fundamental laws are to be enacted, changes made in the fundamental laws of the Confederation, measures adopted relative to the Federative Act itself, and organic institutions or other arrangements made for the common interest, the Diet shall form itself into a General Assembly, and, in that case, the distribution of votes shall be as follows, calculated according to the respective extent of the individual States:

Austria, Prussia, Saxony, Bavaria, Hanover, Würtemberg to have 4 votes each; Baden, Electoral Hesse, Grand Duchy of Hesse, Holstein, Luxemburg to have 3 votes each; Brunswick, Mecklenburg-Schwerin, Nassau to have 2 votes each; Saxe-Weimar, Saxe-Gotha, Saxe-Coburg, Saxe-Meiningen, Saxe-Hildburghausen, Mecklenburg-Strelitz, Holstein-Oldenburg, Anhalt-Dessau, Anhalt-Bernburg, Anhalt-Kotthen, Schwartzburg-Sondershausen, Schwartzburg-Rudolstadt, Hohenzollern-Heckingen, Lichtenstein, Hohenzollern-Sigmaringen, Waldeck, Reuss (Elder Branch), Reuss (Younger Branch), Schaumburg-Lippe, Lippe, The Free Towns of Lübeck, Frankfort, Bremen, Hamburg to have one vote each. Total votes, 69.
Article LIX] The question whether a subject is to be discussed by

the General Assembly, conformably to the principles above established, shall be decided in the Ordinary Assembly by a majority of votes. The same assembly shall prepare the drafts of Resolutions which are to be proposed to the General Assembly, and shall furnish the latter with all the necessary information, either for adopting or rejecting them. The plurality of votes shall regulate the decisions, both in the Ordinary and General Assemblies, with this difference, however, that in the Ordinary Assembly, an absolute majority shall be deemed sufficient, while in the other, two-thirds of the votes shall be necessary to form the majority. When the votes are even in the Ordinary Assembly, the President shall have the casting vote; but when the Assembly is to deliberate on the acceptance or change of any of the fundamental laws, upon organic institutions, upon individual rights, or upon affairs of religion, the plurality of votes shall not be deemed sufficient, either in the Ordinary or in the General Assembly. The Diet is permanent; it may, however, when the subjects submitted to its deliberations are disposed of, adjourn for a fixed period, which shall not exceed four months.

* * *

Article LXI} The Diet shall assemble at Frankfort on the Main. Its first meeting is fixed for the 1st of September 1815.

Article LXII} The first object to be considered by the Diet after its opening shall be the framing of the fundamental laws of the Confederation, and of its organic institutions, with respect to its exterior, military and interior relations.

Article LXIII} The States of the Confederation engage to defend not only the whole of Germany, but each individual State of the Union, in case it should be attacked, and they mutually guarantee to each other such of their possessions as are comprised in this Union. When War shall be declared by the Confederation, no member can open a separate negotiation with the enemy, nor make peace, nor conclude an armistice, without the consent of the other members.

* * *

Article LXV} The ancient United Provinces of the Netherlands and the late Belgic provinces, both within the limits fixed by the following Article, shall form, together with the countries and territories designated in the same Article, under the sovereignty of his Royal Highness the Prince of Orange-Nassau, sovereign prince of the

United Provinces, the kingdom of the Netherlands, hereditary in the order of succession already established by the Act of the Constitution of the said United Provinces. The title and the prerogatives of the royal dignity are recognised by all the Powers in the house of Orange-Nassau.

* * *

Article LXVII] That part of the old Duchy of Luxemburg which is comprised in the limits specified in the following Article, is likewise ceded to the Sovereign Prince of the United Provinces, now King of the Netherlands, to be possessed in perpetuity by him and his successors, in full property and sovereignty. The Sovereign of the Netherlands shall add to his titles that of Grand Duke of Luxemburg.

* * *

Article LXXIV] The integrity of the nineteen Cantons . . . is recognised as the basis of the Helvetic system.

Article LXXV] The Vallais, the territory of Geneva, and the principality of Neufchâtel, are united to Switzerland, and shall form three new Cantons.

[*Articles LXXVI–LXXXIV* further concern Switzerland.]

Article LXXXVI] The states which constituted the former republic of Genoa are united in perpetuity to those of his Majesty the King of Sardinia . . . .

Article LXXXVII] The King of Sardinia shall add to his present titles that of Duke of Genoa.

* * *

Article LXXXIX] The countries called Imperial Fiefs, formerly united to the ancient Ligurian Republic, are definitely united to the states of his Majesty the King of Sardinia.

* * *

Article XCIII] In pursuance of the renunciations agreed upon by the Treaty of Paris of the 30th May 1814, the Powers who sign the present Treaty recognise . . . the Emperor of Austria . . . as legitimate Sovereign of the provinces and territories which have been ceded, either wholly or in part, by the Treaties of Campo-Formio of 1797, of Lunéville of 1801, of Pressburg of 1805, by the additional Convention of Fontainebleau of 1807, and by the Treaty of Vienna of 1809. . . . Istria, . . . Dalmatia, the ancient Venetian isles of the Adriatic, the mouths of the Cattaro, the city of Venice, with its waters, . . . the Duchies of Milan and Mantua, the principalities of Brixen and Trente, the county of Tyrol, the Voralberg, . . . the government and town of Trieste, Carniola, Upper Carinthia, Croatia on the right of the Save, Fiume, and the Hungarian *Littorale,* and the district of Castua.

Article XCIV] His Imperial and Royal Apostolic Majesty shall unite to his monarchy, to be possessed by him and his successors, in full property and sovereignty, 1] Besides the portions of the Terra-Firma in the Venetian states mentioned in the preceding Article, the other parts of those States, as well as all other territory situated between the Tessin, the Po, and the Adriatic Sea. 2] The valleys of the Valtelline, of Bormio, and of Chiavenna. 3] The territories which formerly comprised the Republic of Ragusa.

* * *

Article XCVIII] H.R.H. the Archduke Francis d'Este, his heirs and successors, shall possess, in full sovereignty, the Duchies of Modena, Reggio and Mirandola . . . .

Article XCIX] H.M. the Empress Maria Louisa shall possess, in full property and sovereignty, the duchies of Parma, Placentia, and Guastalla . . . .

Article C] His Imperial Highness the Archduke Ferdinand of Austria is re-established . . . in the Grand Duchy of Tuscany and its dependencies. . . .

Article CI] The principality of Lucca shall be possessed in full sovereignty by her Majesty the Infant Maria Louisa and her descendants, in the direct male line. The principality is erected into a Duchy.

* * *

Article CIV] H.M. King Ferdinand . . . is restored to the throne of Naples, and H.M. is acknowledged by the Powers as King of the Two Sicilies.

Article CV] The Powers, recognising the justice of the claims of H.R.H. the Prince Regent of Portugal and the Brazils, upon the town of Olivença and the other territories ceded to Spain by the Treaty of Badajos of 1801, and viewing the restitution of the same as a measure necessary to insure that perfect and constant harmony between the two Kingdoms of the Peninsula, the preservation of which in all parts of Europe has been the constant object of their arrangements, formally engage to use their utmost endeavours, by amicable means, to procure the retrocession of the said territories in favour of Portugal. And the Powers declare, as far as depends upon them, that this arrangement shall take place as soon as possible ...

[*Articles CVII–CXVII* concern the navigation of rivers and the levying of customs.]

Article CXVIII] The Treaties, Conventions, Declarations, Regulations, and other particular Acts which are annexed to the present Act, *viz.* 1] The Treaty between Russia and Austria of the 21st April (3 May) 1815....] The Additional Treaty relative to Cracow, between Austria, Prussia and Russia, of the 21st April (3 May) 1815. 4] The Treaty between Prussia and Saxony of the 18th May 1815. 5] The Declaration of the King of Saxony respecting the rights of the House of Schoenburg, of the 18th May 1815. 6] The Treaty between Prussia and Hanover of the 29th May 1815. 7] The Convention between Prussia and the Grand Duke of Saxe-Weimar of the 1st June 1815. 8] The Convention between Prussia and the Duke and Prince of Nassau of the 31st May 1815. 9] The Act concerning the Federative Constitution of Germany of the 8th June 1815. 10] The Treaty between the King of the Netherlands, and Prussia, England, Austria, and Russia, of the 31st May 1815. 11] The Declaration of the Powers on the Affairs of the Helvetic Confederation of the 20th March, and the Act of Accession of the Diet of the 28th May 1815. 12] The Protocol of the 29th March 1815, on the cessions made by the King of Sardinia to the Canton of Geneva. 13] The Treaty between the King of Sardinia, Austria, England, Russia, and France, of the 21st May 1815. 14] The Act entitled 'Conditions which are to serve as the bases of the Union of the States of Genoa with those of his Sardinian Majesty'. 15] The Declaration of the Powers on the Abolition of the Slave Trade, of the 8th February 1815. 16] The Regulations respecting the free navigation of Rivers. 17] The Regulation concerning the precedence of Diplomatic agents — shall be considered as integral parts of the arrangements of the Congress, and shall have throughout the same force and validity as if they were inserted, word for word, in the General Treaty.

Article CXX] The French language having been exclusively em-

248

ployed in all the copies of the present Treaty, it is declared, by the Powers who have concurred in this Act, that the use made of that language shall not be construed into a precedent for the future; every Power, therefore, reserves for itself the adoption in future negotiations and Conventions of the language it has heretofore employed in its diplomatic relations; and this Treaty shall not be cited as a precedent contrary to the established practice.

Article CXXI] The present Treaty shall be ratified, and the ratifications exchanged in six months, and by the Court of Portugal in a year, or sooner if possible.